FAMILY VIOLENCE IS A FACT OF LIFE IN AT LEAST ONE IN TEN HOUSEHOLDS IN THIS COUNTRY. BUT ONLY RECENTLY HAS THE MAGNITUDE OF THE PROBLEM BEEN BARED. MOST BATTERED WOMEN DIDN'T KNOW THERE WERE OTHERS WHO SHARED THEIR EXPERIENCE.

"One night when I was sixteen or seventeen years old, I was returning from a movie. No one was in sight, except for a man and a woman staggering towards me across the street. Suddenly, the man cocked his right arm and punched the woman in the face. . . . I still cannot forget the sound of the blows striking that woman or the painful and hunted look in her eyes.

"In 1984 I saw that look again in the eyes of Jane Marie Stafford as she told about her years of anguish as a battered wife in rural Nova Scotia. She was telling her story before a camera for a documentary on CBC's "fifth estate" program. The soundman thought there was a problem with his equipment until he realized the sound he heard through his earphones was the pounding of Jane Stafford's heart, picked up by a chest microphone as she related particularly harrowing or brutal incidents."

—Brian Vallée

"I want this book to be written not for myself but for all of those others out there who are living that same hell as I did. I hate to think how many other women are out there this minute, living that same fear, and how many kids are being abused, all behind closed doors. . . . My healing is not complete. I still see a therapist. I still have hurts. Some wounds will never heal. I cannot erase the scars. I cannot forget—but I can get on with the rest of my life."

—Jane (Stafford) Hurshman

◇ W9-COH-229

LIFE WITH BILLY

Brian Vallée

SEAL BOOKS
McClelland-Bantam, Inc.
Toronto

LIFE WITH BILLY

A Seal Book / published by arrangement with
CBC Enterprises.

Seal edition / August 1986

Cover photo courtesy of Royal Canadian Mounted Police files.
Insert photos provided by the fifth estate, CBC.

ISBN 0-7704-2239-X

Seal Books are published by McClelland-Bantam, Inc. Its trademark, consisting of the
words "Seal Books" and the portrayal of a seal, is the property of McClelland-Bantam,
Inc., 105 Bond Street, Toronto, Ontario M5B 1Y3, Canada. This trademark has been
duly registered in the Trademark Office of Canada. The trademark consisting of the
words "Bantam Books" and the portrayal of a rooster is the property of and is used with
the consent of Bantam Books, 666 Fifth Avenue, New York, New York 10103. This
trademark has been duly registered in the Trademark Office of Canada and elsewhere.

PRINTED IN CANADA

COVER PRINTED IN U.S.A.

U   18 17 16 15 14 13 12 11 10 9

For Maggie, my mother, who taught me from an early age about the worth and equality of all human beings.

FROM THE AUTHOR

One night when I was sixteen or seventeen years old, I was returning from a movie in my hometown of Sault Ste. Marie. No one was in sight, except for a man and a woman staggering towards me across the street. Suddenly the man cocked his right arm and punched the woman in the face. There was a sickening crack when the blow landed.

The woman pleaded with him to stop.

The man drew away from her slightly and kicked her hard between the legs. The woman screamed and doubled over, her hands grasping her crotch. Without thinking, I was across the street holding the man in a bear hug from behind. I yelled at a mechanic who was watching the scuffle from a nearby garage to call the police, who arrived in what seemed like seconds. The man, obviously drunk, abused the officer and cursed me. I explained what I'd seen and was shocked when the woman denied the man had attacked her and told the police that she had tripped and fallen on the pavement.

"But I saw him punch her and kick her between the legs," I insisted. "I'll be a witness in court."

I was not accustomed to violence; and my body was trembling with anger, fear, and frustration. The police officer lectured the man and, with his arm around my shoulder, walked me a short distance away from the couple.

"I know how you feel," he said, "but there's nothing we can do if she doesn't want to press charges."

I still cannot forget the sound of the blows striking that woman or the painful and hunted look in her eyes.

More than twenty-five years later, in 1984, I saw that look again in the eyes of Jane Marie Stafford as she told about her years of anguish as a battered wife in rural Nova Scotia. She was telling her story before a camera for a documentary on the Canadian Broadcasting Corporation's *fifth estate* program. As she discussed incidents that had occurred two and three years before, her eyes widened to unnatural proportions. The CBC soundman, Jerry King, thought there was a problem with his equipment until he realized the sound he was picking up through his earphones was the pounding of Jane Stafford's heart, picked up by a chest microphone as she related particularly harrowing or brutal incidents.

In the quarter of a century between those two incidents, the plight of more than half a million Canadian women who've been kicked, punched, whipped, burned, knifed or shot each year has gone all but unnoticed. It's conservatively estimated that family violence is a fact of life in one of ten households in Canada. But it's only in very recent years that the magnitude of the problem has been bared. The majority of battered women didn't know there were others who shared their experience.

The first shelters and transition houses for battered women and their children in Canada opened in the early 1970s, but it's only in the past four or five years that they've really burgeoned, to the point where there are now more than 225 of them spread around the country. Another 35 programs offer therapy to men who beat their wives. The progress has been significant, but many more shelters are needed, and those in operation are unevenly distributed and often underfunded, understaffed, and overcrowded. It's estimated that two women are turned away for every one who finds a place in a home. Interim Place in Mississauga, Ontario, for example, houses six hundred people a year but in one eight-month period had to turn away nine hundred. A recent report prepared for the federal government says that only 10 percent of wife-assault cases are even reported to police; for every ten thousand violent incidents that *are* reported, only two prosecutions result. Another report urges laws be changed to permit police to remove violent men from their homes, with the courts requiring abusive men to submit to therapy as a condition of parole or probation. It also pointed out the serious lack of facilities and legal protection for immigrant, native, and rural women.

The law has been getting tougher with wife-bashers, but police, prosecutors, and the courts are still reluctant to deal vigorously with them. This lack of enthusiasm was outlined in a report released last August by the Ontario government. It said that despite a 1982 directive to police and the legal system to crack down on abusers and treat domestic violence as a serious criminal matter, hundreds of battered women still live in fear of calling the police. They continue to be intimidated by threats from their spouses, and they misunderstand what will happen if they do go to court. Police are often reluctant to lay charges against wife-beaters because of a lackadaisical attitude on the part of judges trying domestic violence cases. (Progressive Conservative Member of Parliament Dave Nickerson was fined $350 in September 1985 for assaulting his wife, Madelaine. He admitted beating her at their Yellowknife home, bruising her chin, left breast, and wrist and causing her left eye to swell. Nickerson said it "was a private matter" and laughed when asked if he felt any pressure from his colleagues to resign. Calls to resign, sprinkled with hisses and boos, greeted Nickerson in the House of Commons following his conviction, and many people were angry that Prime Minister Brian Mulroney didn't throw him out of the caucus or order him to seek therapy.)

The Ontario report said that 80 percent of rural battered women surveyed feared their husbands would beat them again if they called police, and 50 percent weren't sure if their cases would end up in court if they reported their husbands to the police.

I decided to write this book because I believe the issue of wife-beating is important, but I proceeded only after Jane Stafford agreed to co-operate in its preparation. The book is based on written responses to more than sixty questions I submitted to Jane Stafford, plus court transcripts, and numerous interviews with people involved in the case. I sent Jane a copy of *The Burning Bed*, the tragic story of Francine Hughes, a Michigan housewife who after years of abuse at her husband's hands poured gasoline around his bed as he slept, dropped a match, and left him to die in flames. She was found not guilty by reason of temporary insanity. I asked Jane to read the book before answering the questions I sent her. Jane's response in part:

> I know what that woman went through. It brought my own past back to me in shocking detail. We both realize how impossible it must be for so-called normal people to understand the dilemma of our lives. I haven't cried in years, but Francine Hughes gave me the opportunity to cry for her and with her, and finally for myself.

> Brian Vallée

From Jane Stafford

I couldn't understand why I was being beaten. At first it was a black eye now and again or bumps and bruises that could be covered up. I started wearing tinted glasses, long-sleeved shirts and blouses, turtlenecks, and slacks. As all this was happening, I tried to figure out why. It always ended up with Bill telling me it was my fault. I began to believe him, thinking all the while that things would get better. They didn't. As time went on, I lost everything: my confidence, my self-esteem, my pride—with time, I even lost the ability to care or feel. Bill took everything from me, a bit at a time, until there was nothing left but a shell.

Billy Stafford's parents, my parents, other family members, and the entire community (including the RCMP) knew him and what he was capable of. Yet everyone was helpless. They couldn't do anything to help. My situation became hopeless. I knew nothing about women's crisis centres. Even if I had known, I had no telephone or transportation. Once, I purposely attended a court hearing in Bridgewater, Nova Scotia. It was for a guy who beat his wife and put her in the hospital. His sentence was a two-hundred-dollar fine and a peace bond put against him. Seeing that, I knew I could never report Billy Stafford. He would've considered such a sentence a pat on the back.

My life has been filled with many different emotions—

heartache, disappointment, pain, tears, anguish, sadness, loneliness, suffering, and evil. But most of all, guilt. Guilt for what the emotional and physical abuse did to me and guilt for what it drove me to do. To think that one so-called man could instill so much hate and resentment into another human being . . . I felt like a wild animal that had been cornered or caged, and I fought back the only way I knew how.

The first time my parents ever told me they loved me was when I was arrested and spent the weekend in jail in Halifax. When I came to court from the jail, my dad was there to take me home. He put his arms around me and held me. "I love you, Janey," he said. "Come now, I'm taking you home." It was while I was staying with them at that time that my mother first said the same three magic words, "I love you." I waited thirty-three years to hear my parents tell me that. It's terrible to think that I had to kill someone to get the love from my parents that I always wanted. We've become a very close family and this book is going to hurt them a lot, but it's something I feel must be done.

I want this book to be written, not for myself but for all of those others out there who are living that same hell as I did. If even one person picks up the book and is helped by it, that will be reward enough. I hope it also helps professionals understand the dynamics of abusive relationships.

I hate to think how many other women are out there this minute, living that same fear, and how many kids are being abused, all behind closed doors. I don't think a day goes by when I don't get up with that thought going through my head: I wonder who and where, right at this minute, it's happening to.

My healing is not complete. I still see a therapist. I still have hurts. Some wounds will never heal. I cannot erase the scars. I cannot forget—but I can get on with the rest of my life. Ultimately, time does heal. For me there is a future. There is hope. There are beauty and happiness and love out there, and I'm going after them.

Jane (Stafford) Hurshman

I

Queens County lies midway between Halifax and Yarmouth in the Canadian province of Nova Scotia, jutting into the Atlantic Ocean like a giant, jagged foot. The livelihood of its people depends largely on the changeable fortunes of the fishing, lumbering, and papermaking industries. Its largest town is the seaport of Liverpool, which has a population of about four thousand. Much of the county's population lives in outlying towns and hamlets, such as Charleston, Greenfield, and Riverdale. The small settlements are strung along the fast-flowing Medway River, which runs to the sea from its headwaters at Ponhook Lake near Greenfield. The churning Medway is famous for its trout and the prized Atlantic salmon. Many wealthy residents of Halifax, the province's capital city and its largest, own cottages along its shores. The river's reputation was royally enhanced a decade ago when Prince Charles, heir to the British throne, took time off from a royal visit to try his luck at fishing there. Volunteer fireman Freeman Bolivar was working on the lawn of the new house he built next door to the Greenfield fire station when he saw a provincial Fisheries Department

1

car driving past. "I knew the officers so I waved to them and they waved back," he recalls. "What I didn't know until later was that they had Prince Charles in the car with them. They took him out in a boat for a while but he didn't catch anything."

People raised in the small hamlets along the river have a unique way of speaking. To outsiders, their accent seems barbed with a hillbilly nasalness and twang. The hamlets on the west side of the river are accessible only by River Road, which twists and winds along the course of the Medway.

Other than Harry Freeman's family sawmill operation at Greenfield, the only work available along the river is at Teleglobe Canada, a satellite tracking and relay station built in 1964 near Charleston. It provides work for fifty people and sends satellite TV signals and telephone calls from Europe and other parts of the world to the rest of Canada. Locals know Teleglobe as simply the satellite station.

River Road is paved as far as Teleglobe. The remainder, running about ten miles north to the hamlet of Bangs Falls, has never been paved. With the spring thaw it becomes a treacherous stretch of washouts, muck, and potholes.

A strong stone's throw from the satellite station is a faded, ramshackle frame house and small barn owned by Carl Croft. The place could pass for a movie set for a Ma and Pa Kettle movie. Croft lives there with his wife and teenage daughter. On March 12, 1982, a Friday, Carl Croft was up as usual at four in the morning to feed the animals—a German shepherd, a horse, and a few sheep. Folding his arms against his chest to fight the chill, he entered the small living room and switched on the overhead light. The woodstove was lukewarm to his touch. He opened the door and jabbed at the embers with a poker until they began to glow. He added a few sticks of kindling and a log from the woodbox beside the stove. Closing the door, he opened the draft halfway and watched as the kindling began to crackle and burn. By the calendar, spring was a week and a half away, but Carl knew he'd be using the stove well into May.

Croft was the youngest in a family of six boys and three girls, all raised in the small house. The others moved away from home over the years but he continued to live there, staying on after his parents died. Now he was sixty-three with less than two years to retirement from his labourer's job in Liverpool at the Steel and Engine Company, which specialized in repairing fishing-boat engines and refinishing hulls. It was only at this time of the year, with the cold rains and the ground thawing, that he felt his age. The dampness sometimes caused his bones to ache. Five days a week he walked from his house along River Road, past the satellite station to meet a ride in Charleston at the bridge crossing the Medway River.

On this day Carl left his house at 7:15 A.M. His ride was seldom late, regardless of the weather. He picked up his pace slightly, pulling the collar of his winter coat tight at the throat. It was cold and misty and he could smell the sea. Approaching the satellite station turnoff, he noticed a half-ton Jeep pulled off to the side of the road. He thought the truck might belong to Chester Harlowe because it was near the entrance to the long driveway that led through the woods to Harlowe's place. Harlowe was a young commercial fisherman who operated his own boat out of Liverpool. Perhaps, reasoned Carl, he left the truck there because the driveway was too muddy. In his own words, "But I get close to it and I see it wasn't Ches Harlowe's old truck there. I still didn't pay much attention to it but I come along and got close to the truck and I see there's blood all over the door and I looked around the highway. I thought someone must have had an accident or something, but there was nothing tore up nowhere."

Moving closer, Carl saw a form lying inside the cab against the door on the driver's side. He noticed "a lot of blood and stuff. I looked at him and I knowed he wasn't all there. I know he wasn't living because he didn't move. So I run up to the next-door neighbour, up to John Babin, and I told him about it."

John Babin is a private person. A shorter, slighter version of British actor Michael York, he has deep-set eyes, full sideburns, and a Beatles-style haircut. Some years earlier he left the isolated fishing village in the Gaspé where he was born and travelled around the country working at a variety of jobs before settling in Nova Scotia. "My choice in the Gaspé was to work in the family plumbing and heating business or to work in the woods or at sea. I wanted a different life than that." He married his wife, Coleen, in Nova Scotia. They moved into a storey-and-a-half frame house on River Road in 1974. Initially, John worked as a sheet-metal worker in the construction industry. "I'm a tinker," he says proudly. His trade got him a permanent job in 1978 at the Bowater Mersey Paper Company, a few miles away in the town of Brooklyn, near Liverpool. The Babins had two sons. John likes children and involved himself in the local Scouting movement. He also loves to fish and with the Medway River at his back doorstep, he spent a lot of time in his canoe with a line in the water. His other passions are photography and Basset hounds, which he bred successfully on a small scale.

The Babins lived a normal, ordinary life until a fateful day in August 1981, when their elder son, Danny, a sixteen-year-old, shot himself. The boy had been depressed for some time. He was to enter high school in the fall, leaving behind his grade-school sweet-heart, who was a year behind him. "From December on, he tried to fail his year," recalls John Babin. "But he was an honour student and they told him even if he got zeros for the rest of the year he'd still pass."

John and Coleen had spent much of the day of the shooting scraping the exterior of the house to prepare it for a coat of paint. "Danny was inside lying on the couch. We came in to make some coffee. He got up and went into the bathroom and then upstairs to his room. That's when we heard the shot. I ran up and found him there." Danny had shot himself through the chest, just above the heart, with a .410 shotgun. John Babin was fully trained in first aid but there was nothing he could do. "He died in my arms as I carried him downstairs." He rushed the boy to the hospital in the family station wagon, but it was, as John Babin knew, too late.

The boy left notes for his girlfriend and for his family. He told his parents he loved them and asked to be buried in the village. John Babin wonders to this day if his son really wanted to kill himself or if it was a cry for help. "The shot missed his heart and I wonder about all the TV he watched. There was one soap opera where the victim of a shotgun blast survived and went on and on. He watched that show faithfully."

There'd been a rash of teenage suicides, including one of Danny's friends a few months earlier in Queens County, and John Babin believes that, too, may have influenced his son. "I don't think he would've thought about it without those others." Including Danny's death, there were six suicides in a nineteen-month period in the county. The deaths prompted Staff Sergeant Peter Williamson, in charge of the Royal Canadian Mounted Police detachment, to arrange meetings with parents and teachers. "It was an awful situation," says Williamson. "All I could tell them was to work at keeping lines of communication open with the kids. It was a frustrating thing."

Today, John Babin keeps busy with his job, his dogs, his cameras, and his fishing. His surviving son, Terry, who was fourteen at the time of the shooting, lives with him, but his wife has moved away. "She never got over Danny's death. The stress was too much."

But Coleen Babin was still living at home the day Carl Croft came to their door, eight months after Danny's death. "Coleen had cooked breakfast and I was down cleaning my teeth when he came to the door. I was getting ready for work when I heard the knock. I went to the door and he told me there was an accident or something and somebody was hurt. I could see he was frightened. I thought I'd go and render first aid. I told my wife I'd be right back. We drove down in my station wagon. Croft stayed in the wagon and I walked over. I could see right away he was dead. I thought it might be a suicide. It was prime in my mind."

The scene took John Babin's mind back to a mineral exploration camp in an isolated area of British Columbia where he worked several months before settling in Nova Scotia. One day a camp mechanic took over a shift for a truck driver. He was driving along a logging road with a full load of ore when the truck's brakes failed. The trailer jackknifed and sheared off the cab of the truck just as it broke through the wooden railing of a narrow bridge and plunged into a river. Rescuers, including John Babin, recovered a boot and a hand but no body. The mining camp was so remote that the only access was by air or water. An RCMP officer arrived the next day, but it was three days before the body was spotted, about two miles downstream, trapped in a logjam. It was September and the water was extremely cold. The body hadn't deteriorated. The Mountie pulled it in. Babin helped drag it to shore and wrap it in a blanket and a plastic tarp. The body was taken back to the camp and loaded on a barge. Babin and another worker took it about thirty miles across a lake to the town of Campbell River.

John Babin stared at the bloodied, lifeless form in the truck. "To me it was just one more dead body. In our society, people fear death because they think it's the end, but really, it's a continuation of life. I didn't recognize the truck. There was blood on the door. I didn't have a clue who it was. We went back to my place and called the police."

Rural Nova Scotia is policed by the RCMP. When John Babin called the Liverpool detachment to report what he'd seen, the call was automatically switched to Yarmouth, where officers are on duty twenty-four hours a day. The Liverpool switchboard would not be staffed until the detachment office opened shortly after 8:00 A.M. The dispatcher in Yarmouth checked his list to see who was on call for emergencies in Liverpool. Immediately, he telephoned Constables Archie Mason and Archie Doon. The two single men shared a house on School Street just up the road from their new detachment. They were asleep when the call came. They were left with the impression there'd been a motor vehicle accident with possible injuries. In minutes they were rushing to the scene in their royal blue RCMP cruiser with its familiar white markings. They radioed for an ambulance to meet them there. Mason and Doon got as far as Mill Village, about four miles from Charleston, when their cruiser blew its transmission.

"We'd broken down," recalls Mason. "We called for someone to take us to the scene, but the ambulance came by first and we flagged it down." John Babin, meanwhile, returned to the truck and blocked the road with his station wagon while awaiting the police. "The ambulance came beatin' down the road and I thought, 'Isn't that the way, they get here before the police.' I was surprised to see the policemen get out of the ambulance. I told them there was a body in the truck—minus a head."

Archie Mason was a thirteen-year veteran of the RCMP. A quick glance inside the truck assured him that he was investigating a shooting, not an accident. He radioed for a coroner and a senior officer. A blood spot on the road near the truck was covered with a shovel and a yellow emergency blanket. Constable Robert Hillier was next to arrive. He wrote in his notebook: "I arrived at the scene at 7:35 A.M. and observed a grey AMC motor vehicle, with Nova Scotia license 52 47 7B, at the left side of the road approximately two hundred feet past the Satellite Road." He also recorded the arrival of the coroner "and at 8:15 an unknown person seated in the vehicle was pronounced dead. The unknown male was seated in the cab of the pickup; he had been decapitated. It would appear to be some shotgun gauge due to the fact a piece of fibrous wad was laying on the seat. It was cold with misty rain and it was just early morning."

A police photographer noted later the cab of the truck was splattered with blood, brain particles and lead, and wads of a firearm. "It was everywhere. It was just like an explosion in there." The keys were still in the ignition, and outside on the ground near the driver's door there was more brain matter and a set of false teeth.

The most precise report came later from pathologist Dr. James Perry: "In summary, this man died as a result of a gun-shot wound to the head. The entrance wound being in front of the left ear approximately midway between the ear and the middle of the skull and upper face, extreme comminution of the skull bones and pulpification of most of the brain. It is my opinion that the muzzle/skull distance was probably within six inches. The slug fragments found indicated a single slug."

At six-foot-one and 180 pounds, Corporal Howard "Howie" Pike is best described as rangy and raw-boned. He was thirty-five, a veteran of fifteen years with the RCMP, the last four at the Liverpool detachment. He arrived at the scene shortly before 8:30 A.M., just as employees at Teleglobe began arriving for work. They glanced inquisitively at the clutch of police cruisers and officers. Corporal Pike recognized the truck immediately. A license-plate check revealed it was registered to Billy Stafford, who lived ten miles up River Road in the tiny settlement of Bangs Falls. Pike peered into the cab of the half-ton. "There was no face to see, but the clothing and the size of the body made it obvious to me it was Billy Stafford. I'd seen him two or three days earlier up at Freeman's Lumber Mill at Greenfield. He was coming out in his truck when I was going in. He was wearing a light brown sweater, same as was on the body." Corporal Pike had spoken to Billy Stafford only once, when he had pulled his truck over about a year earlier. "His wife was driving the truck. He was under the influence but she was sober. He asked me why I was stopping him. I told him it was just routine and that was it."

Staff Sergeant Peter Williamson has a reputation for being a no-nonsense cop who's had more than his share of scraps with tough guys during his career. A native of Bathurst, New Brunswick, he joined the force in 1960. Married and with two sons, he was transferred to Liverpool in July 1977. Now he headed the thirteen-member detachment. He was responsible for policing the town as well as surrounding Queens County. Although the coroner declared the man in the truck dead before Williamson arrived at 9:00 A.M., nothing had been touched and there was still some doubt whether it was a murder or a suicide. "When they told me it was Billy Stafford," says Williamson, "I admit I thought to myself, 'It couldn't have happened to a better guy.'" He walked around to the passenger side of the truck and opened the door. He was looking for a gun.

"Okay, boys," he said after a careful look, "there's no gun. We've got a homicide here. No gun, no suicide. Call in a dog man. If someone threw the gun away, a dog might be able to pick up the scent."

Williamson put Corporal Pike in charge of the investigation. "Howie, you look after the file. Hillier, you stay with the body and look after the exhibits."

Williamson told Constable Mason to work with Pike and then returned to the detachment. "I advised my superiors in Halifax we had a homicide, and by the end of the day I had nine or ten men on the case. We didn't have a suspect. Knowing Billy Stafford, it could have been anybody. There were a lot of people who felt threatened by him. He intimidated most everyone he knew."

After making a note of the clothing Billy Stafford was wearing, Howie Pike and Archie Mason decided to drive up to the Stafford residence in Bangs Falls. They stopped at every house along River Road, asking residents if they'd heard or seen anything unusual the night before. No one had. The drive to Bangs Falls was tortuous because of the washouts and mudholes brought on by the spring thaw. The Stafford house is on a gentle slope beyond a single-lane bridge that crosses the Medway River and joins River Road. A low, white board fence flanks the long driveway and leads to the yellow frame bungalow. Directly below the house, about halfway to the bridge, is a weathered small barn with a sagging roof. It belonged to Margaret Joudrey, the Staffords' closest neighbour. She lived in a trailer and used the barn for storage. Smoke was rising from the Stafford chimney when Pike and Mason drove across the narrow bridge. The driveway was too muddy to attempt in their cruiser. As they got out of the car they noticed a woman leaving Margaret Joudrey's trailer.

"That's her, that's Jane Stafford," said Pike.

The woman was walking towards the house. She turned to the officers as they approached. She was a slim brunette of medium height with lightly freckled, attractive features. Pike did the talking.

"Mrs. Stafford?"

"Yes?"

"I'm sorry to bother you, but I have a few questions to ask you."

Jane Stafford nodded.

"When did you last see your husband?"

"He left in his truck last night," she answered softly. Pike noticed her eyes seemed somewhat vacant, that she was staring off into the distance.

"You haven't seen him since?"

"No."

"Did he have a gold watch?" She nodded yes.

"Do you remember what he was wearing?"

"Blue jeans. A light brown sweater."

"Work boots? A studded belt?" Again she nodded affirmatively.

"Mrs. Stafford, I'm sorry to inform you, we found your husband deceased in his truck this morning."

Jane Stafford fainted.

II

Peter Williamson first met Billy Stafford in the summer of 1977, shortly after Williamson was transferred to

Liverpool from the RCMP detachment in Chester, Nova
Scotia. Then forty years old, Williamson was soon to
take over the detachment as its staff sergeant. He was
working in a small office around a corner from the main
public reception area. Two female stenographers were
working at desks behind a counter set up for the public.
Billy stormed into the office in an ugly mood. The
women were taken aback when they looked up to see
him glaring at them across the counter. He stood slightly
over six feet tall and weighed over 250 pounds. He had
a broad face with a receding hairline. His thinning,
light brown hair was slicked back. He had protruding
eyes and thick lips. His moustache and long sideburns
were neatly trimmed.

"What in Christ is this notice you sent me suspending
my license?" he shouted.

"Do you wish to file a complaint?" asked one of the
women politely.

"These bastards are always after me," said Billy,
moving closer to the counter.

Williamson was out of sight of the counter but
within earshot. "I could hear him mouthing off and
yelling at the stenographers," he recalls.

At 220 pounds on a solid six-foot frame, Williamson
wasn't afraid of a scrap. His reputation for toughness
grew through his years with the RCMP. He was short-
tempered and good with his fists. Billy Stafford was
somewhat startled when Williamson appeared from around
the corner and in one motion vaulted across the counter
to face him toe-to-toe.

"You've got a bad mouth, mister," said Williamson,
his square jaw inches from Billy.

"You've got no goddamn right suspending my license again."

"You want to lodge a complaint, do it," said
Williamson with a growl. "But you're going out of here
fast or you're going to jail, and I don't need anyone to
help me put you there."

Billy Stafford glowered at Williamson but backed
away and turned for the door.

"He left cursing and swearing all the way out,"

recalls Williamson. "I was warned about Billy Stafford when I first came to Liverpool. Over the years it became an involvement with him, almost on a regular basis. Mostly he'd be driving without a license, or driving with too many points under the Motor Vehicle Act. He'd be suspended and then the boys would pick him up for driving when his suspension was in effect. He was well known and he was feared. He was an intimidating individual. He was a big man and he worked on that premise. He pretty well did what he wanted out there in Queens County. His neighbours feared him and they knew that if they went to the police, they'd have to go to court and then he might take some retribution later. He was very obnoxious and resented the law. When a summons was given to him, he'd just tear it up, leave it there, and then say, 'If I go, I go.' He never bothered me after that first confrontation and I had about seven big guys he stayed away from. We weren't afraid of Billy but we were cautious. We enforced the law. He wasn't blatant enough to come up and threaten us. He knew that we'd take him to court. He was sort of a bully."

Peter Williamson took Billy Stafford very seriously when it came to the safety of his men. Whenever he sent them to deliver a summons he ordered them to go in pairs and armed. 'I believe that Billy Stafford would be pushed to a certain point, or we would go out there sometime when he was under the influence of alcohol or whatever, and he would, no doubt in my mind, would have shot one of us. He was that type of individual. We knew he had a lot of loaded firearms."

Anyone who knew Billy Stafford well knew about his affinity for firearms. He had a reputation around Queens County as the ultimate "deer jacker," a hunter who shoots deer out of season, or without a license, or who exceeds the quota during the regulated deer season. Billy Stafford was generous with his seemingly endless supply of illegal venison. It found its way to many a table and freezer in the county. The RCMP and the provincial Lands and Forest Department were well aware of Billy's illegal activities, but he always managed to elude them. The one time he was charged for deer jacking he persuaded a friend to go to court and take the blame for killing the animal. The friend perjured himself and Billy got off.

Some friends of Billy Stafford say he always had a mean streak, but others, such as Calvin, Timothy, and Leslie Anthony, say he was kind and generous. Billy was close to their parents, Allen and Leona Anthony. When the two separated, Billy lived for a time with Allen Anthony and his sons in Milton. When the boys moved in with their mother at Mill Village on River Road, Billy was a regular visitor. Timothy was about eight years old and Leslie twelve when they first met Billy Stafford, then in his early thirties. Billy worked on ships sailing out of Liverpool, and when he returned from sea, he gave the boys money, as Timothy recalls, "to buy clothes and cigarettes and stuff." As the boys got older, they often went hunting with Billy. Timothy says as far back as he can remember Billy Stafford nearly always carried and used drugs. Calvin Anthony says Billy "used me pretty good" over the years—it was Calvin who lied in court to help get Billy acquitted on the charge of deer jacking.

Lamont William "Billy" Stafford was born on Thursday, February 13, 1941. But as he grew older, he claimed he was born on a Friday. He was the second oldest of five children, three girls and two boys, in the family of Lamont and Winnie Stafford. The couple later adopted a sixth child, a boy. The family lived in a modest but comfortable home in Liverpool's upper end. Lamont Stafford ran a successful scrap iron and "junkyard" business, eventually retiring to a larger home in nearby Hunt's Point.

Alfie Warrington knew Billy from the time they were children. "Billy and I used to work for his dad in the junk-collecting business. His dad used to give me a few bucks for helping once in a while. His was the only junkyard and I think he did pretty good at it." Today, Warrington does a bit of farming at his home in Middlefield, a hamlet on Highway 8 not far from Greenfield and Bangs Falls. He's been living on welfare and a small disability pension since 1974, when a drunk driver rammed his car, leaving him with permanently damaged disks in his back. "I've been unable to do much of anything since then." Warrington, a black, channels his energies into improving race relations in his province. He's a member of the Human Rights Commission, the Black United Front Movement and the Cultural Society in Dartmouth. When the news of Billy Stafford's grisly death spread through Queens County, Warrington says the first reaction was, "Oh, my God, isn't that awful." But the people who really knew him didn't say anything.

Warrington says he and Billy were friends "but he's always been sadistic." He recalled an incident in their late teens when he and Billy were riding in the rear of Lamont Stafford's truck. "We were helping his father, who had bought a bunch of strands of guy-wire ends. Billy started whipping them across my legs. I told him to stop because it hurt but he kept doing it. He didn't stop until I struck him with a piece of metal. After that he gave me a wide berth."

Billy Stafford had a strict upbringing. People who knew the family say that as he grew older Billy became abusive towards his parents, particularly his father.

In 1962, at age twenty-one, Billy Stafford married Pauline Oickle. She was pregnant by him at the time. Six years later, Pauline was granted a divorce on the grounds of cruelty. Billy had begun beating her soon after they moved into a small two-room apartment, and continued when they moved into her mother's home in Milton.

"He was very cruel to me in the six years that I was married to him," recalls Pauline, who now lives in Ontario. "He beat me quite often, with anything he could get ahold of—a beer bottle, broom handle . . . his fists, mostly. I was really afraid of him, so I more or less kept my mouth shut unless I was spoken to. I treated him as well as I could. Even with respect. . . even after the beatings I took and my children took. I always did everything that he wanted me to do because if I didn't, I knew what was going to happen."

Pauline and Billy Stafford had five children during their short marriage. Pauline was pregnant with her third child in 1964 when Billy administered a particularly severe beating. Billy had been drinking with Pauline's mother when he suddenly appeared on Pauline's side of the house and began beating his wife with his fists until her face was a bloody pulp. It was during the winter. Somehow Pauline managed to free herself of Billy's grasp and ran out into the snow wearing only slippers and a nightgown. "I ran down to my uncle's house with no jacket or nothing. By the time I got there I was in shock and they had to take me right to the hospital. My face was all cut and black and blue. He kicked me so bad they thought I was going to lose the baby, but I didn't."

Pauline Stafford laid asault charges against her husband, and photographs of her injuries were taken as evidence. She said she agreed to drop the charges against Billy when his father assured her that Billy had signed a peace bond ensuring that he wouldn't beat her again. Billy Stafford came home, and two weeks later the beatings resumed. They became progressively worse. He once tried to drown Pauline by submerging her head in a bucket of water. She credits her grandmother with once saving her life by pulling Billy off after he had choked her into unconsciousness. Pauline still bears marks on her body where Billy bit her. His pattern of violence became all too familiar to Pauline and her children. The beatings came whether Billy was drunk or sober, and the children, no matter how young, didn't escape his wrath.

"He could be nice one minute," says Pauline, "and the next minute he'd turn right on you and just start beating you for no reason at all. He would really get wild-looking. His eyes would be just glaring and the spit would fly and froth from his mouth. He never treated the children with love at all. I'd say from the time they were about six months old, he started beating them. When you put them to bed at night, they didn't dare cry or he'd go up and beat them, right in the crib. I think he just hated them all, yet I kept having a child every eleven months because I was not allowed to do anything to keep from getting pregnant. He wouldn't allow me to take the pill or anything. I used to say to myself after every beating that I was going to leave. But I was always in pretty bad shape so I more or less just stayed hid in the house."

Billy Stafford's brutality against his wife and children continued until the spring of 1968, when Pauline's cousin, who lived in Ontario, returned to Nova Scotia for a visit. The cousin, who hadn't seen Pauline in fifteen years, immediately realized what was going on in the Stafford household and told Pauline she could always come to stay with her in Ontario if she ever decided to leave Billy. Until then, Pauline, sickened by Billy's treatment of the children, knew she had to get out but had no place to go. She had watched helplessly as Billy sat the children on a stairway leading to a bedroom. He would light up cigarettes, stick them in their mouths, and make them sit there until the tobacco burned away. Then he forced them to eat the butts. He was particularly brutal to Elizabeth, their second oldest daughter. Pauline remembers Billy forcing the child to stand against the house while he threw knives at her to see how close he could come without hitting her. "And he used to sit her out on the back porch in the dark at night. Today she's still terrified in the dark. They were all terrified of him. As soon as he came home they all just went and sat. They had to sit there all day without moving. They couldn't even speak properly when they went to school."

The incident that pushed Pauline into leaving Billy occurred as he was leaving to work on the fishing boats one morning. She watched horrified as Billy took their youngest daughter, Darlene, into the backyard and beat her with a wooden rocker from a rocking chair. The small girl was lying on the ground face down with Billy's foot on her back. "He beat her from the waist down until she messed herself," recalls Pauline. Without a word, Billy picked up his seaman's bag and prepared to leave. Dutifully, Pauline went up to him and kissed him.

"Good-bye," she said. "I'll see you in two weeks."

Billy Stafford grunted and left. When he returned from sea his family was gone. Enraged, he beat Pauline's mother in an attempt to find out where she went with the children. A year later Pauline returned to Nova Scotia for a visit. Billy begged and pleaded with her to return to him. Pauline agreed to think it over. "But when I went back to Ontario, my cousin sat me down and talked to me. She said he would never change. So I just went out and started divorce proceedings." It was a decision she's never regretted.

By 1971, Billy Stafford was living common-law with another woman, Faith Hatt. Their relationship was to last two years. Initially, Billy treated Faith well and she saw no evidence of his dark side, but within a few months she became the victim of his unprovoked physical attacks. "For no apparent reason, he would take hold of me and pound me with his fists. You never knew. He could be good one minute and the next minute—snap! He actually frothed at the mouth when he came at me, like a mad dog. There were occasions that he beat me when he wasn't drinking, but most of the time it was when he was drinking."

Living with Billy Stafford's unpredictable moods was turning Faith Hatt into a nervous wreck. For her own sanity she knew she had to get out. Then she discovered she was pregnant, and she wasn't sure what to do. Billy decided for her one night when he returned from sea aboard a fishing boat. He and Faith were staying in a cabin adjoining his parents' house. She was three months pregnant. Billy was drinking heavily and all evening he verbally pestered Faith, asking her if there were something she'd forgotten to tell him, something she was withholding. Faith Hatt had no idea what he was talking about, but that didn't stop Billy. When they retired to the cabin "he kept dwelling on this and finally he started pounding on me and then he grabbed hold of me and started choking me." She believes Billy would've killed her, but he was so drunk she managed to free herself and run from the house. He chased her down the street, but she managed to elude him and stayed the night with a neighbour. The next day Faith's family scraped together enough money to pay her way out of town. "I knew I couldn't just break off with him and stay here in town because he probably would've haunted me to death." She moved all the way to Calgary and did not return to Liverpool for seven years.

Faith returned to live in Liverpool in the summer of 1979. She stayed with her sister while looking for an apartment or house for her and her young son, Rodney. On a warm July day, about two weeks after her arrival, Faith was driving to take a look at a place she'd heard about in nearby Brooklyn. She was startled when Billy Stafford pulled up beside her in his truck. "He started talking to me," recalls Faith, "and he said he wanted to see Rodney. I really didn't want him to. But I was back in town and I planned on staying and I didn't want any more trouble. So I figured the best thing to do was to let him see him. He saw Rodney one time and that was it."

Billy Stafford was pleased to think that he was born on Friday the thirteenth, even though it wasn't true. He said it was lucky for him. He often bragged that he was sent by the devil or that, in fact, he was the devil. He believed in astrology and horoscopes and kept a book handy to see what the stars held for him each day. At a fair in the town of Bridgewater, Billy once paid for a "personal" computerized handwriting analysis and horoscope reading. The computer said he was well adjusted mentally, easily influenced, secretive and idealistic, and philosophical and considerate. It described him as sarcastic and shrewd and not easily discouraged. It also said Billy had a magnetic personality with strong likes and dislikes. His dislike—hatred, really—of the RCMP was legendary in Queens County. "He was always on about them," remembers longtime friend Alfie Warrington. "He'd chew the heads right off them. He used to tell me that if they ever stepped a foot in his house, it would be the last time they stepped anywhere."

By his thirty-third year Billy Stafford had two broken relationships behind him and six children, none of whom he supported. He was a merchant seaman and looked the part. He was big and burly with crude tattoos on each forearm just below the elbow. A lot of people went out of their way to avoid him. Those who drank with him say he could be considerate and good-natured one minute and fly into a rage and take a swing at you the next. He had a reputation as a bully who preyed on people who feared him. One man who feared Billy Stafford was young Jimmy LeBlanc, a Liverpool fisherman who died mysteriously while out to sea aboard the *Mersey Enterprise*, a fishing vessel, in the winter of 1974. Billy Stafford was also aboard the boat on that trip. On February 14, the day after Billy's thirty-third birthday, it was reported that Jimmy LeBlanc either fell or jumped overboard. He was twenty years old. Billy Stafford bragged years later that he threw the young seaman over the side following a heated argument. He claimed that after the argument LeBlanc went into the galley to make up a mug of tea, and Billy went in behind him, dragged him out, and threw him overboard.

Jimmy LeBlanc was the second oldest of Myrna LeBlanc's six children. He was five feet, seven inches tall with a medium build. His mother remembers Jimmy telling her he was afraid of two people "and one of them was Billy Stafford. Jimmy told me a lot of people were afraid of Billy Stafford. I know my son did not commit suicide or fall overboard. Jimmy didn't know how to swim a stroke. There have been so many different stories over the years—if only somebody would come forward and tell me the truth."

There's been a distinct reluctance among the *Mersey Enterprise* crew members who were aboard that day to talk about Jimmy LeBlanc's death. The RCMP Liverpool detachment may reopen the investigation into the tragedy. Staff Sergeant Peter Williamson said that if the crew was intimidated into silence by Billy Stafford "that's one thing, but now that Billy's dead they'd better not be hiding the truth." For Myrna LeBlanc, whose husband deserted her and their six children twenty years ago, her son's death has been a nightmarish ordeal. "The day I found out, a neighbour called and asked me if it was true about Jimmy's death. I had to call Mersey Seafoods and ask if he'd drowned. They told me it was true. I had nothing in writing from them and I still have nothing. Even if I had a death certificate it would make it more real, even though in the back of your mind you know he's dead. I always think of him. He was quiet and shy and he would give you the shirt off his back. He was happy-go-lucky and he loved the woods and hunting. We've been a very poor family but we're a close family. I've always had a suspicion that Billy was involved in my son's death. When I heard about Billy's death, I looked up at Jimmy's picture on the wall. It was almost as if he was smiling—revenge at last."

III

January 25, 1949. The unforgiving North Atlantic smashed waves against the rugged Nova Scotia coast. It was a bitterly cold afternoon. In the small coastal town of Brooklyn, a few miles from Liverpool, Gladys and Maurice Hurshman were welcoming their second child into the world. They were pleased it was a girl, a sister for Douglas Edward, born sixteen months earlier. They named their daughter Jane. Her first recollections of their house in Brooklyn are of its huge size, and how cold it was in winter. There was no bathroom, no running water. Her father, who worked in a nearby sawmill, carried wood home on his back each night in the cold months. With the outbreak of the Korean War in June 1950, Maurice Hurshman joined the Canadian Army and after basic training was sent to Korea to help fight the Chinese and North Koreans. He served thirteen-month and six-month stints before returning home

permanently in 1952. He decided to remain in the
army, and because he liked to cook, eventually became
an army chef. Two more children were born to the
Hurshmans during their stay in Brooklyn: Mona Dianne
in April 1953, and Sandra Rose ten months later.

When Jane was five years old, she was exposed to a
side of her father's nature she was unfamiliar with. The
day began happily enough when her mother took her
and her brother to see their first movie. It featured the
Three Stooges and the zany, make-believe violence that
kids then and now seem so taken with. But what Jane
saw that day when she left the movie house was anything but make-believe.

"There was a commotion taking place outside. It
was my father fighting with the town cops. They were
trying to get him in their car to take him to jail. He'd
been fighting in a restaurant. I'm sure that's when I had
my first feelings of being a lost little girl—not knowing
what to do or where to go. I was very frightened and
confused. I didn't know who was hurting who. All I
know is that they were taking my daddy away."

Life in the Canadian Army usually meant a lot of
moving around. It was no exception for Maurice
Hurshman and his family. In May 1954, he was transferred to the base at Truro in north-central Nova Scotia
near the head of Cobequid Bay, an arm of the Bay of
Fundy. A railway, lumber, and factory town, it was
formerly an Acadian settlement called Cobequid. The
Acadians were expelled and the town destroyed in
1755. A few years later, settlers arrived from New
England and Northern Ireland. They named the town
for Truro, England. The Hurshmans lived off the base
in a two-storey house with a spacious backyard. Jane
remembers a wide staircase leading to the upstairs
bedrooms. Her brother had his own bedroom, and Jane
and her little sisters shared another. The wide staircase
became Jane's favorite place, a hideout of sorts.

Jane's father drank more heavily in Truro, and it
made him irritable, unpredictable, and often mean.
Soon he began beating his wife. He never abused his
children, but Jane remembers, "He was very strict with

us. We couldn't leave things lying around or out of place. At night I used to sit alone on the stairway, especially when they were fighting. I could see them but they couldn't see me. He would stay up all night drinking, go to work, do his job, and come home and start the vicious cycle again."

Whatever his faults, Maurice Hurshman saw to it his family was never hungry or without proper clothing. With four children, money was tight—their clothing usually was secondhand, purchased from a thrift shop. Gladys Hurshman was an accomplished seamstress and often made her children outfits from old clothes. Jane was tickled one day when her parents bought her a new blue dress and white knee stockings. She smiled about it all day. That night, she heard her parents fighting and came out to sit in her secret spot on the stairway. When the fighting and shouting ended, Jane went to bed, forgetting her new stockings on the stairs. Her father found them there later and burned them in the woodstove. He told Jane it was her fault for not putting them away.

In Truro Jane began her schooling in a two-room schoolhouse where grades one to eight were taught. It was new and exciting, and she took to it immediately. She loved to learn and study, and she wanted desperately to please her teacher. She often volunteered to clean the boards and brushes after school. She liked the praise that came with the chore. It made her feel needed and loved. That feeling was short-lived. Jane was caught up in the anticipation that first graders feel with the approach of Christmas. Her teacher talked about decorating the classroom and brought out a bundle of Christmas cards to be used for that purpose. Jane stayed on after the bell rang to clean the boards and brushes as she usually did. The Christmas cards were lying invitingly on the teacher's desk. Jane was dazzled by the bright colours. She wanted to display them, to share her pleasure with her fellow students, and, most important, to please the teacher. She noticed a bottle of glue on the teacher's desk and stuck all the cards to the blackboard. She was brimming with pride. She couldn't wait to see how happy everyone would be when they saw the cards the next morning. But nothing was said and the teacher didn't look at all happy.

"Would whomever put these cards on the board please come up here," said the teacher, unsmiling. "I have something for you."

Jane, somewhat confused by the sombre mood, stood and walked to the front of the class.

"I did it. Aren't they beautiful?" she asked.

The teacher stared at her coldly and without a word, reached for the strap in her desk drawer. Six-year-old Jane was dismayed, hurt, and bewildered. "She never explained why I was being punished. I wouldn't cry. I just went back and took my seat and did my work. I never told my parents that I got a strapping. I vowed at that time that I'd never get another one, and I never did." Jane had the same teacher for three years, and for three years she tried to make up for a wrongdoing she didn't understand. She was an honour student but she stopped trusting people and became quiet and withdrawn. Never again did she volunteer to help out around the school.

Jane cherishes her few fond memories of the three years the family spent in Truro. "Mom used to take us picking blueberries. We would pick all day and then sell the berries. We were never given allowances, so the berries provided us with some spending money. Sometimes in the winter we helped make ice cream. Those were the nice times but they were very scarce." She had no regrets when, in 1957, the family was transferred again, this time to Camp Gagetown in neighbouring New Brunswick. They moved into a three-bedroom brick bungalow with hardwood floors. Her mother kept it spotless and filled it with plants. The best thing, from Jane's point of view, was the army school on the base. It was much larger than the school in Truro, and each grade had its own teacher. There was even a gymnasium. Jane continued to reap A's, and she excelled in gym class. She became an avid reader and began studying French. There were even pluses in her home life. Her parents bought her her first bicycle, a solid secondhand one with a large frame. Jane was very proud of it.

About the same time, another army family moved in next door. They had a daughter, Valery, who was Jane's age. What Jane found unique about Valery's family was that her parents didn't drink, smoke, or fight. She loved visiting their house, and she and Valery became inseparable.

Her friend's home became an oasis for Jane, a respite from the continuing violence and pain in the Hurshman household and in the homes of many of their friends and acquaintances. Drinking, arguing, and physical abuse were commonplace. "Except for Val's parents, it seemed everybody we knew lived that way. There were all-night drinking sessions and poker games with Dad and a group of men. There was always loud music playing."

During one poker game a neighbour, obviously drunk, declared he was going out to get something to eat. He was killed instantly when his car slammed head-on into a truck. He left behind a wife and six children. Jane sensed the depth of the tragedy—the waste. "I was sad, yet I was secretly thinking, 'Now maybe Dad can see what drinking can do. Maybe he'll stop.' But he never did."

Jane never felt prouder of her parents than the night they dressed up in their finest clothes to attend a dance. They weren't arguing when they left the house, and Jane thought they were about the most beautiful couple she'd ever seen. But when she heard them come in a few hours later, her father was cursing in a loud voice. "They just got in the door and he ripped Mom's dress almost off. He pushed her to the floor and was cursing at her and hitting her." Gladys Hurshman pleaded with her husband to stop. She was crying and worried he would awaken the children.

"Fuck the kids!" shouted Maurice Hurshman, striking her again.

Jane and her brother ran downstairs, pleading with their father to leave their mother alone.

"Get the hell in your beds where you belong!" he ordered.

The children retreated to their rooms. Jane was ten or eleven at the time. She shared a double bed with her younger sisters. "I went in and they were crying, wanting to know what was happening. I held them and kissed them and sang to them." Usually when Jane's father abused her mother, she took her sisters to the basement. "I don't know why. It just seemed to be safe there. I never wanted them to see what was going on. So we sat in the basement. I held them and sang to them until there was no more fighting or noise. I always sang the same song. They still know it today." The song:

> One fateful night, the car was stopped
> Upon the railroad track.
> I put you out and you were safe,
> Yet you came running back.
> Sweetest angels, can you hear us?
> Sweetest angels, can you see us?
> Are you somewhere up above?
> Are we still your own true love?
> Sweetest angels, sweetest angels,
> Answer us please!

Maurice Hurshman's violence wasn't restricted to his wife. Jane remembers a military police van in the yard of their home at the Gagetown base one afternoon after school. The police were forcing her father into the van.

"Where are they taking you?" asked Jane.

Her father stared at her hesitantly.

"Good-bye," he said with a sigh.

Running into the house, Jane asked her mother what was happening.

"Your father is just going away on a scheme again for a while."

"Scheme" was a euphemism for manoeuvres. Jane learned later her father had struck an officer in a fight. Sending him off on manoeuvres was his punishment. Seeing her father whisked away by police was traumatic for such a young girl. She felt a sense of loss, even though his absence meant temporary peace in the Hurshman household. Equally devastating for Jane was the departure of her best friend, Valery, whose father was transferred to the Canadian forces base at Hemer, West Germany. The two had been closer than sisters, sharing their innermost secrets. They'd even found pleasure in New Brunswick's soft summer rains. "We'd get out our bathing suits and play in the rain. I can remember how nice it felt, hitting my hot skin. It made me feel new—all fresh and clean. To this day I love walking in the rain."

As it turned out, the loss of her friend was temporary. A month after Valery left, the Hurshmans found themselves on their way to the same Canadian base in Germany. The family sailed to Europe from Québec. Jane had never been on a ship, but her excitement waned just hours out to sea. She took to her bed, severely seasick, and remained there for most of the eleven-day journey. "The doctor gave me a needle every so often. We hit the tail end of a hurricane and I thought the boat would sink. Everything got thrown around and broken. It was then I realized how powerful the ocean is. I have great respect for it. It fascinates me. To this day I can't swim and I won't go in any boats, big or small."

The ship landed in Southampton, England. Travelling by train to the Channel, across France, and into Germany, the family carried only their personal belongings. Their apartment at Hemer was in a long row of grey cement buildings. The austere uniformity wasn't restricted to the exterior. Inside, each apartment was laid out exactly the same and identically furnished, right down to the curtains and bedding. Each apartment had a balcony, small kitchen, dining room, living room, and three bedrooms. Jane's parents had one room, her brother another, and she and her sisters shared the third.

The Hurshmans had no television, no telephone, and no car—but for a drinking man the place was a godsend. Across the street was a pub where beer was cheaper than soft drinks; to have beer delivered the Hurshmans had only to place a card in the window. "The beer truck always stopped at our place," recalls Jane. "The card was a permanent fixture in our kitchen window." Servicemen were also issued ration cards entitling them to purchase liquor and cigarettes duty-free on the base.

Jane was happy to find Valery living in the same complex. It also proved to be a bonus for Maurice Hurshman. Since Valery's parents didn't drink or smoke, they gave him their ration cards. His supply of tobacco and alcohol was virtually limitless. Jane remembers her father often being drunk, and he always had friends in drinking. He bought a floor-model stereo and played loud music constantly. When he wasn't drinking at home, he was drinking in the pub.

Like the pub, Jane's school was directly across the street from their apartment building. The school was "huge and beautiful," with a winding staircase leading up from the main entrance, its black wrought-iron railing festooned with plants. The Hurshmans stayed in Germany for three and a half years, which for Jane meant grades seven through nine. Academically, she continued to excel. She took up volleyball and basket-ball, but her favourite sport was cross-country running. She won several ribbons and medals.

During one track and field meet involving schools from Canadian bases at Hemer, Soest, and Werl, Jane's basketball team won a first-place ribbon; her volleyball team a second-place ribbon; and she won a medal for placing second against one hundred competitors in a seven-mile cross-country run. Jane started a diary in which she kept her ribbons and medals and recorded her most personal thoughts. During the school year she picked up extra money by baby-sitting and by "washing heads" and cleaning floors and sinks at a hairdressing shop. A lot of her income was spent on Elvis Presley and Beatles records, but she wasn't allowed to use her dad's record player to play her music. On weekends, Jane and Valery often went into the record shop in Hemer, where they chose several records at a time, took them into a booth, put on earphones, and listened to their favourite songs.

Jane became fluent in German, and in the summers found light work in a factory. Jane and Valery spent a lot of time in a teenagers' hangout called the Slop Shop. It was at the rear of a pub owned by a German family. As they got older, the inseparable friends began travelling on their own. "We used to catch a bus or train, with no specific destination in mind, and just go. We travelled all over Germany that way. We even went by bus to Holland several times, exploring old castles and caves." Friends who owned a car once took the Hurshman family on a day trip to a castle and huge dam. It was the only family outing Jane remembers. While working at the hairdressing shop one day after school, Jane asked if she could have her hair done in lieu of pay. They back-combed her hair, which was the style then, and applied a touch of makeup. "They transformed me into a new person. I went home and went right into the bathroom, where I stood gazing at myself in the mirror and thinking how pretty I looked. Dad was drinking as usual. I could hear music and men talking. Mom was running around waiting on them hand and foot. I walked into the room hoping that someone would comment on how nice I looked." Her father looked at her.

"Who in hell do you think you are?" he yelled. "You made-up whore, get in that bathroom and wash that shit off your face and comb your hair."

Jane was fourteen years old. She was hurt and humiliated. "My mother has never in her life worn anything but lipstick. And to this day I seldom wear makeup. When I do, there's so little, it's barely visible. That's how much of an impression that day made on me."

A few days after that incident, Gladys Hurshman entered Jane's bedroom and handed her a brown paper bag.

"Hide this in your closet. You'll need it soon if you don't already," said her mother in a hushed voice.

"What is it?" asked Jane.

"You'll know someday."

Jane closed the door and opened the bag. Inside was a sanitary napkin and belt. "I didn't know what they were for but I thought they must be bad because my mother told me to hide them." Several months later at Valery's house Jane didn't feel well and she went into the bathroom. "When I saw all the blood I thought I had some disease and was going to die. I stuffed toilet paper in my panties and ran home." Lying on her bed, she wondered what was wrong with her. The bleeding continued at school the next day. For the first time ever, she asked to be excused from gym class.

"You don't look very well. Are you sick?" asked her teacher.

"I'm bleeding and I'm going to die."

Comforting her, the teacher explained what was happening.

The drinking and abuse continued unabated in the Hurshman household. Returning from school one afternoon, Jane heard her father shouting. She bent down and peered through the mail slot in the front door. "Dad was drunk and had vomited all over everything. He was yelling at Mom to 'clean up this Jesus mess.' Mom, as usual, did what he ordered." Jane sat outside on the steps praying silently: "Oh, Lord, please let it get better. I can't stand this." Moments later her father staggered out of the house and slumped down on the step beside her. Eyes glazed, he stared at Jane.

"I hate you!" he suddenly declared.

Jane sat stunned. "I like to believe he was so drunk he didn't know who he was talking to or what he was saying. But at the time, and for years to come, it left an awful impact. I thought, 'If my own father hates me, then who will ever love me?'"

Maurice Hurshman had a younger brother, James, who had come to live with them during their stay in Gagetown. He was eight years Jane's senior. She looked up to him and thought of him as a big brother. He later joined the Canadian Army's Black Watch. Jane hadn't seen him since the family left Canada. She was baby-sitting one night at the Hemer base when there was a knock at the door. It was her uncle James in full uniform, including a kilt. "I opened the door and got the biggest hug . . . I was so happy to see him. He had a male friend with him." Jane allowed Sandy and Mona to get up and see their uncle.

When the girls returned to bed, James and his friend began drinking. She was shocked. She'd never seen Jim drink before. He seemed different. He fell asleep. Jane's parents were partying up the street at a neighbour's apartment. She joined her sisters in their room and locked the door. Before long, there was a knock on the bedroom door. It was Jim's friend, and he wanted in. He banged loudly on the door, and Sandy and Mona began crying. Jane quieted her sisters and told them to hide under the bed. She was terrified. Somehow she found the strength to push and pull a large wardrobe against the door. She told the girls she was going for help. Directly below the bedroom window was a stairway leading to the basement of the apartment building. Climbing out the window, Jane tried to balance herself on the thin steel railing around the stairwell. If she slipped, she would fall to the cement stairs below. Somehow in the darkness she managed to climb down and ran to the neighbours to get help.

"Dad was drinking. I told him what was happening and he left in a rage. The guy had the bedroom door open and was pushing his way into the room when Dad arrived. The kids were terrified but they remained silent, still hiding under the bed. Dad grabbed hold of the guy and threw him down the apartment steps and out of the building. Dad was raving mad at Jim, who was awakened by the noise but didn't have a clue about what had happened." Jane snuggled into bed with Sandy and Mona. By this time, the party had moved to the Hurshmans' apartment. Jane knew it was going to be another long night when she heard her father shout to her mother, "Get me a drink, squaw, and get some music playing."

Jane considered her mother to be the backbone of the family and, even though she seldom expressed outward affection, "it seems as if we knew she loved us. She made sure we went to Sunday school and church. She always had a strong belief in God, and she instilled that belief in us. I feel certain that God always had a special angel watching over my mother."

Returning from school one day, Jane found her mother in bed, which was most unusual. She was too ill to get up. Her body was hot and the bedclothes were soaked in blood. Maurice Hurshman arrived shortly after Jane.

"Jesus Christ!" he said. "What the hell happened?"

He rushed his wife to the hospital. Jane stayed behind to look after her sisters and prepare supper. There was no telephone, so she had no way of checking on her mother's condition. She put Mona and Sandy to bed and waited, her insides churning. Later in the evening she kept her mind occupied by reading to her sisters in bed. She heard a car pull up and her father's voice. Fearing he might be drunk, Jane stayed in the bedroom. She heard him talking and thought he'd brought someone with him. She listened intently but heard only his voice. It was then she realized Maurice Hurshman was praying; she never forgot his words: "Dear God, let Gladie live, please. I don't know what I'd do without her. I love her and I'll never lay a hand on her again."

Gladys Hurshman suffered a tubal pregnancy. The doctors were afraid the massive bleeding would induce shock and death. Later that night there was a knock on the Hurshman door. Jane heard a male voice urging her father to go immediately to the hospital. They didn't think his wife would live through the night. Jane stifled a sob and did her own praying as her father left the apartment for the hospital.

Gladys Hurshman recovered and was home in a few days. Jane can't remember her father ever striking her mother again. The drinking, cursing, and arguing continued, but there was no more physical abuse.

Jane was fifteen when she left Germany. During her last eight months overseas she had a boyfriend, Joe. He was in the service and was several years her senior.

She met him at a Salvation Army recreation centre and restaurant set up for Canadian servicemen and their families. Joe had a motorcycle and a car. Jane was impressed. She wasn't supposed to date Joe but she did anyway. She loved riding with him on his motorcycle. It gave her a feeling of freedom. Joe was good-natured and made her happy. "We often drove—no place in particular. We walked in the rain, talked about anything and everything. He would hold my face in his hands and kiss me ever so gently, as if I might break." On Jane's fifteenth birthday, Joe threw a party for her at a pub, complete with birthday cake and candles. He gave her a delicate watch, which she cherishes to this day. When Jane arrived at home that evening she showed the watch to her mother.

"My boyfriend gave it to me," she said proudly.

"Don't tell your father."

Her father stormed into the room. "Don't tell your father what?" he demanded.

"Jane has a boyfriend and he just gave her a watch for her birthday."

Maurice Hurshman eyed his daughter.

"And what did you give him in return?" he asked curtly.

Jane didn't understand the question.

"We've got two more weeks over here," said her father. "Then we go back to Canada. You're grounded until we leave."

Jane was crushed. Joe was waiting for her the next day after school. "I told him what had happened. He was as heartbroken as I was. For the next three days I played hookey. Joe would pick me up in the afternoon and we just drove around on his motorcycle." When she came home for dinner on the third day, Jane knew she was in trouble. Her father was sitting at the table, her brother Douglas beside him.

"Just ask her, Dad; just ask her," said her brother. "She hasn't been to school in the last three afternoons. I saw her get on that guy's motorcycle and drive away."

"Is it true?" asked her father sternly.

"Yes, it's true," said Jane.

Her father removed his belt. "That was the only time my dad beat me. I was so hurt. I felt so defeated but I wouldn't give him the satisfaction of crying." When Joe arrived at school during the noon break the next day, Jane explained what had happened. He was close to tears.

"I'll stay away," he said. "I don't want you to be punished for seeing me."

But Jane wanted to see him again, more than anything she'd ever wanted in her life. They made plans to meet on the coming Saturday night—her last night in Germany. "As usual, Dad was drinking that night. I put Sandy and Mona to bed early. I told them I was going to sneak out the window to see Joe. They agreed not to tell. Joe was waiting for me down the street. There was a heavy mist in the air, but it was warm." They drove into the country in his car, stopping on a deserted cobblestone road. They left the car and walked in silence. There were grassy fields on either side of the road. "So much was passing between us without a word being said. I asked him to hold me and kiss me. He lifted me right up in his arms and kissed me while he was still walking along." They stopped and stared into each other's eyes.

"Joe, will you make love to me?" asked Jane softly.

"Janey, you're so very special, so pure. I can't hurt you like that."

"Please, Joe, I want one good memory to last me forever."

Jane could feel her heart pounding when he laid her down in the damp, soft grass. They made love in the darkness. "I was a virgin; it wasn't what I expected it to be. It hurt a lot. I wanted to cry but I didn't. I told him it was nice." Afterwards, Joe held her gently in his arms.

"I love you, Janey," he whispered. "I'll be returning to Canada in six months and we'll be together again."

"I can't wait for that day."

Arriving back home, Jane asked Joe to come in, not knowing what to expect. He agreed. "My dad was still drinking, but he appeared to be in a good mood. I was so happy that Dad didn't make a scene. I don't even remember the conversation. I was so proud to have Joe sitting beside me. My mind kept flashing back to what we'd done earlier. I wondered if anyone could tell by looking at me." Joe stayed about an hour and Jane walked him to the door. He kissed her gently on the lips.

"Good night, my angel," he whispered. "I'll see you tomorrow before you leave."

On the morning of February 5, 1964, the Hurshman family's belongings were packed and ready to be loaded on the bus that would take them to the airport. There was no sign of Joe. Jane waited anxiously, but he wasn't there when the bus arrived. It was a cold, grey, rainy day. Jane felt deep sadness on the bus. "I didn't want to board that plane. It was going to take me away from the only person who ever said he loved me." There was a large crowd at the airport. Jane heard a voice calling her name. "I searched the faces and there stood Joe. I was so happy. We said our good-byes in the rain, with Joe reassuring me that he would write and we'd be together again when he returned to Canada."

Maurice Hurshman's new posting was at the Canadian Army base at Winnipeg, Manitoba. The family flew from Germany to Trenton, Ontario, where they were put up in a motel for two days before catching a train to Winnipeg. Jane remembers stuffing herself with treats that were unavailable in Germany. They ate a lot of ice cream, banana splits, and red licorice and spent considerable time before the television set. Jane remembers watching *The Beverly Hillbillies* for the first time.

The train trip from Trenton to Winnipeg was a nightmare for the Hurshman family. The army bungled their reservations and they were forced to share a single compartment. Jane was crushed between her brother and sisters and slept fitfully on the overnight journey.

It was still dark when they arrived in Winnipeg. It was the heart of winter. The snow was deep and the temperature was forty below zero. Jane had never experienced such cold. "I couldn't breathe. The air was so cold it hurt to take a breath. I thought I was going to die. We weren't prepared at all. We were dressed in spring clothing. The winters in Germany weren't near as cold. At that moment I began hating Winnipeg."

There was no room for the family on the army base, and they were forced to live in a motel with housekeeping units for a month. There was no respite from the subzero temperatures, and Jane's breathing problems continued. "We all thought it was just the weather, until one morning I bent over to tie my shoe; the pain was more than I could stand. Mom took me to a clinic where they found I had three fractured ribs." The ribs were fractured in the cramped compartment on the train nearly three weeks earlier. "They strapped my ribs up with tape and I can remember the doctor saying, 'Young lady, you sure must have a high pain threshold.' At the time I didn't know what the doctor meant, but I was to find out in the years to come."

After a month of searching, Maurice Hurshman found a four-bedroom house for his family off the base in the city. Jane had her own bedroom for the first time. Although happy to have her own room, she missed the company of her younger sisters and the comfort they had provided each other each night for as long as she could remember.

Jane wrote often to Joe in Germany, but until they found a house and a permanent address, he couldn't respond. "When I sent him my new address, I got a beautiful letter from him and a pair of white leather boots. I had admired them once in a shop window in Germany. It made me so happy. But it was the first and last time I heard from Joe. I put his letter in my diary. I still wrote him but never got a reply. I figured he had just forgotten about me. I was very hurt."

In Winnipeg, Gladys Hurshman found a job doing housework. "It was the first time she ever had a job. It was different, coming home and Mom not being there. I used to make lunch for the kids and I'd have supper started by the time she got home. It must have been difficult for her, walking to and from work in all that cold."

Jane began feeling desperate and lonely. Because she lived off the army base she enrolled, midway through the year, in a civilian high school. Joe wasn't writing to her, and although her friend Valery had moved to Winnipeg when her family was also transferred from Germany, she lived on the base and went to school there. "I didn't see much of her. For the first time ever I hated to go to school. I just didn't fit in. Everything just seemed so wrong, and I was so very lonely. Once again I started feeling like that lost little girl. I kept up my grades at school but I never made any friends there. I knew my marks were good, so I never worried about passing. It was sure a shock and surprise when I got my report card in June 1964 and it said I failed. I couldn't believe it. That was the last straw. I wasn't the only one who failed that year. They failed everyone who came back from Germany. They said they failed us because we were behind a year, according to their standards. To me it was just a feeble excuse."

Spring sunshine melted the snow and warmed winter-weary bones but did nothing to soothe Jane's disappointment over failing. She felt trapped in an unhappy home life with no friends. She wanted out, and when she saw a way, she jumped at it. "Some friends of Mom's and Dad's were being transferred to Nova Scotia, and I wanted very much to go. It was summer now and the summer in Winnipeg was as hot as the winter was cold. Mom and Dad said. I could go—at least for the summer. When Dad came to the train station to see me off, I knew in my heart I'd never return there to live." The couple Jane travelled with had two young sons. She looked after them on the long trip to Nova Scotia, while their parents drank and fought. They were both drinkers, but the husband was an alcoholic who often beat his wife. They went as far as Kentville, Nova Scotia. Jane stayed with them a few days, "but it was just one big drunk with lots of physical abuse on the part of the husband to his wife. Eventually one of his relatives drove me to my grandmother's house in Liverpool. I remember thinking when I arrived, 'I'm in a safe place now.'"

IV

Jane's "safe place" was the home of her paternal grandmother, Mildred Hurshman, known affectionately as Gramma Mill. She was an energetic, stocky woman who lived in a large house in Liverpool. A path from the house leads through a gentle, tree-covered slope across a rail line to the rocky shoreline, where the Mersey River empties into the Atlantic Ocean. Salt water from the ocean mixes with the fresh river water, making children's bodies more buoyant when they jump from the nearby train trestle during the warm summer months. Gramma Mill worked at a nursing home, usually in the evenings. She was separated from her husband and lived with a fisherman, big George Whynot, who operated his own boat out of Liverpool. Jane remembers George being more of a grandfather to her than her real grandfather. She had her own room in the house, and Gramma Mill, who loved to bake, always prepared hearty meals.

Jane spent a lot of quiet moments sitting on the rocky shore watching the tide. Sometimes she walked along the shore to a small sandy cove. Big George, Gramma Mill, and Jane lived downstairs in the house. Her Uncle James, whom she hadn't seen since Germany, lived upstairs with his wife and young son. James was out of the service and worked on a Liverpool scallop dragger. The house was a gathering point for many of James's fishing and drinking buddies.

At one of James's parties Jane met a man we'll call Marty for this book. Nine years her senior, Marty owned his own car and reminded Jane of Joe, the boyfriend she'd left behind in Germany.

"He was a nice-looking, quietly spoken, very talented man. He filled a very lonely spot in my life. I needed him—needed someone. He happened to be the one to come along. He told me he cared. I'm sure I would've clung to anyone who showed interest or affection. I don't honestly know if I loved him or not. I was still a child myself. When I first went out with Marty he took me to visit friends of his—a married couple. There was drinking but it was a different kind of drinking. Everyone was happy and having a good time. There was no fighting, no hollering, no abuse of any kind. Marty could play any kind of stringed instrument, and he could sing very well. It was all very nice. We went to a lot of house parties like that one. Marty had a very placid nature. It wasn't in him to be violent or abusive. His grandparents raised him as if he was their own son. They were devoted to him and they catered to his every wish. When I started going with him he had a good job at the Power Commission. His grandmother was the real motherly type and I got along with her very well. She never drank or smoked. His grandfather had quit drinking years before, and they didn't allow any drinking in their house. That was a form of security for me. They had a big house which was well maintained, but it had no bathroom or running water. It was heated by a woodstove. I loved going there. It was homey."

Jane began dating Marty on a regular basis. The first time they had intercourse was in his car. He'd been drinking. When it was over, Marty asked Jane if she'd "come." She had no idea what he was talking about "but I figured I was supposed to say 'yes,' so that's what I said."

There was a county fair that summer of 1964. It was at Caledonia, about twenty-five miles from Liverpool. Marty asked Jane to go as his date. Jane asked Gramma Mill if she could go. She was shocked by the response.

"No, you can't go," she said sternly. "And I don't want you to see Marty anymore. I'm going to write your parents and tell them you're being bad and I don't want you here anymore."

Jane promised not to see Marty again. She didn't want

to return to Winnipeg. But she had no intention of keeping her promise and saw Marty whenever she could. In September she started back to school, repeating ninth grade.

"Mill knew I was still seeing Marty. I came home one evening and went directly to my room. I'd been out with Marty and we'd had sex. I didn't want to face anyone. When I entered my room, I saw my diary laying on top of my dresser. I knew someone had been at it. I was so very hurt. I felt I'd been violated. My diary was sacred to me, and now even that wasn't mine alone anymore. I couldn't accept that Mill had actually read my diary. But I knew it was her. My hurt turned to anger and I ripped up every page and threw them and my ribbons and medals from Germany into the garbage. When I went into the living room Mill was trying to get in touch with Mom and Dad by phone. I didn't say a word to her. I just went back to my room and packed up my belongings and hid them under the bed. Then I laid down and waited for morning to come."

Jane's maternal grandparents, George and Ger trude Westhaver, lived nearby, across the railway tracks. She arrived on their doorstep with her suitcase the next morning. "I told them what had happened and asked them if I could live there. They'd had hard times. My grandfather didn't work, and their house was small—it had no bathroom or running water. There were still four boys and a girl living at home, yet they said I could move in.

"My grandma was a tiny, very quiet, hardworking woman; much like my own mother. She would always do without to give to us kids. My grandpa, who I always called George, was a big man with a deep, loud voice. When he spoke, you listened. He drank a bottle of wine every day, but I never once saw him get violent or abusive. He would just drink his wine and go sleep it off. They were very poor but they were good to me. Freddy was the youngest of their boys and he and I became very close. He was six years younger than me. We played a sort of a game every day when we walked to school. We always asked each other what would be the first thing we'd do when we grew up. He always said he'd never eat bologna and I said I was going to have a padded toilet seat—no more rough boards or splinters in my bum. We'd always laugh but Freddy doesn't eat bologna anymore, and when I got my first bathroom in 1980, the toilet had a padded seat."

The Westhavers didn't mind her dating Marty. He was allowed to come to their house to pick her up for dates. On school nights she had to be in by 10:00 P.M. Marty often brought a bottle of wine over for George, and the two of them would sit and talk while he drank it. Jane felt secure and content—part of the family. Then came a surprising letter from her mother. Joe had returned from Germany and had come to Winnipeg to visit her. "He told Mom he hadn't written to me because he'd been involved in a serious motorcycle accident and was hospitalized for a long time. I don't know what I felt when I read that letter but I knew I didn't want to go to Winnipeg ever again and I was involved with Marty. That was the last I ever heard about Joe. I still think of him every so often. I hope he has a happy life, wherever he is."

Other letters passed between Winnipeg and Halifax. Gramma Mill became vindictive towards Jane, even though she no longer lived with her. "She wrote my parents and told them I was running wild with an older man. She told some terrible lies about Marty." Gramma Mill claimed Marty impregnated a fourteen-year-old girl and then abandoned her. Gramma Mill also claimed he had syphilis. "I got a letter from Mom telling me I had to come home because of what Mill had told her. I told Marty what was going on and he was very hurt, very upset with Mill. He even went to a doctor to prove her wrong. It was all a pack of lies." Jane wrote her mother and assured her the stories were not true and that she had no intention of returning to Winnipeg.

Two months after her sixteenth birthday, a doctor confirmed Jane was pregnant. She was numbed by the news and worried how Marty might react. His grandparents left that weekend to visit their daughter in Halifax. Marty asked Jane to spend the weekend with him. They were lying in his bed in the darkness on a Friday night.

"Marty, I went to the doctor today and he said I'm going to have a baby."

Jane couldn't see his face. He was silent for several minutes.

"Well that's something, ain't it," he said finally. "I guess I have to marry you. When do you want to get married?"

"I don't know. When do you think we should?"

"I dunno either. Go to sleep now and I'll decide tomorrow."

Marty fell immediately to sleep. Jane lay awake, thoughts and questions bombarding her mind. "How was I going to tell Mom and Dad? What would I do with a baby? Would I be a good mother? I knew I wanted this baby very much. It would be mine and I would love it."

In the morning, Jane called her mother. It was their first conversation since her departure from Winnipeg the previous summer. Her father wasn't home. He was on a six-month posting at the Canadian forces base at Alert in the Northwest Territories, two hundred miles from the North Pole. "I told Mom I was pregnant and we were getting married. She said she'd write and tell Dad." Her mother asked when the wedding would take place. Marty checked the calendar and decided on Saturday, April 24. She told her mother the date and that was the end of the conversation. They broke the news to Marty's grandparents when they returned from Halifax Sunday afternoon. They hugged her, and Marty drove Jane home to tell her grandparents.

"Does your mother know?" asked her grandmother.

"Yes, I called her and she said it was okay."

It was settled and Jane was relieved. She went to school until the day before the wedding. "Marty took care of everything. His sister loaned me a blue dress. Marty bought me some flowers, and my Aunt Judy and her new husband stood up for us." They were married at 7:00 P.M. at a minister's house. Friends of Marty gave them a small reception in their apartment. Jane didn't know most of the people and she doesn't remember who held the reception. Neither Marty's grandparents nor Jane's parents attended the wedding—nor did they send gifts. Marty got drunk at the reception. They went back to his grandparents' house and went to bed. Marty vomited and immediately fell asleep. Jane lay in bed thinking about her life. She didn't really know what love was or what the future held. "I was pregnant. When you got pregnant, you got married. You make your bed; you lie in it and make the best of it. I didn't blame anyone. I was going to be a mother and Marty a father."

Jane and Marty moved in with his grandparents. The baby wasn't due until October. The ensuing six months were uneventful and boring for Jane. Marty's grandmother did everything for him. It was as if he didn't have a wife. She made up his lunchbox for work; made his breakfast in the mornings and even woke him to get ready for work. She did all the housework. Jane got up when Marty did and made the bed. That was the extent of her chores. Marty turned his paycheck over to his grandmother. She paid whatever bills he owed and gave him the rest. He didn't give Jane any money unless she asked for it, which she seldom did. "I really didn't need any. I had plenty to eat, clothes on my back, and a roof over my head. I felt I was just there as a convenience for Marty—giving him sex whenever he wanted it." Jane centered her existence on her baby. She weighed only ninety-eight pounds the day she was married but she didn't begin to show until her last two months. As her pregnancy progressed, Marty ignored her more and more. Being married didn't change his life-style. He came and went as he pleased. Sometime he asked Jane to go with him, but usually he went alone. When she asked him where he was going or who he was with, Marty would say, "It's none of your business."

Jane knew she would love her child, but she was also looking forward to the birth to end the monotony of her day-to-day existence. "I needed something to fill the growing void inside me. I didn't know anything about having babies and I didn't know anybody I could ask about it. I didn't know what to expect when my time came." She awoke one morning, a few days after her due date, with a pain in her lower back. She'd never had a day of illness during her entire pregnancy. The pain persisted through the day. Marty came home from work at 5:30 P.M. He cleaned up and ate supper.

"I'm going out," he announced.

"Can you drop me off at Mill's? I want to take a bath."

Marty drove Jane to Gramma Mills without a word.

"Where can I reach you if I need you?" she asked as he was about to leave.

"I don't know, but you can try the tavern."

Jane had a soothing hot bath, but the pains persisted. Gramma Mill made her a hearty snack. By 11:30 P.M. the pains had worsened considerably. She looked imploringly at Gramma Mill.

"I think I'm going to have my baby. The pains are really bad now."

"This is your first one, so it could take a while."

Jane sat back and gritted her teeth as they watched television. Shortly after midnight a severe contraction caused her to double up in pain. She jumped to her feet.

"Call someone to take me to the hospital!"

Marty was telephoned at the tavern. He wasn't there. A friend of Gramma Mill's drove Jane to the hospital. She was admitted shortly after 1:00 A.M. on October 9, 1965. She was alone and terrified. They prepared her for the delivery room and left her alone again in the cold, unfamiliar surroundings. Jane got up to go to the bathroom when her water broke. She didn't know what was happening. She yelled for the nurse, who appeared immediately. Jane apologized for making a mess. She was taken to the delivery room, and the doctor arrived shortly after. He did his best to put her at ease.

"It won't take long now, Jane," he said soothingly. "Do you want a boy or a girl?"

"I want a boy. I'm sure it will be a boy."

The pain got worse. The baby was coming. The doctor urged Jane to push harder.

"I see the head now. Keep pushing."

Jane pushed as hard as she could.

"It's a boy, Jane," announced the doctor. "You got your wish."

It was 5:05 A.M.

Jane was drained but ecstatic.

"Does he have all his fingers and toes and everything?" she asked.

"Hey, slow down," said the doctor with a smile. "Here, you can see for yourself."

He placed her seven-pound, fifteen-ounce baby in her arms. "At that moment I was the happiest person alive. I felt so much love. There was a lot of pain but I'd had a very easy delivery." Jane decided to name her son Allen. Marty's sister had suggested the name to her months before. When she left the delivery room, Jane called Marty to tell him the news. His grandmother answered the telephone.

"Marty is asleep and I don't want to wake him," she said.

"Well, tell him we have a son and ask him to bring my suitcase when he comes to visit us tonight. It's all packed under our bed."

"I'll do that. Good night."

Marty arrived at the hospital after supper that day. He left Jane's suitcase at the nursing station "and he told them to tell me that he had a cold and couldn't come to see me or the baby. He never did come to visit us. Not once. Nor did I have any other visitors. Marty's grandfather came to pick us up when we were ready to come home. It didn't matter how much I was ignored—I had my baby. I devoted all my time to him. I talked to him and sang to him right from the time he was born." Marty's grandparents now had a great-grandchild and, once home, they doted on him. Jane never went anywhere without Allen. He became her whole world.

Jane and Marty lived with his grandparents for a year and a half after their wedding. The house was on the main highway in Milton, a town three miles from Liverpool. After Allen was born, Marty and Jane began thinking about getting their own home. They bought a piece of vacant land a half mile from his grandparents.

When Allen was about six months old, Jane found a job at a Liverpool grocery store. She worked every day but Sunday. It was a nine-to-five job except for Fridays, when she worked twelve hours. She earned twenty-nine dollars per week. Either Marty or his grandparents would drive Jane to and from work. Most of her meager paycheck went into a savings account for a new home. Marty's grandparents baby-sat for Allen when Jane worked. When an old building was torn down, Marty bought the lumber from a Liverpool dealer and used it to build a home on their vacant lot. It was a small, two-bedroom structure with grey and white siding. Jane remembers the house was simple but comfortable. She left her job at the grocery store to spend more time with Allen and to decorate their home.

Jane doesn't recall much of the next few years, except that Marty was drinking more and more and life was monotonous. He never abused her physically, but he was seldom at home, and when he was, he was usually half drunk or asleep. They had sex at his whim. The act became mechanical for Jane. "One night I got enough nerve to ask him what he'd meant when he asked if I'd 'come' the first time we had sex."

"Good God," he replied, "you wasn't any virgin when I first had sex with you. You must know what 'come' means. You ain't really that stupid, are you?"

"Oh, I was just joking—never mind me," said Jane, embarrassed.

She remembers one night when they'd been married about three years. "It wasn't Marty's usual on-and-off sort of sex. It lasted a long time. That was the first and only time in our ten-year marriage that I had a climax. It was different. It felt good. It was then that I knew what he meant when he asked, 'Did you come?'"

When Allen was old enough to go to school, Jane decided to upgrade her education. In September 1970, she enrolled in adult classes at a Liverpool school. She found it fulfilling and attended classes regularly to the end of the school year in June 1971. She completed grade ten with straight A's. Allen also did well in school. That summer she took him with her to visit her parents, who were now living at the Camp Borden base in Ontario. Marty refused to make the trip with them.

"After we came home from that visit, I got a letter containing a photograph of a nude woman. It was cut up in pieces and you had to put it together like a jigsaw puzzle. The face was missing. The letter said, 'Guess what Marty was doing while you were away?' I asked him about the photo but he denied knowing anything about it. I didn't mention it again but I didn't dismiss it from my mind, either."

With the summer over and Allen back at school, Jane found herself with too much idle time. In January 1972, she enrolled in a typing course in nearby Bridgewater. Marty was no longer working. He'd quit his job with the Power Commission for a better-paying one at the Bowater-Mersey Paper Company, but that ended in the summer of 1971 "because of his drinking. He was sick a lot. It was a vicious cycle for him. He'd get drunk, sober up, get sick, turn back to the booze, and the cycle went on. He went into hospital to dry out. He had major stomach surgery for bleeding ulcers—all due to booze—yet he kept on drinking." The family was living on unemployment insurance and the $50 a week Jane received from Canada Manpower when she enrolled in the typing course. She drove to and from school in Marty's 1964 Ford Fairlane.

Shortly after she started the typing course, Jane discovered she was pregnant again. "I considered having an abortion, but when I thought about it seriously, I knew I couldn't. About two months before the baby was born I heard about a guy at the paper mill who had some pictures taken at our house while I was visiting my parents in Ontario the previous summer. I got the guy's name and address and went to his house. Apparently when Marty left his job at the paper mill he gave the pictures to him. Marty had kept them hanging in his locker at the mill, thinking I would never find out about them. The guy's wife answered the door when I went there. I introduced myself and told them I knew about the pictures. I told them I wanted them and if they didn't give them to me I would call the police to come and get them. I told them it was illegal to have that type of picture in their possession. I didn't expect the reaction I got. They were scared. They told me to come back at 1:00 P.M. to get the pictures."

Jane returned and they handed over the photographs. Looking at them made her nauseous. "They were disgusting photos of a naked woman lying on my bed, in my bedroom, in my house. There was a bottle of wine between her legs with the neck shoved into her vagina. I couldn't believe Marty had actually done this to me. I felt used and dirty. And here I was, seven months pregnant. My world was crushed. My husband was not only a drunk but a liar and a cheater as well."

Jane soon learned that Marty was still seeing the woman in the photographs. He drove Jane to school one Friday afternoon and was supposed to pick her up at 10:30 P.M. "He never showed up. Here I was thirty miles from home and pregnant. I knew of no way to get home. I started walking and after about ten miles a car full of young guys stopped and offered me a ride. They drove me right to my door. It was around midnight. The house was in darkness. My first thought was, 'Oh, God, where's Allen?' I rushed next door to Marty's brother and they had Allen. They told me Marty was in jail. He'd been picked up for impaired driving after being with that woman."

Jane's second son, Jamie, was born October 17, 1972. Allen was seven years old at the time. It was an easy birth, but afterwards Jane began hemorrhaging and required blood transfusions. Four years later, when she went to donate blood at a Red Cross clinic, it was discovered she had a rare blood type and had been given the wrong type of blood after Jamie's birth. Marty, with Allen in tow, came to visit Jane and the new baby only once in hospital. Jane was despondent about her marriage but resigned to her fate. She decided, because of the new baby, to stay and try to make a go of it. But by the time Jamie was three years old, she could take no more. Her father had been transferred once again by the army, this time only a hundred miles away, to Cornwallis, Nova Scotia. A few days after the

New Year in 1976, Marty came home half drunk. He'd been out all day. He came in about 10:00 P.M. and set a forty-ounce bottle of rum on the table. Jane had had enough. They'd shared nothing in their relationship for more than a year—not even sex. Jane eyed Marty and the bottle.

"It's either me and the kids or that bottle," she said.

Marty picked up the bottle and kissed it.

"I guess you lose," he said with a smirk.

Entering the bedroom, Jane threw her clothes and the children's clothes into a garbage bag. She woke Allen and Jamie and they left in the car for her parents' home. "It was very cold and it was snowing hard. The car broke down in the middle of nowhere. It was late and I was scared. I didn't know what to do. But it was so cold I knew I had to do something. You could see your breath when you talked, and frost was forming on the inside of the windows. I put the boys in the back seat and put the garbage bag of clothes over them. There was no traffic on the road and I didn't know which way would be shorter to go for help. My parents didn't know we were coming, so they wouldn't be expecting us, and Marty would be too drunk by now to care about us. I left the boys in the car and gave them strict orders not to sleep or to get out of the car. There was about a foot of snow on the road. It was still coming down and blowing hard. I had no hat, gloves, or boots. It seemed like I walked forever. Then I saw a light in the distance and kept walking towards it. I couldn't feel the cold anymore. I heard dogs barking. There were two German shepherds, and they came at me. I was already too scared for my boys and myself to be frightened of them. I just walked right past them and pounded on the door of the house.

"An elderly man and woman opened the door and let me in. I was hysterical. I told them what happened and that my boys were still in the car in the cold. The man got dressed, went out on his snow machine, and brought my boys back. They were so very cold. The milk in Jamie's nursing bottle had frozen. He was crying and said, 'Look, Mommy, it don't work' as he held up his bottle. He'd wet himself, and his snowsuit and pants were frozen stiff. We were all so happy to be where it was warm. They gave me hot coffee and let us stay the night. The next day the man got my car going. It was so cold the gas line had frozen up. I thanked the people and we continued on to my parents'. As I drove I thanked the Lord for keeping us safe. I vowed I'd never go back to Marty again.

Jane stayed a few days with her parents before driving back to Milton to have it out with Marty. Allen was reluctant to leave his father until the school year was over. Jane agreed to let him stay with his dad during the week. He would stay with her on weekends and any other time he wanted to come to her. She and Jamie went to live with friends. Marty begged her not to leave him, but her mind was set. Jane didn't expect (or ask for) any help from him. She went to the Queens County welfare office. She was told they couldn't help her unless she was legally separated or divorced. She wanted nothing less than a divorce. The welfare office set up an appointment for her with a legal aid lawyer. The welfare director told her she could leave Jamie with his secretary while she saw the lawyer. Returning from the lawyer's office, she discovered Marty had taken Jamie.

"Well, since you don't have any dependents, we can't help you," said the director, shrugging.

Jane rushed back to the lawyer's office, who told her there was nothing she could do because Marty had as much right to Jamie as she did. Jane was convinced the welfare director had set her up to save the county some money. She was shattered and frightened but angry. "I went to Marty's house, but no one was there. Then I went to his sister's house. I could hear Jamie crying, 'Mommy . . . Mommy,' but no one would answer when I pounded on the door. There was nothing I could do. There was no fight left in me. My boys were gone. I was falling apart." She was convinced Marty had taken Jamie as a ploy to get her to return to him. Desperate, she returned again to the lawyer's office.

"Marty doesn't want a divorce," said the lawyer. "And as far as I can see, you don't have grounds for one."

Jane was furious. She still had the photographs Marty had taken of the woman in their bed, but she thought they were too disgusting to use as legal grounds for a divorce. They made her feel used and degraded. Thinking of the photographs made her more determined to be free of Marty. She stared coldly at the lawyer.

"I'll be back in a week," she declared. "And I'll give you grounds—grounds that'll even make Marty want to divorce me."

Leaving the welfare offices, Jane walked directly across the street to a doctor's office. He had a reputation for providing women with ready access to birth-control pills. He prescribed Jane a three-month supply. "My own doctor wouldn't understand why I needed the pill unless I went into a long explanation, and I didn't want to do that. After Jamie's birth he advised me not to have any more children, and he was able to convince Marty to have a vasectomy." Jane needed the pills because she decided to have an affair to give Marty grounds for a divorce. But she didn't want to get pregnant. The man she chose for the affair was Billy Stafford, one of Marty's many casual friends. Marty had so many people in and out of the house Jane didn't take much notice of any of them. But she did take notice of Billy Stafford, and she got to talk to him after a 1976 New Year's party. Marty got drunk at the party and wanted to visit Jane's parents. He invited Billy Stafford to join them. Billy agreed and suggested they take his car. Jane did the driving. On the way there Marty went to sleep. Jane and Billy got to talking. She told him she'd had enough and was going to leave Marty. She was taken by Billy's engaging smile and found him to be a perfect gentleman.

"If you ever need any help or if there's anything I can ever do for you, just let me know," offered Billy.

Jane thanked him for being so kind and said she'd call him if she needed anything. At her parents' place, Marty drank while Jane and Billy talked. He seemed concerned, and she was very taken with him. They drove home the next day, and a week later, Jane left Marty.

Jane called Billy and reminded him of his offer to help. "I remember, and the offer still stands," reassured Billy. "Is there some way I can help?"

"Well," said Jane, somewhat embarrassed, "if I slept with you and you were willing to testify in court, it would be grounds for Marty to divorce me."

"I'll do whatever you want," said Billy.

By the end of January 1976, Jane and Billy Stafford were living together. Her divorce from Marty was final by May. "I was full of hope for a new and better life when I went off with Bill. He was my knight in shining armour. He was always telling me he loved me."

"We'll have a good life together," promised Billy. "I will protect you always. You won't be hurt anymore."

V

In the first weeks and months Jane was with Billy Stafford, he was charming and attentive. She felt safe and secure living with him, but there was a large void in her life. Her sons were still with their father. The question of custody didn't arise at the divorce hearing, and she believed Marty wouldn't want to bother with the children once the divorce was final. It didn't work out that way. She learned years later that Marty didn't allow her name to be spoken in his house, and he told his sons to stay away from her. He would keep Jane's children from her as punishment for her leaving him to live with Billy Stafford. While she agonized over the loss of her sons, Billy continually reassured her she'd eventually get them back.

"Don't be bothered about it," Billy would say. "Let them get used to the situation as it is. They'll have their fill soon enough. Let him see what it's like trying to raise two kids."

Initially Jane and Billy rented a bachelor apartment in Liverpool. It was small but comfortable. Living with Billy exposed Jane to a life-style she'd never imagined. When he wasn't out working on the fishing boats, Billy was always on the go. He couldn't sit still and always took Jane with him. Billy seemed to have an endless supply of friends to visit for drinking, card playing, or partying. "Even in my marriage to Marty, I was never a person to go visiting. I knew a lot of people but I didn't have any special friends. Marty's brother and his family lived next door to us in Milton for eight years but I didn't go to visit them more than three or four times, and that was at Christmas, when it was appropriate. I was never like a lot of women who went around visiting; having tea and catching up on gossip. My mother never did those things, either. But with Billy it seems we were always out visiting somebody."

In March 1976, while Billy was out on the fishing boats on a typical two-week run, Jane went to visit her parents. Returning to her apartment in Billy's car, a 440 Dodge Monaco, she hit an icy spot, and the car spun into a telephone pole, which snapped in two. The upper portion, including a transformer, crashed onto the car's roof. Jane was stunned but unhurt.

Severed, live electrical wires were laying over the car's vinyl roof. She was told later she could have been electrocuted if the roof had been metal instead of vinyl. The car was totalled, and Billy had no collision insurance on it. She went to the wharf to meet Billy when he was due in. Before she could explain what happened he walked towards her, reached out, and hugged and kissed her.

"You wrecked my car, didn't you?" he said with a smile.

"How did you know?"

"I had a feeling about it. Don't worry about it—I can always get another car, but never another you."

Billy picked up his paypacket and they went home. "He went out for a while and returned with a dozen roses—my first·ever—and a beautiful pair of earrings with my birthstone set in them. I was just floating on cloud nine. I was really enjoying all this love and affection. We made love that night. It was the second time in my life that I reached a climax during sexual relations."

During a visit with friends of Billy in Charleston, a hamlet a few miles from Liverpool, Jane noticed a big vacant house. She asked Billy if he'd like to live there.

"No one has lived there for over twenty years," he said, laughing. "The people who own it won't rent it."

"Do you mind if I check into it?"

"I don't mind. If it makes you happy, do it."

Jane contacted the woman who owned it who, much to everyone's astonishment, agreed to rent it to Jane for twenty-five dollars a month. It was an old house, very dirty. She gave Jane the key, and when Billy returned from fishing, he went with her to see the place. Billy shook his head and laughed when he glanced over the interior.

"Why, it's a wreck. You can never get this place fit to live in," he said. "They should pay us to live here."

Jane was not discouraged. Billy stood back and watched as she wandered from room to room. She loved the house and believed it had potential and a lot of character.

Billy could see her mind was made up.

"All right, hon," he said finally, "I'll give you five hundred dollars to spend however you want. If you think you can fix it up while I'm out on my next trip, then fine, we'll move in."

Over the next two weeks Jane cleaned, painted, papered, laid floor coverings, hung drapes, and moved their furniture into the house. "No one, including Bill, could believe what I did. It was lovely and anyone would've been proud to live in it. Bill was very impressed with what I accomplished. I thought we would be very happy there."

Although her life with Billy was somewhat fulfilling, the guilt Jane felt about her sons gnawed at her continuously. "The emptiness from their loss was growing deeper and deeper. It was especially hard when Bill was out fishing. I longed to see them, to touch them, to hold them in my arms. I felt guilty about not seeing them, but there was nothing I could do. Several times I went up to Allen's school just to get a look at him." To help fill the void, Jane bought a miniature poodle. "She was coal black. When I first got her she was so small I could hold her in the palm of my hand. When the sun shone on her she looked blue from the rays. So I named her Blue. She helped fill my time. I took her everywhere."

While they were still living in their first apartment Billy discovered Jane was on the pill. She kept them on the refrigerator beside the kitchen sink so she wouldn't forget to take them.

"How long have you been taking these?" he asked.

"I started taking them when I knew I was going to go out with you."

"Why?"

"I didn't need them with Marty because he had a vasectomy. I had complications after Jamie was born and I was advised not to get pregnant again."

"I wish you wouldn't take them, hon. Just let nature take its course. If you did get pregnant, wouldn't it be great? Wouldn't you like to have a little girl?"

"No. I don't know why, but I never wanted girls. I always wanted boys."

"Well, hon, you can't have a boy or a girl taking those things."

Jane was standing by the sink holding the pills in her hands. "Do I dare take the chance of getting pregnant?" she asked herself. "I'm scared, but Bill wants a baby. Bill reached out, took the pills, and dropped them in the garbage. They were never mentioned again, and as each month came and went, I breathed a sigh of relief." But there was no sigh of relief when she missed her period in August 1976. They were living in their big house in Charleston by then. "After a couple of months, the doctor confirmed I was pregnant. I wanted the baby very much but I lived each day in fear, wondering what would happen to me and the unborn baby. I had myself believing something drastic was going to happen to us. I never expressed my fears to anyone, especially to Bill. I just figured I didn't say much when he threw my pills away, so now I had to suffer the consequences."

Because of Jane's rare blood type she had to undergo regular blood checks in the latter part of her pregnancy to ensure she wasn't producing antibodies that would endanger the fetus. She also had an ultrasound examination of the baby. "It made me feel better. I could hear the baby's heart beating and feel it moving. It took my fears away for a short time, but they always returned. It seemed like I was always at the hospital getting poked with needles so they could examine my blood. The more I went to the hospital the more my fears grew." Jane also had problems controlling her bladder because of the pressure from the weight of the baby.

Overshadowing all of her fears and physical problems was a sinister change in Billy's attitude towards her. Although she and Billy didn't discuss marriage after her divorce from Marty, Jane took his surname. She was Jane Stafford and in Billy's mind, now that she was carrying his child, his ownership was complete. Signs of his true self, the side that Jane didn't know existed, began to surface. She wouldn't learn of his penchant for physical violence towards women until several months after the birth of their child. But as her pregnancy progressed, her gentle, sympathetic, and physically imposing protector and benefactor became threatening. Jane was confused and bewildered. This was, after all, the man who had promised she would be safe with him, the man who had promised she would never again be hurt as long as he was around. Jane couldn't understand Billy's resentment. It was Billy who said time and again he wanted her to get pregnant. The more her pregnancy showed, the less he took her out. He spent more and more time away from home, drinking. When he was home he made snide remarks about how big she was getting. He called her a "cow," and when he was drunk, the verbal abuse intensified. Billy turned particularly mean when, because of her pregnancy, Jane was unable to control her bladder.

"Jesus Christ!" he would shout, "I can't dress you up and take you anywhere. You piss wherever you sit. Can't you control yourself? It ain't bad enough you're big as a barrel, now you have to be like a dog and go around pissing on everything. Fuck you, I ain't taking you anywhere until you have that kid." Billy was true to his word.

Jane went into false labour on May 24, 1977. She was in the hospital for three days. Billy left on the boats the day after she was released. She went to his parents' to be near someone if the baby came while he was away. On May 30, Jane awakened at 3:00 A.M. with severe pains. Billy's father, Lamont Stafford, drove her to the hospital. They took her to the maternity floor in a wheelchair. They didn't have time to finish prepping Jane. She was only partially shaved when they wheeled her to the delivery room. An eight-pound, nine-and-a-half-ounce boy was delivered at 3:45 A.M. "I knew Bill wanted a girl but I was happy it was a boy. After the birth I began to hemorrhage again, just as I did after Jamie's birth." Before the birth Jane's doctor advised her to have a tubal ligation within three months of the delivery. Her baby was born on a Wednesday. Two days later she went in for surgery. Hospital officials said her husband would have to sign a form approving the operation.

"He's out at sea," said Jane. "I'm sure he'll sign them when he comes to visit."

They went ahead with the operation. "I was secretly happy about the surgery. I knew I couldn't get pregnant ever again. Nine months of never-ending fear and worry was enough. I didn't ever want to go through that again."

Billy Stafford returned from fishing the day after the operation but didn't come to visit Jane until the following day—a Sunday. He didn't ask how she felt and he made no mention of the baby's health.

"Well, you got what you wanted, didn't you," he said sarcastically. "You got your boy."

Jane eyed him passively.

"Well, old woman, you can damn well look after him. He's all yours. I've been on a party since I got in Saturday morning and now I'm going back to party some more."

"Before you go, you're supposed to sign a form for my surgery."

"Fuck that. You expect me to sign for an operation that makes you no fuckin' good anymore? No way, old woman, no way. Don't call me until you're ready to come home. And I'm sailing on Wednesday, so you make sure you're out by then."

After Billy's outburst at the hospital, Jane wasn't looking forward to going home, but she hoped he'd feel differently once she arrived with the baby. That afternoon Billy's parents came to visit her. She asked them to help her choose a name for the baby. She couldn't decide between Jason and Darren.

"Call him Darren," said Billy's mother, Winnie. "Darren—Darren Edward. Edward is Lamont's middle name."

Jane agreed, and the baby was named Darren Edward Stafford.

The following Tuesday morning, Jane called Billy at his mother's house. He was in a surly mood when he came to pick up her and the baby, and it didn't change in the car.

"Because of my surgery, they told me not to do any lifting or any strenuous work for six to eight weeks. I've still got my stitches in. Can the baby and I stay at your mother's for the next two weeks while you're out to sea?"

Billy stared at her incredulously.

"To hell with that idea, old woman. It was you who agreed to that operation, not me. So you just get your ass home and get back to keeping house and looking after that bastard you got there in your arms."

Jane didn't dare speak again during the drive home. She was shocked at what she saw when she entered the house. "I am a spotless housekeeper and I couldn't believe the mess. The sink was stacked full of dirty dishes. There were booze bottles and cigarette butts all over the place. The ashtrays were filled to overflowing. Your feet stuck to the floor where booze and pop had been spilled. The bedroom smelled like a pigpen. Bill had been drunk-sick and vomited over the bed and floor and just left it there. In the bedroom was a bucket he'd used as a toilet. He'd been too drunk or too lazy to walk outside to the outhouse."

"Well, what the hell are you waiting for?" Billy said with a sneer. "Can't you see all the work that needs doing around here? Put that little bastard in the crib and get busy."

There was no running water in the house. It had to be drawn up from a well by bucket, carried to the house, and heated on the woodstove. There was no washing machine, and the laundry had to be done by hand.

"Can you please get me a few buckets of water so I can wash the bedclothes and do the dishes and floors?" asked Jane.

"What in fuck is wrong with you? Crippled or something? Get your own fucking water."

Jane was bewildered and hurt, but she sensed there was no point in arguing with him. Despite the pain, she drew the water and cleaned up the entire house. "Between doing all of that, I had to cook supper, prepare Darren's formula, and change his diapers. I finished about 10:00 P.M. I was so exhausted, my whole body ached and my stitches hurt. Bill was already in bed when I crawled in. It seemed like I just got to sleep when it was time to get up to feed Darren. I was glad Bill was going on the boat. I needed the rest. A couple of days after Bill sailed, I went to visit his parents. I told them how Bill was acting towards me and Darren." Lamont Stafford was silent.

"Janey, dear," said Winnie, "you have to understand his side. He's had you all to himself for a year or more and now he has to share your time. Give him time, dear. Let him adjust to all the changes. He'll be just fine, you'll see."

Billy was at sea for two weeks. On his return he demanded Jane have sex with him. Jane had been to the doctor to have her stitches removed, but she was in no condition to have intercourse. She'd just finished feeding and bathing Darren when Billy came through the door.

"Go into the bedroom and strip," he demanded. "I want to screw you. I haven't touched you since you started getting big, and now I want it."

"But Bill, it's too soon. I just got my stitches out."

"I don't want to hear none of that. Just get your ass into the bedroom."

Jane went into the bedroom and undressed. "He came in and stood there glaring at me."

"Just look at you! What a hard-looking mess! A scar across your guts; stretch marks all over you; legs that look like two broom handles—the only good thing I got out of this is that your tits got bigger."

He reached out with both hands and squeezed Jane's breasts until they began to drip milk.

"I'll get something that little bastard won't get. I'll just help myself to a little drink of this."

Jane stared in disbelief as Billy began suckling her breasts.

His mother's advice echoed in her mind: "Give him time, dear. Let him adjust to all the changes." Billy pushed Jane to the bed and entered her roughly. "I thought I was being torn apart. He wasn't gentle, and since he'd been drinking, it took him longer. To me it seemed like forever. When he finished he just rolled over and went to sleep. I just laid there feeling used and dirty. I wished we had a bathtub so I could take a hot bath to soothe my hurting body and wash away the awful feeling."

Jane and Darren were home from the hospital less than a month when the woman who owned the house ordered them to leave so that her mother could move into the house. "We offered to buy the house but she refused to sell. I loved the house and it hurt to have to move out. I'd put so much work into it." Jane was despondent about leaving the house, but their situation wasn't entirely desperate. From her years with Marty she'd met a kindly woman, Margaret Joudrey, whose husband, Stan, was a longtime friend of Billy's. They lived in a house ten miles up River Road in Bangs Falls, and the couples often visited each other. The Joudreys came to visit Jane at the hospital when she had Darren, and when they learned they were being forced to move out of their Charleston home, they offered to sever a piece of their land and give it to the Staffords at no cost, other than surveyor fees. They took the land and bought a cabin for a thousand dollars and had it moved there. From the time they moved out of the Charleston house in June 1977 until the cabin was made liveable on their new lot, Jane and Billy moved in with Lamont and Winnie Stafford. "It was fine living there. His parents had a beautiful big home and I got along well with them. They loved Darren and they were very good to me. Lamont never got abusive or violent. He would drink until he had enough and then go to bed. Winnie and I would sit and talk and have a few drinks."

Billy and Jane moved to their own house in Bangs Falls at the end of August 1977. A few days later, Jane began working at the Hillsview Acres County Home for the elderly. "It was a good job, and it was close to home. I figured I would have my own money and I would be able to clothe Darren and buy whatever he needed. Bill didn't mind me getting the job there. The staff were all women, and the patients were all elderly." Jane was hired as a domestic, but within a month she was promoted to cook. "Right from the start, my wages bought groceries and paid bills. If I managed to have a few dollars left, he would steal it right out of my purse." The first time Jane confronted him, Billy went into a rage.

"Did you take some money from my purse?" she asked.

"No goddamn way!" he shouted.

"It's only you and me here in the house. Who else could take it?"

"I told you I didn't take it. Are you calling me a liar? You're so fucking stupid you probably spent it and you want to blame me for stealing it."

Jane, staring incredulously as Billy's face reddened and eyes bulged, knew it was pointless pursuing the matter. In eighteen months Jane had seen her common-law husband change from being kind and loving to verbally abusive. In November 1977, she was to learn about his penchant for physical abuse. "Darren was six months old. It was my day off and I'd gone to town to do my shopping. There happened to be a photographer in town taking baby pictures. I had Darren's taken. On the way home I stopped to pick up some Kentucky Fried Chicken for supper. When I left the house Bill was installing some kitchen cabinets I'd purchased. He had a friend, Richard Coombs, helping him. It was late afternoon when I got home. I bought the chicken because we didn't have a stove—only a hot plate—and the guys were working in the kitchen. By buying supper I wouldn't be in their way." Billy glared at her when she came through the door.

"Where the hell were you all day?" he demanded. "I'm starving. Get me something to eat."

Jane could see Billy had been drinking. She served the chicken. Billy didn't say anything until after Richard left. By then Jane had Darren in bed and the kitchen cleaned up. It was a beautiful night. She went out and sat on the veranda. She was gazing at the stars when she heard Billy come out of the house behind her.

"Here, come and sit beside me and watch some of this beauty," she said.

Billy walked over to her, put his hand on her head, and pulled her into the house by the hair.

"You fuckin' whore!" he shouted. "You slut! You tramp! I'll give you beauty. I saw you giving Richard the eyes. You just bought that chicken to impress him, didn't you?"

Jane struggled against the pressure of his grip on her hair.

"Answer me, you no-good whore. Didn't you?"

"I . . . I don't know what you're talking about. I just don't know."

Billy slapped her face and began punching and kicking her. "That was my first real beating, and I didn't know why." Billy was sheepish the next morning at breakfast.

"I'm sorry," he said. "I'll never do it again. I promise."

The beating planted a seed of fear in Jane and gnawing doubts about herself. "Doubt about myself and whether it was my fault. I wondered, 'Did I look at Richard like he said I did?' Just maybe I did. To me, no one got that angry or violent without a reason. So I must have been the reason. I prayed a silent prayer, 'Please, Lord, help me to be better so this doesn't happen again.' But it did happen, over and over again, and it always ended up being my fault. The scene was repeated every time a man came to the house after that. It got so I wouldn't even come out of the bedroom when he had male company, but he still accused me of the same thing and beat me for it."

About the time the Staffords moved into their home at Bangs Falls, Billy found himself blacklisted on Nova Scotia fishing boats. Details of the incident that caused the blacklisting are sketchy, but it resulted in Billy being charged with mutiny. He'd been hired for a trip aboard the scallop dragger *Kathy and Susie* out of Lunenburg. When he returned home, he told Jane he'd been in an argument with the skipper and first mate. "He wanted them to turn the boat around and bring him home," recalls Jane. "He said if they didn't he would wreck the boat. He beat up the mate, held a knife to him, and said that if they didn't, he would tear everything to hell on the boat. They did bring him in. He was blacklisted, and the Mounties charged him. Two of them came to the house and served him the papers. He slammed the door in their faces and told them to get out. While they were walking back to their car, which was parked by our picture window, Bill got a fully loaded automatic rifle and came to the window. Bill pointed it right at one of them as he was getting into the car. They ducked down and backed the car out of the driveway with the driver's door open so that they could see where they were going." Billy, meanwhile, was into one of his patented rages.

"You fucking pigs!" he screamed, jabbing his middle finger into the air several times. "I'll get you one day."

Billy continued his diatribe long after the police cruiser was out of sight. No one would testify against him, and the charge against him was dropped. "I know he went to court about it, but nothing happened. He wasn't sad about it. He wasn't sorry. To him it was a big joke when it was all over. He just got his way again." After he was blacklisted, Billy began collecting unemployment insurance and stayed at home through the winter of 1977-78. He made it clear what he expected of Jane.

"Well, old woman," he declared, "you're working now, so I don't need to work. You can look after me. Besides, you're in debt to me for three thousand dollars."

"What do you mean?"

"You remember when you smashed up my car? Well, that's how much it was worth. Now start paying."

Billy taunted Jane about the car accident from then on. "He forever brought that up to me, and to his death he claimed I never paid that debt."

Billy also completely refused to baby-sit for Darren. In retrospect, Jane believes his attitude was a godsend. Just below their home lived Marie and Morton Joudrey, no relation to Jane's close friend and neighbour Margaret Joudrey. They were a warm, retired couple who agreed to baby-sit Darren while Jane worked. Marie Joudrey is short and heavy-set with a broad face and laughing eyes. She's perpetually good-humoured, and she loves playing bingo. She continued to live in Bangs Falls after Morton died of cancer in August 1984.

"Marie and Morton were fantastic people," says Jane. "When I told Darren of Morton's death he cried for two days. He speaks very lovingly of Morton and always includes him in his prayers at night. They looked after Darren from September 1977, when we moved to Bangs Falls. He was treated as if he were their very own. They loved him. He called Morton 'Daddy' and Marie 'Mommy Marie.' They had an adopted son, Scott. He and Darren are like brothers. I'm thankful that Billy wouldn't baby-sit Darren. According to psychiatrists, Darren's way of coping with a negative situation was helped very much by being put into a normal atmosphere every day. When I came home from work at 3:00 P.M., I'd stop to pick up Darren at Marie and Morton's—but he didn't want to leave." Marie Joudrey said Darren would often run and hide when it was time to go home. "He'd hide until Jane would say, 'You'd better come out, your father's waiting for us.' He was scared to death of Billy."

Jane said Darren's' eyes filled with fear whenever she mentioned his father was waiting for him. "He would run and get his coat and hat, kiss Marie and Morton good-bye, and look at me as if to say, 'Well, Mommy, if we must go—let's go.'" Why was Darren Stafford so frightened of his father? Jane says that as far as Billy was concerned, "Darren was just something to be abused and used and taught to make it through life as a man from the day his feet could touch the floor. He could laugh when he was told. He could talk when Bill told him to. Being a man, he couldn't cry. If you've done that from the time you were about six months old, it's like brainwashing. Through the middle of the night, as any baby does, he would cry, and I would get up to feed him. Well, by the time he was six months old, Bill used to go to the crib and I'd never hear another word. But I wasn't allowed to get up and go to him. I used to wonder all night long, is he dead? There was never a sound came out of there. It was like stories you read about Hitler training kids. Darren had the same kind of training. He didn't cry."

When Darren was about three years old, Jane was outside working in the garden when she heard Billy hollering. "Our bedroom was in the front of the house, and he just stuck the gun out the window and he fired a shot. It was close enough to me that it lifted the ground up beside me."

"Get in here, old woman!" shouted Billy. "You've got a mess to clean up!"

Jane went quickly into the house. Billy was standing in the kitchen, his face flushed.

"It's in there," he said, pointing to the bedroom.

Jane entered the room. "It was like a nightmare. My little boy was lying on the bed naked and his body was covered in welts from his neck to his feet." Billy had broken a piece off a mop handle and used it to beat the child. Darren was trying unsuccessfully to stifle his sobs, his tiny body quivering like a wounded animal. He had defecated during the beating and there was blood and feces all over the bed and floor. Darren lay on the bed, quivering. Jane began weeping. Billy heard her, came into the bedroom, and punched her in the face.

"Get this fucking mess cleaned up, old woman. We're going out. And get the kid dressed. He's going, too."

Obediently, Jane cleaned up herself and Darren as best she could. They went out to the car and drove down to Margaret Joudrey's trailer. "We picked up Margaret and we all went for a drive. It was just as if nothing had happened."

In the winter of 1978-79, Billy Stafford found temporary employment on a Canada Works Program project at Buckfield, a few miles north of Bangs Falls. He couldn't get work on a fishing boat, but in 1980 he began sailing on the Irving Company's oil tankers— Kent Lines Limited—out of Saint John, New Brunswick. Later he worked on Irving's gypsum boats. The final trip he made was aboard the SS *Gypsum Countess* in the fall of 1981. He was supposed to stay for three months, but he quit after one month and came home. Jane says Billy got into some kind of trouble during that trip, either with the crew or with drugs. She said he came home with a large quantity of drugs. When he came through the door after that trip, he had an announcement for Jane.

"Old woman, I just quit. I'm not working anymore." He also announced that an alcoholic friend of his, Ronald Wamboldt, was coming to live with them. Jane had no say in the matter. Wamboldt was also a wife-beater. Alcohol had taken its toll on his body; when he moved in with the Staffords he was a shell of a man and much smaller than Billy. Wamboldt's wife, at the urging of her children, left him and moved to Toronto in August 1978. He failed to meet his mortgage payments, and the bank took his house in September 1981. He said he knew he was stupid to move in with Billy but had nowhere else to go. Wamboldt was given a separate room, the room where Billy kept his guns. Wamboldt had known Billy for twenty-five years. Billy often punched him and slapped him around. He usually called Wamboldt "Dummy" and one time he shot at him, just missing. "He didn't shoot right at me . . . you see, if he did, he'd never miss because he was a good shot." To earn his keep, Wamboldt did chores for Billy and helped with various animals Billy kept on occasion. Wamboldt says that if he failed to follow Billy's orders, "I'd get another smash." He said it never entered his mind to go to the police after Billy's assaults because "I was afraid I might get more." Wamboldt often saw Billy beat Jane and Darren. He said Billy often knocked her down and always referred to her as "old woman." Jane, he said, was "a beautiful mother. She worked hard and she was clean. Kept the house clean . . . clothes, and a good cook." Wamboldt remembers Darren being "very afraid and some nervous. It was unbelievable."

One evening Jane prepared dinner for herself, Darren, and Margaret Joudrey. Darren reached for something and fell off his chair, striking his mouth on another chair. It drove his top teeth through his lip. The cut bled profusely, and Darren cried aloud from the pain. He was two or three at the time. Jane tried to calm him, and Margaret Joudrey applied an ice pack. It was an hour before the pain subsided and he was able to sleep. His lips were swollen. Billy came home later that night. "The first thing he did was go in and wake Darren up and when he saw his sore mouth he asked him if he cried," recalls Jane.

"Yes, Daddy, I did cry," said Darren.

Billy gave the child three sharp punches in the face. "Blood was flying everywhere," said Jane.

"Don't dare cry again or you'll get more of the same," warned Billy.

"The next time Bill was gone, I took Darren to the dentist, who wouldn't touch him. He sent me to a children's hospital. They put him asleep and drilled the nerves out of his two front teeth and five others. They didn't want to pull them out at his age. His two front teeth are black and they'll stay that way until he loses his baby teeth."

Billy Stafford often picked his son up by the hair of the head and held him suspended off the floor. He once gave Darren three dollars and the boy lost them. Bill picked him up by the hair, put a butcher knife to his throat, and told him that if he ever lost any more money, he'd cut his gizzard out. At other times he held him upside down by the feet and pointed a loaded .30-.30 rifle to his head. He'd tell him if he was a bad boy, he'd splatter his brains all over the place.

When Billy came home, mealtime was traumatic for both Jane and Darren. "Darren couldn't even hold a cup in his hand without spilling it, he would shake so badly. Mealtime was just so full of hate at our table. Darren had to eat at the same speed as his father did, and lots of times he couldn't do that. So Bill would take the spoon and just keep shoving it into his mouth. Darren would vomit right on the table, and Bill would just take Darren's plate and scrape the vomit into it and keep on feeding him until it was gone. It all had to be eaten. Nothing was ever left. Sometimes Bill would just reach out and hit Darren or myself on the side of the head for no reason at all. Or he might hit you over the head with a cup or knife, or whatever he had in his hand. If I complained about how he treated Darren, he would just knock me to the floor. Bill's parents were there for dinner one day with his sister Cathy, her boyfriend, and their two children. I had come home from work, and his mother had started supper already. Everything was ready to be served, and it was on the plates. For some reason Bill just went berserk. He got a gun and smashed the plates around. He took everybody's plate and scraped everything into the garbage. He hit Cathy's boyfriend on the side of the head with the gun. Her kids were screaming and crying, Cathy was crying, and everybody just got in their truck and left."

Although Darren had a lot of toys, he was never allowed to play with them when Billy was around. At Christmas, the boy wasn't even allowed to open his gifts. "Bill would open them for him. He'd pass them to Darren and put them back under the tree, where they had to stay. Darren could just look at them. He was never allowed to play with them. One time I bought Darren a battery-powered motorcycle, one you could really drive. Because Darren liked it so much Bill gave it away to another little boy. Darren was heartbroken but couldn't show any emotion. If Bill happened to be away and I let Darren play with his toys, Bill would come home and throw them in the garbage or run over them with his truck. The only time Darren was happy was when Bill was away on the boats—but even then, he was always afraid of his father coming home. The only thing Bill ever taught Darren was to 'be a man' —to fight and hate. He didn't know how to play with other children. All he could do was show them his muscles and fight with them."

When Darren was two years old he took very sick one night. He had a high temperature and a bad cold and he had trouble breathing. Jane, seriously worried about Darren, asked Bill to drive him to the hospital. "Bill literally dropped us off at the door of the hospital. I stayed with Darren all night and sponged-bathed him to get his fever down. A bad infection in his ears caused the high temperature. About 10:00 A.M. the next day I called Bill at his parents' to come and get us. He picked us up and we went back to his parents'. Darren was very irritable. Although he didn't cry, he whined a bit, which was understandable. Bill gave him a beating and put him to bed, all alone. Billy's mother, Winnie, didn't like what she'd seen."

"Don't do that, Billy," she said. "The baby is sick." Billy glared at his mother.

"You just go about your work and mind your own goddamn business," he told his mother. When Billy was away at sea, Jane often stayed with his parents on her days off. "It was nice. Lamont would baby-sit for Darren, and Winnie and I would go to bingo. When we got home we would sit and talk and sometimes have a few drinks. It was nice and peaceful. No Bill around, yelling and hollering—just the peaceful sound of silence. It was like everyone became their normal selves when Billy wasn't there."

In October 1980, Jane's elder son from her previous marriage, Allen, came to live with her and Billy in Bangs Falls. He was fifteen years old and had been in trouble with the law for breaking and entering. He was on probation at the time. While Billy was at sea in March 1981, Allen got into more trouble. As soon as Jane found out, she contacted his parole officer. "I was so scared that Bill would find out about this and get off the boat and come home that the worry of it nearly drove me crazy. I knew that if Bill found out he would kill him.

"During this period of stress, Margaret Joudrey asked me to take her to Bridgewater to do her shopping. We went that evening, and since I was there, I decided to get some Easter shopping done for the children. I was so worried about Allen I walked right out of the store with a shopping cart and everything in it. I didn't even realize it. The next thing I knew the man from the store had me by the arm and I was being arrested for shoplifting. The court took it easy on me and gave me fifty hours of community work and a year probation. I was worried about what Billy might do if he found out about Allen, and now with this happening I had all that much more to worry about. I went to a psychiatrist at the time. I told her I could never tell Bill what had happened but I couldn't tell her why. I did my community service hours and I reported to my probation officer and on February 24, 1982, I appeared in court and got an absolute discharge. Billy never did find out about it. Allen was sent to the School for Boys in Shelbourne, and he remained there until the end of August 1981. When he got out he went to live with his father, Marty."

In January 1982, the Social Services Department from Liverpool called Jane at work and asked if she and Billy would be willing to take Allen back again. Jane was against it because she feared how Billy might treat him, but Billy insisted he come and live with them. It was Allen's choice. He wasn't getting along with his father and decided to move in with Jane and Billy. He did pretty much as Billy told him to avoid his wrath. That strategy didn't always work. "I used to get hit all the time, like Ronny Wamboldt. It was normal. We just got used to that." Billy treated the two of them like his personal slaves. When they went to cut wood in the bush, Billy used the saw and Allen and Ronny did the carrying and loaded the truck. "He just did the easy stuff. Me and Ronny did the rest of it."

Allen remembers the night friends of his, who were also Billy's friends, came to the house at Bangs Falls. "They all sat at the table in the kitchen and I went over to talk to them to see what was going on in Liverpool and in Milton. Just like that, Bill hit me so hard that I didn't feel it at first and he said, 'Go sit on the chesterfield.' So I went over and sat on the chesterfield." Ronny Wamboldt says Billy treated Allen like he was ten or twelve years old and not sixteen. From time to time Billy gave Allen spending money or a marijuana joint. These small rewards didn't come close to compensating for the atmosphere of fear he, his mother, Darren, and Ronny Wamboldt were forced to live under.

Allen vividly recalls one of the mealtime episodes when Billy went berserk. "I used to eat my supper real fast. Well, my little brother, he couldn't eat very fast. So one day Billy started feeding it to him himself, spoonful after spoonful. Darren threw up and Bill just scraped it all back in the plate and made him eat it again. And then Mom said, 'You know he can't eat very fast, hon,' and Bill just got up and smashed all the plates and cracked me on the head and went over and started beating Ma with his fists. Then he went over and gave Darren a good beating. He said to my mother, 'When I'm talking to these fucking kids, I don't want your mouth to open.'" Allen said Jane often called Billy "hon" or "dear" to calm him because she was afraid of him. He often saw Billy beat Jane, Darren, Ronny Wamboldt, and even their pets and other animals. He would beat Wamboldt "because Ronny wouldn't go to bed or he'd go to the washroom and miss the toilet. Bill kicked him in the stomach one night and put him outside. When Ronny woke up the next morning, he was in bed in the house. Bill told Ronny he fell outside on a cement brick but he kicked him in the stomach that night." Because he was drunk much of the time, Wamboldt doesn't remember many of the beatings he took from Billy Stafford. "I got hit," he said, "but I never hit back. There's a good many times he cracked me."

Billy was also cruel to Jane's dog, Blue. She'd been a house dog from the day Jane brought her home. But one day Billy decided to keep her outside. "She wasn't used to that," said Jane. "Then he started kicking her around and he'd hold her up by the back of the neck and bite her nose. It broke my heart to see this but I knew not to say anything because if I did he would just do it all the more. If I acted as if I didn't care, he'd usually stop doing it."

At one time, the family also had a St. Bernard that became vicious because of Billy's mistreatment of it. "Bill used to grab him by the jaws and bite him on the nose or kick him under the chin," recalls Allen. "He was right crazy from being beat all the time. I took it for a walk one day and this old woman was coming down the road in her car down in Greenfield and he charged right up on her roof. He'd bite anybody. It was just craziness." In a small barn at the rear of the Stafford property they kept a horse and two cows. Allen said when he went out to feed the horse "it was right up on its hind legs. It was right wild from being kicked and whipped by Bill."

Billy Stafford's obsession with horoscopes, the devil, and astrology played a large role in determining what he would or would not do on any given day. He kept up-to-date horoscope books in the house and expected Jane to read the daily predictions for his zodiac sign.

"Okay, old woman, let's see what today holds in store for me," he would say.

Jane would read his horoscope and Billy would sit back and think about it. He would smile smugly if the reading was positive. "Well, the old devil is going to be with me today. I can do as I please and nothing will happen to me." He would scowl darkly if the reading was negative. "The old devil gave me my warning. I'll be good today." Being good meant he usually stayed around the house getting drunk or high. Jane dreaded the negative readings because they meant she and Darren would be abused more than usual. "Being cruel to us gave him a sort of satisfaction or revenge for having to stay at home."

On one of those days that Billy Stafford stayed home, Jane was bent over putting wood in the stove when a shot rang out and struck the wall inches above her head. The stove was in direct line with the open bedroom door. Billy had fired a .22 bullet at her while lying in bed.

"Don't worry, old woman," he said with a chuckle, "if I wanted to hit you, I wouldn't have missed."

Jane's heart was beating wildly and the blood drained from her face. "If I'd stood up, I'd be dead," she said later of the incident. "I really thought I was going to have a heart attack."

Billy Stafford often said he'd never die. "I have the power—right from the devil."

It's perhaps appropriate that Billy Stafford should use the word "power," for many researchers agree that it's a conscious or unconscious quest for power over their wives and their households that cause men to batter. Such men have a desire for absolute control over every aspect of a woman's behaviour and life, including her job, household chores, caring for children, and her social life and all contacts outside the home, including her own family. There are, of course, many other reasons why men become batterers. The violence is learned, with a man much more likely to beat his wife and children if he was beaten as a child or if his father abused his mother.

Alcohol and drugs play a role in wife-battering, but most experts agree they aren't causes by themselves, but rather act as facilitators. It's estimated that more than 50 percent of batterers have alcohol or drug problems but, as in the case of Billy Stafford, a man who beats his wife when he's drunk usually beats her when he's sober as well. Assaults against wives often begin after the birth of a child. Some battered wives believe this happens because their husbands don't want (or can't handle) the responsibility, financial or otherwise, for their children. Typically a wife-beater tends to suffer from low self-esteem, relying strongly on a dutybound wife. Low self-esteem certainly didn't seem to be a problem for Billy Stafford. He believed he was invincible, a power unto himself.

Jane Stafford was optimistic when she and Billy moved to Bangs Falls. They had their own home, which Billy put in Jane's name because he owed considerable income-tax arrears and feared the government might take it from him. Her dream of a happy, normal married life was soon shattered. It was in the Bangs Falls house that Jane was to see Billy Stafford's true nature surface in all its brutality and ugliness. "It was there," says Jane, "that all the fighting and abuse took place. Where my children and I lived in fear, where Billy Stafford reigned over his kingdom like a dictator. I was very much like my mother, always having faith things would get better. For Mom it did. For me, it kept getting worse."

Billy Stafford's total income for the five years from 1977 to 1981 was only $22,000, and that included unemployment-insurance payments. Everything that went into turning the Bangs Falls home from a cabin to a proper house came from Jane's wages. "And I did a lot of the actual work on the repairs, remodelling, and rebuilding, along with a friend of ours, Dempsey Hatt, who I hired to help me. That included a new roof, an addition to the house, and construction of our small barn. I worked harder than any man. We had no well, and until 1980 I brought water from where I worked or carried it from a spring half a mile from our house. I carried all the water for cleaning, cooking, and laundry. There was no stove in the house until I got a second-hand electric one at the end of 1979. We also got a woodstove about that time for heat. Before that, I cooked on a single-burner hot plate and did my baking at Margaret Joudrey's."

Jane Stafford loved her job at Hillsview Acres because it gave her precious time away from Billy and the home she'd come to view as nothing more than a torture chamber. Her home life was made more miserable by Billy's slovenly personal habits. Often he purposely messed up the house because he knew it bothered Jane, who was a perfectionist in her housekeeping. Drunk or sober, it was routine for Billy to get up several times during the night for a snack. He would bring the food into the bedroom, turn on the light, and sit on the bed smacking his lips and slurping loudly while he ate. He always made enough noise to keep Jane awake. If he ate grapes, apples, watermelons, or peaches, he spat the seeds and pits around the bedroom. Particularly revolting to Jane was Billy's habit of urinating in a pot he kept beside the bed. Sometimes he ignored the pot and simply wet the bed. "When that happened, he'd start to hoot and holler until I got up and stripped the bed and changed the sheets. He knew I needed my sleep because I had to work. He slept all day while I worked, but he did his best to keep me awake at night. To get to work was a pleasure, tired or not. It was when I came home that my work really started."

In retrospect, the shot Billy Stafford fired at Jane while she was filling the woodstove was a turning point in her life. It was the last time in their relationship she was able to voice anger, to rebel against his brutality.

After the shock and fear subsided, Jane stared hatefully at him while he lay in bed laughing, the rifle across his thighs.

"I'm going to leave you," said Jane firmly.

"You can leave me anytime you want, old woman," said Billy, laughing. "But I told you before I won't be a third-time loser. If you go, you'll be coming back, and you'll bring that little bastard with you because I'll start shooting that precious family of yours, one by one."

Jane's anger subsided and she was overcome with deep despair. She felt there was no way out, no hope. "I realized I just couldn't stand any more. I totally withdrew from that point on. I built a protective wall around myself. I didn't have the strength or the will to deal with it. I resigned as a wife, a mother—a human being. I had always found the strength to deal with whatever came along. No more. I'd had it. The limit was reached. My mind went limp, blank, and drained of emotion. I became a robot and believed that only in death would I find peace."

The metamorphosis was now complete. Jane Stafford had become a perfect example of the so-called battered-wife syndrome. Blamed so often for the attacks against her, she comes to believe they're her own fault. With the last of her fight gone, she becomes passive and demoralized, feeling no self-worth and believing she's not worth saving. She stays only because she fears her husband will kill her, her children, or her family. Besides, she has no money and nowhere to go.

VI

Billy Stafford's reign of terror wasn't restricted to his Bangs Falls home. Many people—friends, relatives, even strangers—around Queens County had had run-ins with him over the years. Marilyn Fisher met Billy in the fall of 1978. One day her dog came home bleeding from a bullet wound. The bullet had passed right through the dog's neck. The dog survived and Marilyn Fisher's son, Barry, followed the trail of blood across the river to the driveway leading to Stan and Margaret Joudrey's and Billy Stafford's homes. Marilyn took her dog to a veterinarian "and when I came home from there I went into the RCMP headquarters. That was on a Monday." Billy Stafford showed up at her door the next afternoon. "There was a knock at my door. I can't remember the words that he used. He was standing there with both fists doubled up, shaking them at me. He was hollering about my husband, Cleveland, and my son, Barry." Several woman friends were visiting her at the time and she was embarrassed and frightened.

"Are you Mr. Stafford?" she asked.

"You're goddamn right I am!" screamed Billy.

"Well, it wasn't my husband or my son who reported you to the Mounties. It was me."

"I didn't shoot your fucking dog. Why did you say I did?"

"My son followed the blood."

"How do you know Stan Joudrey didn't shoot it?"

"I know Stan well enough that he'd never do something like that."

Billy went into a rage and began screaming and cursing at her. "He looked like a wild man. His face was red, his eyeballs were bulging out of his head. He scared me. I was terrified, so I said, 'Good-bye, Mr. Stafford,' and shut the door in his face." Marilyn Fisher's husband was furious when he learned about Billy's visit. "My husband talked to him and told him if he ever came near us again he'd kill him." Billy Stafford never bothered them again.

In the spring of 1979, Marsha Freeman was walking down the road near Greenfield, pushing her child ahead of her in a baby carriage. Billy Stafford was driving on the same road. He drove his car right at them, swerving at the last minute. "He gave me a good scare. I thought he was going to hit us with his car. And it was deliberate." Marsha Freeman reported Billy to the RCMP and he was taken to court, fined, and put on probation. At the time, Marsha and her husband, Kevin, were building a house directly across the river from Billy Stafford's place. They built it slowly, as time and money permitted. It took them four years in all.

Before Billy had tried to frighten Marsha with the car, the Freemans had hired a man to do some backhoe work. "The fellow left his backhoe in our yard with oil drums in the bucket, and it was facing the Stafford house. When he came the next day there were holes, bullet holes in the oil drums." The Freemans didn't call the police because "at the time we didn't know whether it was accidental or exactly how it happened. We just assumed that it was maybe some child had a gun." At that time they had no reason to connect Billy to the holes in the oil drum. But they later found a bullet hole in the house they were building. "We have no proof as to who did it but it was from the direction of his [Billy's] house." The RCMP investigated that incident. Allen remembers Billy shooting at the Freeman house while it was under construction. "On New Year's Eve night, he never used to shoot off his gun at twelve o'clock, he'd shoot it off about three o'clock in the morning. He used to shoot at a house that a fellow was building there."

One summer day in 1980 Allen was home when two of Jane's cousins, Victor Westhaver and Doug Parnell, dropped in to visit Jane and Billy. "I was watching TV and I don't know what happened. Dougie was talking to Ma or something. Bill had a forty-ouncer, and he was talking. Suddenly he jumped up and grabbed ahold of Dougie and threw him over against the sink." Victor Westhaver, who was sitting in a chair at the time, remembers asking Billy what was going on.

"Don't hold your head up to me or I'll put it down!" Billy shouted at Victor.

"It'll take a lot more than you to put it down," replied Westhaver.

Allen says as soon as Billy heard that, "He just cracked him. His head hit the wall and when it come back he was all full of blood." Billy turned to Jane.

"Get the gun, old woman. I'll get rid of them."

Obediently, Jane took a .22 from the gun rack and handed it to him. He aimed it at them.

"Get the fuck out of here or you'll be carried out!" screamed Billy.

"Come on, let's go," said Westhaver to Doug Parnell as they rushed for the door. "I headed for my truck," said Westhaver, "and I heard a shot go off. I wasn't looking back to see if he was shooting at me or up or down or where. But I heard the shot so I just jumped in my truck and Dougie jumped in the other side and we just drove off. I thought he was crazy." Allen was scared and ran from the house at the same time. He said Billy fired in Westhaver's direction "and parted Vicky's hair, I guess."

Ivan Higgins, from the small town of Brooklyn, near Liverpool, once sold Billy Stafford a woodstove. Billy invited him, his wife, and two-year-old child to visit his house in Bangs Falls. "It wasn't any real party by any means. We got there and Billy had just installed the new woodstove and we were sitting around talking to him. Maybe about an hour had gone by and the next thing you know, Billy was quite upset with me. I really didn't notice anything too different about him, but I had to be real careful what I said to him. Maybe he had a few too many beers or something, I don't know. Next thing you know, he turned on me. He was quite grumpy and gruff." Higgins is not a big man. Suddenly he found himself sitting in a chair with the threatening form of Billy Stafford looming in front of him. Higgins got to his feet.

"What's wrong, Billy?" he asked, backing away.

Billy punched him in the mouth with no warning. "I'm hardly a man to stand up to him; after I realized he really intended to do some harm to me, I scooted out. Some people grabbed his arm. He was quite upset with me. I couldn't make out why or what. Somebody said I should just get out." The Higgins' child was asleep in another room. "I'll be grabbing the kid," said his wife. Higgins was sitting barefooted and didn't even have time to get his sneakers on. "A couple of friends just sort of kept him at bay and I zoomed out of there. He came in a few days later, very apologetic, saying such things as, 'I wouldn't be much of a man if I couldn't apologize for something like this.' Ever since that we got along fine, but I never went to any more parties of his."

Ronny Wamboldt's brother, Gene, stands six feet tall and weighs about 210 pounds, not as big a man as Billy Stafford but quite capable of handling himself. He once had a fight with Billy, and it ended in pretty much a draw. He knew Billy for about twenty years and considered him his friend. "Well, if you stood up to him, you didn't have any trouble with him," says Wamboldt. "But if he thought you were scared of him, he'd keep it that way. He had an awful temper. He'd fly off the handle some quick. It grew worse as he got older." He saw Billy once in a while when he went out to Bangs Falls to see his brother. He noticed Billy was smoking a lot of dope, and he warned Ronny Wamboldt that if he stayed he was going to get himself in trouble.

Billy was using a lot of dope, and the RCMP suspected him of buying and selling it. Initially, he used mostly marijuana, but as he travelled to ports in Europe, Jamaica, and Mexico he began bringing home hash and acid. Jane said when he came home from his last trip "he brought some kind of pills and he made me and Ronny a pot of tea and put some of them in it. I was in another world for a couple of days and Ronny almost went crazy." Her son Allen was watching TV and saw Ronny's reaction. "I think it was acid or something. About an hour later Ronny said he saw a truck with no wheels on it going around out in the yard. And he saw a duck lay a golden egg on the floor and he was like that for three days. Bill just sat back and had a good laugh."

But Billy Stafford wasn't laughing when he mixed acid and alcohol. "It was bad enough when he drank," said Jane, "but when he did both at the same time, you could see murder in his eyes. He had a spell for three nights in a row where he brought one of the wooden kitchen chairs into the bedroom and used two of his belts to strap me to it. He would load up the shotgun and lay on the bed with it pointing at me. Those were three long nights. I didn't know if I was going to see daylight or not. He just raved on and on through those nights. When the alarm went off, he'd get up, unstrap me, and tell me to get ready for work." Before freeing Jane on one of those mornings, Billy Stafford urinated over her head.

Ronny Wamboldt's estranged wife, Andrea, has a pleasant face that hides a lot of bad memories. She was married to Wamboldt for twenty-one years, and she left at her children's urging. Ronny was drunk most of the time, and he used to beat her. Andrea grew up with Billy Stafford's first wife, Pauline, and went to school with Billy in Liverpool. She and Jane Stafford got to know each other—and became the best of friends— through their husbands. Andrea lived with Ronnie in a house in Milton before she left him and moved to Toronto. They saw Jane and Billy at least once a week. Andrea also worked with Jane at the Hillsview Acres County Home for three years. She remembers visiting the Staffords in 1978 or 1979. Margaret Joudrey was also there. "Billy and Ron were drinking and suddenly Billy got up and started beating Jane around the head and face. He was calling her 'Pauline' and beating on her. I had to holler at him. I said, 'That's not Pauline,' and he snapped right out of it." Andrea knew Billy had mistreated Pauline, but at first she didn't know Jane well enough to warn her about him. "Billy and Jane got along well when they first started living together, but things changed after Darren was born. I saw him beat her up many a time."

Andrea never thought about going to the police to complain about Billy's treatment of Jane, or of Pauline before her. She was also being beaten at home, and "if I went to the police, what would Billy have done to Pauline and Jane? He would have killed the pair of them. He threatened to a good many times. There's no protection. There's no protection whatsoever for women that are being beaten. Pauline had to leave or he would have ended up killing her. But he told Jane, I heard him say it many times, 'Old woman, get it out of your head. Don't think you're leaving me, because I'll kill you. I'll find you and kill you.' He never got over Pauline leaving him, which is why he threatened Jane. Telling a woman to leave a situation is easier said than done. You've got a lot of things to think about. You're scared. You've got kids to look after. You don't know where you're going to go, who's going to look after you. And Jane was really afraid of Billy. She was scared of Billy. Really frightened. She wanted out of that situation. Every other week she had bruises—on her face, on her body. I didn't like Billy. I was very scared of him. When Pauline took her kids to Ontario, they couldn't talk. They had to get speech therapy, he had them so scared."

When Andrea Wamboldt returned from Toronto on her vacation in February 1980, she went to Hillsview Acres to surprise Jane and her other former workmates. It was a Wednesday and Jane was off for the next two days. Andrea agreed to stay with her in Bangs Falls while she was off. On Thursday they went into town and bought a quart of rum to celebrate their reunion. Billy was home quietly drinking and went to bed shortly after Darren and Allen went to bed. The women sat up, talking about old times. At about 2:00 A.M., Billy suddenly appeared in the bedroom doorway with a .30-.30 rifle. He pointed it at Andrea Wamboldt's head.

"You're just like Pauline," he said with a sneer. "Leaving your husband like that. You never should have left Ron." He turned to Jane and began beating her on the head and face with the gun.

"Don't get it in your head to leave me, old woman!" he screamed. Billy grabbed both women by their throats, ripping the neck of Andrea's sweater and glaring at her.

"Now get the fuck out of here or I'll blow your fucking head off."

Andrea fled the house without her coat. It was dark and windy and the temperature was below zero.

She walked three miles in the cold to Hillsview Acres, where she called her brother, who drove out to pick her up. "Jane brought my coat in the next day and apologized for what happened. She wanted me to come back out for supper that night because Billy wanted to apologize to me. I said, 'No way.' I never saw Billy after that."

After Andrea had left the house the night before, Billy continued beating Jane with the gun until she was unconscious. It was daylight when she came to, lying on the kitchen floor. Her clothes were wet. Allen heard the beating but waited until Billy was snoring before checking on his mother's condition. "When I found her she wouldn't wake up." He didn't dare turn on a light for fear of waking Billy. Feeling his way in the darkness, Allen went to the kitchen, filled a cup with water, and poured it on his mother's face. "And I shook her a few times but still couldn't wake her. She just laid there. I was nervous about Billy, so I just went back to bed. By the time I got up the next morning, Ma was in bed and there was no water on the floor or anything." Several days later, Allen told his mother he thought she was dead that night because he couldn't rouse her.

Jane Stafford's parents moved to Danesville, about a half hour's drive from Bangs Falls, after her father retired from the armed forces in 1977. It was the same year Jane moved in with Billy. Maurice Hurshman quit drinking in 1980. Jane wasn't close to her family, and she hadn't really spent any time with them since her midteen years. Now that they were living so close to each other they would visit and socialize from time to time. Maurice Hurshman sometimes drank with Billy Stafford. "He wasn't too bad a fellow when he was sober," Maurice Hurshman said of Billy. "You could sit down and talk to him and joke and carry on. But if you was having a drink with him, you had to be very careful what you said because he'd get very violent." He saw an extreme example of that violence one day and avoided Billy Stafford after that. They lived in a spacious trailer home on a landscaped lot with trees and flowers. Jane and Billy were visiting one evening. "We were having a few drinks," recalls Maurice Hurshman, "and I don't know what I said, something jokingly. He thought I called his house a shack or something and he really went into one. He went just like he was crazy, like a madman. He frothed from the mouth and went right into a rage, just that quick." Maurice Hurshman wears glasses. His complexion is ruddy and his thick, steel-grey hair is combed back off his forehead. At five feet, eleven inches and two hundred pounds he wasn't in bad shape for his age. He's kept in condition since his retirement by hiring on as a crew member for fishing boats sailing out of local harbours. But he was no match for Billy Stafford. "He hit me; knocked the window out of the house. He kicked the door. Drove a hole through it. Broke the latch off the outside aluminium door. There was nothing I could do. He knocked me down. The wife and Jane jumped in between. He struck Jane and knocked her back against the wall. Then he said, 'Come on, woman, we're going home,' and they left. After what I saw Billy was like, I never came around them that much. He'd come down to the house after that sometimes and I'd be scared just to hear him come in the yard."

Maurice Hurshman didn't know the extent of the abuse his daughter was suffering at Billy Stafford's hands. "Jane never mentioned it to me. I guess if it would have got out, well, he'd probably have killed her for sure. Jane used to wear dark glasses, but I didn't know this was going on. If she had a bruise or something, I'd say, 'How'd you do that, Jane?' She'd tell me she bumped it or something."

Billy Stafford drove like a man possessed. Jane was terrified when she drove with him. "He was a maniac. You took your life in your hands when you got in a vehicle with him. He was a speed freak. He had to pass everything on the highway. He'd drive as fast as he could. It didn't matter what the weather conditions were or whether he was drunk, sober, or stoned. He had more accidents than you can count on your fingers and toes. I had to take the blame for several of them because he was drunk. He forced me to say I was driving. He lost his license several times for motor-vehicle offenses like speeding and reckless driving. He was a real hazard on the highway. It's a miracle he didn't kill someone or seriously injure them."

Billy usually had a gun with him in his truck when he drove around Queens County, and if he saw a deer, he shot it. It didn't matter what time of year it was—hunting season or not. During the 1981 deer-hunting season Billy really didn't have to worry about bagging one. He'd shot nine deer before the season even opened. He gave some of them away because his freezers were full. It's difficult to understand why Billy Stafford thought the police were out to get him, were picking on him. He was buying, using, and probably selling drugs. He was a deer jacker par excellence. He was often drunk while driving. He disobeyed most traffic laws. And he let it be known on countless occasions that he hated the police.

If it had been publicly known how he treated his animals, he could have been charged under animal welfare laws as well. One of his two cows died after Billy abused it. Jane and others saw him push a shovel handle up the cow's rectum. "One morning after I'd seen him do that, he went out to feed the cow and it was dead. He couldn't get it out of the barn, so he tied a rope around its back and hooked the rope to his truck. He got the cow out and put it on the back of the truck. About that time a friend from Buckfield came by. He knew cattle and he took a look at the cow. He thought it must have had a heart attack but he didn't know what really had happened. Bill took the cow way back into the woods and dumped it off the truck and left it."

Billy Stafford hated the RCMP in general and Constable Gary Grant in particular. Grant first met Billy in 1977, shortly after he was transferred to Liverpool from a posting in a small town in rural Newfoundland. Today Grant has slimmed down considerably, but in his three years in Liverpool he carried 250 pounds on his six-foot, three-inch frame. Grant looks affable enough. His light brown hair has receded enough that he can properly classify himself as bald on top. He has a neatly trimmed moustache and dimples in his cheeks. The lines at the corners of his mouth, from a distance, make it look like he's perpetually smiling. Gary Grant has a quick wit, but he can be tough when he has to be.

"I spent five and a half years in Newfoundland. On Friday nights we put on old clothes because we knew we'd be out breaking up fights. We had five clubs to police and there was only two of us, but in those days people showed some respect for the RCMP. It was a small town and the people would line up for their mail at the post office. We'd line up right along with them but they always insisted we go ahead of them. It was almost embarrassing but it was a courtesy they wanted to show us."

He had his baptism of fire in the Newfoundland town when he got into a slugfest at the scene of an accident with half the town watching. His opponent was a local tough, a big man who was drunk. Grant finally got the better of him and was putting the cuffs on him when a man in the crowd stepped out and helped him. When he or his partner were called to a club to break up a fight "we always put the sirens on a half mile away" to give the participants fair warning that they were coming. "If they were still at it when we arrived we always took one of them away or they'd be at it as soon as we left. They knew we meant business but they knew we were fair. If there was a crowd around the fight, they always cleared a path for us. We were both a good size but we had to be. We had no backup for sixty miles."

Gary Grant joined the RCMP in 1969. He now heads the drug squad in Bridgewater. "When I arrived in Liverpool Billy Stafford was a topic of conversation. We were warned about him. He was a person we had to keep an eye on. I was made aware of Billy Stafford by word of mouth. There was nobody like him. Two or three months after I got there, I stopped him to size him up. I wanted to know about him and I wanted him to know I was in town. I was friendly that first time but even though I'd never met him, he was totally hostile. He was one of those guys you'd look into his eyes and see the hate, like he wanted to tear your face off. There wasn't even an attempt to cover his hostility. He was the kind of guy you'd never let think you were afraid of for a second. You had to have that approach with him or you'd lose. If he thought you were intimidated, he'd own you. You never knew with Billy Stafford. He was helter-skelter. The people who lived out there couldn't really enjoy the place knowing he was around. I used to stop him every two or three months. He never crossed the line but he always went right to it. He knew the police were looking at him and we took verbal abuse every time."

Grant and two other officers were once sent out to Billy's house to search for illegal venison. "My role was to take care of Billy Stafford and let them do the search. I was half thinking, maybe today was the day I'd find out what the guy was made of. I was prepared. Let's get at her—pitter, patter."

The Mounties parked their cruiser at the foot of the driveway and strolled towards the house. They weren't in any rush. It was deer meat they were after, and it would be difficult to conceal quickly. Grant knocked on the outside door. There were a few chickens squawking in the yard.

"What the fuck do you want?" shouted Billy from behind the door.

"These hens are all virgins," said Grant, trying to ease the tension.

"You're wrong—I fucked them all," said Billy sharply. "What do you want?"

"We've got a search warrant here to look for deer meat."

Billy opened the door partially.

"There's no fucking deer meat here. You guys are always trying to get me. You fucking assholes."

Gary Grant was contemplating citing Billy for obstruction of justice when suddenly the door opened.

"Fuck it, come in," he said. "You want to come in and fucking look, come in and look."

Grant went to the centre of the living room "because I figured that's where we'd have it out if there was going to be a problem." The other officers began searching the house. "They were looking for illegal deer meat and we wanted to see what weapons and ammunition he had around. Billy came within two feet of me and came out with a string of obscenities. He was bugged that he couldn't keep his eyes on all three of us at once. He'd stare at me and then glance quickly over to the other two." One of the other officers opened a dresser drawer.

"What the fuck are you looking for in there? Panties?" shouted Billy. "Why don't you sniff them?"

Grant moved towards him when he started cursing at the officer.

"Why don't you grow up and start acting like a man," said Grant.

That threw Billy into a worse rage. "He just went on and on. I got in about ten words. His eyes bugged out. He was red as a beet and started frothing at the mouth. He looked very intimidating. I'd dealt with mental cases in the past and when they explode they become very strong. I thought, 'If he explodes, he's going to be totally awesome to deal with.' I made up my mind: If he made a move for me, I'd kick him in the testicles. I was half scared so I was looking for the quickest way to end it. His spit was hitting me in the face. It was just flying all over. He was like a demon. He never moved more than a foot away from me the whole time.'

"You rotten cocksucker, one of these days you're going to push me too far!" screamed Billy.

Billy didn't complete a single sentence without an obscenity. "He was totally enraged. We'd violated him. We were in his domain. This was his fortress, and we were inside. He continued to abuse us as we left. We looked around outside for power cords in case he had a buried freezer somewhere. We didn't find anything. It was the most distractive search I've ever been on. I never met anyone like Billy Stafford."

Jane Stafford had sat quietly during the search listening to Billy's rantings. He kept it up when they left the house. He stomped through the house hollering and bellowing about Gary Grant. "He hated all cops with a passion but he especially hated Grant," Jane said.

"One of these days I'll get that fucking Grant!" screamed Billy. "I'll get him alone somewhere and I guarantee you, only one of us will be coming out alive. I killed one man already and got away with it. It would be a real thrill to kill that cocksucker."

"What do you mean, you killed one man already?" asked Jane, frightened but curious.

"Do you remember Jimmy LeBlanc? He supposedly jumped overboard a few years back. In fact, old woman, it was Valentine's Day, '74. Well, he never jumped. I threw him overboard. He made me mad and I threw him over the side. And I'm going to kill Grant when I get him alone—no witnesses—just the same as with Jimmy."

Jane sat stunned. "That really put the fear in me," she said later.

Jane was a good worker and well thought of at Hillsview Acres. Her bosses promoted her to chef after only one month at the home, and in June 1981 they approached her and asked if she was interested in attending a cooking workshop in Truro, Nova Scotia, all expenses paid. "My bosses, Raymond and Debbie Fiske, gave me all the information about the workshop and we talked about it all one afternoon. I wanted badly to go. It would have been an interesting learning venture, and Lord knows I needed it. I'd been with Billy for five years at that point and my mind had become stagnant. I still had a secret desire for learning, and I wanted this so much. I told them I'd give them an answer by the end of the week. That gave me four days to catch Bill in a good mood and get his approval. Deep inside I knew it was no good to get my hopes up, but I wanted to go so badly. When I got home that day, Bill appeared to be in a good mood. He wasn't working at the time but he'd received his unemployment insurance cheque that day so he was all set with his booze and his drugs. He didn't yell at me or hit me when I came through the door, and that was a good sign. I never talked unless I was spoken to, so I just walked in and smiled and started about my work. We got through our usual suppertime ordeal and I got Darren settled in bed." Billy sensed something was on Jane's mind.

"Okay, old woman, what is it? You've been going around here like a dog shitting razor blades ever since you got home, so spit it out."

"Well . . . there's this cooking workshop in Truro from June 30 until July 3. I've been asked to attend on behalf of Hillsview Acres. It's all expenses paid. I'd really like to go. It sounds very interesting and I'd learn a lot."

Jane realized immediately she'd made a mistake, telling Billy how important it was to her. "For the next four days he played cat and mouse with me. One minute he'd tell me I could go and I would get excited and happy. Then he'd tell me I couldn't go." Jane was off, as usual, on Thursday and Friday. Billy gave her a black eye during that time. When she was leaving for work Billy told her she could go to the workshop, but she knew he was just toying with her. "When I got to work I told Raymond Fiske I couldn't go because I had too much to do at home." When she arrived home from work Billy met her at the door.

"I made up my mind," he said, gloating, "you ain't going to no fucking workshop. I may have said this morning you could go, but now I say you ain't. And that's the end of it. Now run down to Margaret's and phone that bastard boss of yours and tell him you ain't going'."

"I already told him I wasn't going," said Jane.

"You think you are some fuckin' smart now, don't you. You old bag. Well, I'll tell you something, old woman. You think you can outthink me, eh? It will be one fucking foggy day when you get one step ahead of me. You'll never live long enough to outthink me. I've been sent by the devil. I have the power. And that old grey-whiskered prick up there [Billy pointed to the heavens] can't help you." He began pounding on the table with his closed fist and his voice rising.

Suddenly he was on his feet. He punched Jane

about the head and chest. "He started choking me, squeezing my throat. As I started to pass out I heard him saying, 'I am sent by the devil.' When I came to, he was snoring in the bedroom. I picked myself up and I remember thinking, 'I hate you, Stafford. I hate you'—and I had never hated anyone in my life. Yet there was also a different feeling. I thought about what Bill had said about my never getting one step ahead of him and I knew I had done just that. It was some sort of a small victory."

Billy didn't allow Jane to go anywhere unless it was to run an errand for him. If she went to town there was a time limit. "When I went anywhere, I avoided talking to anyone. I was terrified if someone spoke to me. When that happened I told Bill as soon as I got home. I was that paranoid. Bill was a very jealous man, although he never had any reason to be. As a couple we never went anywhere in public, never to a movie, a restaurant, a dance, or a tavern. When we did go out it was to someone's house to drink or smoke dope. The only entertainment I knew was work, work, work. I wasn't even allowed to attend church or speak of the Lord. I wasn't allowed to have a Bible, and I wasn't even allowed to have any pictures of any members of my family in the house."

VII

In the first months that Jane lived with Billy Stafford, their sex life was normal. But all that changed after Darren's birth. Jane's pubic hair was shaved off for Darren's delivery. Billy found that sexually stimulating. From then on he began shaving Jane's pubic hairs periodically. It got worse for Jane when Billy began sailing on the gypsum boats to ports in Norway, Holland, Mexico, Portugal, Bermuda, and Boston and New York in the United States. "Until he started on the boats, he just kept shaving me. But when he started on the boats he would come home and tie me to a chair and pluck out the hair with a pair of tweezers. He always used to say, 'You won't have to worry, because when I get done with you no man will ever want you.' He would tie me to a chair and pull each hair out one at a time. My legs were spread apart. It was very embarrassing and painful. When he went away on those boats, he would buy me all kinds of weird underwear—things in white, gold, silver, black, and red. And fancy garter belts, silk stockings, and panties without crotches." He also bought her half-cup bras, perfumes, and sheer nighties. Billy also brought home piles of pornographic magazines. Jane believes they incited Billy to indulge in increasingly degrading, bizarre, and painful sexual rituals. "Usually he came home off the boats in the middle of the night. He would wake Darren up, show him what he bought him, give him a beating, and put him back to bed. Then he'd stand me in the middle of the room, rip my nightgown off me, and throw it in the garbage. He'd examine me from head to foot to see if I had any marks or bruises on me, and if I had any, I had to explain how I got them. He would call me every dirty name he could think of, put the stereo on full blast, and run my bath water."

After Jane bathed, Billy would douse her with perfume and dress her up in whatever new underwear he'd brought home with him. "He would lay down on the bed and order me to undress him. While I was doing that he would bite my breasts and pinch the insides of my thighs. It was very painful." Billy then hurled Jane to the bed on her stomach and tied her wrists to the bedrail with heavy string or fishing line. He forced her to her knees and spanked and slapped her buttocks until they were sore and burning. His "games" would vary, but usually he untied her hands from the bedrail and retied them with Jane's wrists together. Then he forced her to masturbate while he watched from above. Untying her hands once again, he'd retie them behind her back and order her to her knees. He would enter her from behind, but after a few minutes of copulation, force himself into her anus. "The pain was always so awful. It was like being torn apart." It was apparently painful for Billy, too, because about the third or fourth time he went through that ritual, he went out to the barn and returned with a piece of solid plastic plumbing pipe, an inch in diameter and four or five inches long.

"This'll fix it so you get used to it," declared Billy as he greased the pipe with Vaseline and forced it into Jane's rectum. She was forced to leave the pipe inside her whenever he was home. She was allowed to remove it only when she went to work or when Billy wanted sex. The entire ritual was repeated for several months until Billy returned from a trip to Mexico. "I came home from work and he was already home, sitting at the table drinking. He brought Darren a beautiful Mexican hat."

"Have you been a good boy while Daddy was gone?" asked Billy.

"Yes, Daddy."

"Then this is for you," said Billy, handing him the hat.

Darren tried it on.

"Okay, now put it away and get to bed," Billy ordered, cuffing the boy.

Billy was on his feet the second Darren's door closed. "He came over to me and slapped me across the face several times. He ripped my clothes off and examined me. As usual, he tied me to a chair and plucked out my hairs and, as usual, it was painful, disgusting, and humiliating. When I was naked and bathed and perfumed, he tied my hands behind my back and put a dog collar around my neck. It had a leash. He led me around the house on my hands and knees, examining me. We finally went into the bedroom, where he made me lay across his knees and he beat me with a hard-bristled hairbrush until I started to cry and beg him to stop." Billy then forced Jane to masturbate while he photographed her with a Polaroid camera. "When he got tired of that he said he had a surprise for me." He went out and went through his seabag and returned with an artificial penis and a vibrator.

"You won't have to masturbate with your hands anymore," said Billy. "This will be better." He plugged in the vibrator and ordered Jane to use it on herself. "My hands were now tied in front of me and I was lying on my back. He had my feet tied to the bedrails with my legs spread wide apart. He took the artificial penis and kept shoving it in and out of my mouth."

"You're such a good cocksucker," said Billy, forcing it into her mouth.

Jane bit on the artificial penis to stop the pain, but that angered Billy.

"You'll have to pay for that," he declared. "I'll have to wash your mouth out with something bad." Jane watched as he urinated in a glass. He approached her, grabbed her by the hair, and forced her to drink it. The degradation continued; he tied all of her limbs to the bed and penetrated her with the vibrator and artificial penis. Later he forced her to perform oral sex on him and ejaculated on her face. Billy fell asleep while Jane lay there wondering what further depravity she would be subjected to. Three hours later he awakened and began pummelling her about the head and shoulders. He dragged her by the breasts into the bathroom, where he forced her to her hands and knees in the tub as it filled with hot water. Jamming her douche syringe in and out of her anus, he screamed obscenities at her and beat her. When she screamed in pain he took a pair of soiled panties from a laundry hamper and shoved them into her mouth. Dragging her back to the bedroom, he again tied her up, abused her with his "toys," and forced her to have anal sex. That scenario was repeated many times, but the worst was yet to come.

Jane was menstruating when Billy arrived home from the boats one afternoon. After the usual bathing and perfuming ritual, he ordered her to mount him. Jane was bleeding heavily and he forced her to lick the blood off him. Then he brought in their St. Bernard dog and tried to force her to fellate the animal. Jane vomited and he forced her to clean up the mess and then copulate with the dog while simultaneously fellating him.

It's difficult to conceive the innocent young teenager who sought love in a soft, grassy field in Germany now being battered and sexually tortured by a monster. That she was able somehow to cope and manage to survive seems miraculous in itself. "To me, I was violated in the most degrading ways possible. Courage is often a matter of learning that you can survive doing things that frighten and hurt you. Do it often enough and the fear gets somewhat tamed, but it's always there, gnawing away at you."

VIII

Jane Stafford felt totally trapped, isolated, and alone. Only she knew the full extent of Billy Stafford's growing depravity. Others around her were probably aware that Billy beat her from time to time—but wives getting slapped around was not all that unusual. With Billy not working, her only respite was her job at Hillsview Acres and her quiet moments with Darren and Allen when Billy was away from the house. Besides the beatings and sexual humiliation and degradation, Jane was constantly denigrated, threatened, and verbally abused. "You hear it so often, that everything is your own fault, that you're always wrong, you begin to believe it." What Jane Stafford didn't realize was that as bad as her life with Billy was, her situation was commonplace for thousands of women living similar hells across the country. She didn't know that about half a million Canadian women each year are threatened, punched, kicked, knifed, or shot. She didn't know that calls to domestic disputes, a euphemism for wife-battering, are the largest category of requests to police for help, even though less than 10 percent of incidents are reported to police. Jane never went to the police about Billy Stafford. She didn't dare. She'd seen how Billy manipulated the law and forced others to take the blame for his crimes.

In a very real way Jane Stafford was the victim of society's patriarchal institutions, including the legal system and religion, which have both entrenched violence against wives for thousands of years. At that time in Jane's life, feminism combined with the increasing participation of married women in the work force were beginning the final push to get wife-battering out of the closet. Despite that push, however, religion and the legal system continued to perpetuate wife-beating by tacitly supporting the preservation of the family unit over the safety of women. Even judges encouraged the belief that if a domestic assault was treated as a crime, it would break up the family. Better to treat it lightly, do whatever is necessary to keep the family together.

When police did respond to domestic disputes, did not actually witness an assault, and the woman wasn't seriously injured—no broken bones or bloodied face— no charges were laid. More often than not, the police would tell the woman to get a lawyer or see a justice of the peace and lay a charge and go to court herself. Crown attorneys seemed to give wife-assault cases a low priority, viewing the problem as less serious than assault between strangers. And when cases actually went to court, judges were loath to send a man to jail because it would break up a family. As a result, courts rarely imposed jail terms or even fines. Typically, they handed out suspended sentences, probation orders, or absolute or conditional discharges. That was despite the fact that 20 percent of all homicides in Canada are spouse slayings, and of 222 women murdered in Canada in 1982, more than half were killed by their spouses or ex-spouses.

Jane Stafford's desperation was compounded by the fact that Billy's two previous wives had fled the province to get away from him. She believed that his threats to kill members of her family if she left were real. Jane came to the conclusion that either she or Billy would die in their house in Bangs Falls. "The older he got, the worse he got. I can remember twice waking up through the night and getting out of bed and getting the shotgun and loading it and putting it to his head when he was asleep. The only thing that kept me from pulling the trigger was the fact that Darren would wake up to see what a mess his father would be in. That is the only reason I never pulled the trigger."

Jane also contemplated suicide but discarded the idea. Leaving Darren to grow up alone under Billy's roof was out of the question. On one occasion Jane drove with Darren to a curve on a highway where cars and trucks would be unable to stop when suddenly confronted by a parked vehicle in the middle of the road. There is heavy truck traffic on that particular road, and Jane figured she and Darren would be killed instantly if one hit them. "I considered that and then I said, 'Hell, no,' maybe I could do it for myself, but not for Darren. My son was the only thing that kept me from death and from losing my sanity. He was my strength, my gift from God, my whole instinct to survive." Billy had beaten Jane into unconsciousness more than once. She knew the time would come when she wouldn't wake up. Her desperation and her instinct for survival started her to thinking of hiring someone, an outsider, to kill Billy. The man she chose for the job was Beverly Taylor, from the coastal town of Riverport, on the LaHave River about an hour's drive away. Taylor was a fisherman who later got a job on an oil rig. He came to the Stafford house in Bangs Falls around Christmas in 1981. "He arrived with a friend of Bill's and they were talking about some dope deals and he mentioned about having a gun and talk along that line. I thought he might be able to help me." She thought about how to approach Taylor over the next couple of weeks. Fellow workers at the Hillsview Acres County Home in Greenfield noticed Jane seemed more withdrawn than usual and she was losing weight noticeably. "It seemed like something was bothering her but I didn't know what," recalled Gail Brewster, who worked with Jane at the home for three years as a domestic. She was also replacement cook on Thursdays and Fridays, Jane's days off. Sometime around Christmas she noticed a bruise on Jane's arm and another under her left eye "but she covered it with makeup." In January, Jane approached Gail and asked her to telephone Beverly Taylor in Riverport.

"I'm having something made for Bill's birthday," explained Jane. "I don't want him to know about it. Call Bev Taylor and ask him to call me at work between seven and three."

Gail Brewster tried for a week to reach Taylor. "I finally got him on a Saturday morning before I went to work."

Eventually Jane talked to Taylor and asked him to visit her at Hillsview Acres. "She didn't really specify why. She just said it meant a great deal of money." After two more calls from Jane he agreed to meet her. He arrived on a Sunday morning shortly after breakfast. The home's assistant matron, Muriel Oliver, answered the door. "I came out to see what he wanted and Jane said 'This is for me,' so I went back in the house." Jane met Taylor at the back door. It was snowing heavily outside. They went to a small room at the rear of the home for privacy.

"What did you want to see me about?" asked Taylor.

"I want to hire somebody to hit Billy. To kill him."

"Why did you pick me?"

"You look like a guy that would help a person out of a bad situation."

"Why do want him killed?"

"I've got good reason."

"Does he beat you?"

Jane nodded.

"He's driving my little boy crazy and he threatened to kill my mother and father if I ever left him."

Taylor noticed the desperation in Jane's eyes.

"What's in it for me?" he asked out of curiosity.

"Twenty thousand dollars," replied Jane. "It's Bill's life-insurance policy. You can have it all."

Taylor was silent for a moment.

"I'm not interested in anything to do with killing Billy," he said. "Why not phone a lawyer or something?"

"There wouldn't be any purpose in that. He'd get revenge on me or hurt my mother and father. I could never run far enough to get away from him."

"What about the police?"

"They can't do anything."

Jane's mind was in turmoil. She felt that an opportunity to do away with Billy was slipping through her fingers.

"Billy jacks a lot of deer. He's always hunting in the bush. You could do it there and leave him. Nobody would ever know who to suspect because he's got so many enemies."

"I can't do that. But Billy trucks dope back and forth on the gypsum boats. Why don't you set him up and have him put away for a couple of years."

Jane pondered the idea for a few moments. She thought it might work. She told Taylor she would be in touch with him about it. When Taylor left Hillsview, he felt uneasy. "I wasn't really sure whether she was serious or not at the time. I thought it might have been Billy putting her up to it for some reason, so I just went down and paid Billy a visit and talked to him. Billy was involved in drugs to the best of my knowledge and that's the only thing I could figure. And when I talked to a few of Billy's friends later, they said that's pretty well something he might very well do."

A day or two later, Taylor telephoned Jane. "He asked me for three hundred dollars so he could get enough dope to set Bill up. I said no because somehow, someway, Bill would have got out of that. One of us, me, Ronny, somebody, would have took the blame for it."

Jane did not give up on Beverly Taylor. She telephoned him two or three more times to see if he would help her "like hiring another guy to kill Billy. She also asked me to get her poison. I said 'no' and after a while she just stopped calling and that was the end of it."

That was the end of it for Beverly Taylor but not for Jane Stafford. "I wanted him dead. I hated him. He was a maniac."

IX

Billy Stafford was all business when he awoke on the morning of March 11, 1982. He had a project under way and he wanted to get at it. By daybreak, he, Allen, and Ronnie Wamboldt were in Billy's truck headed up River Road to Freeman's Sawmill to pick up a load of sawdust. He planned to make three or four runs before lunchtime. The sawdust was being used as fill behind the barn, where Billy planned to build a pigpen. Chuckling to himself, he recounted his confrontation with Margaret Joudrey the night before, when he had informed her he planned to raise pigs. She complained that the stink would be awful. Billy told her he could do as he pleased, and once again they argued over whether or not Margaret owned her land. He knew it further upset her that the land issue was being raised in front of Roger Manthorne, who was in the trailer at the time. Manthorne was frightened of Billy Stafford and sat silently as the argument progressed.

"Old lady, I'd like to burn you out," said Billy as he left the trailer.

About the time Billy's truck pulled into Freeman's Sawmill, Jane Stafford was at home doing the laundry.

It was her day off but she got up to do the washing early because, according to the forecast, the bright sunshine was to give way to fog and rain by early afternoon. "I had to get the laundry done, hung out, and dried before the rain started. They got done hauling sawdust about midmorning and they came in for tea. I made them tea and a sandwich. My laundry was all finished and on the line and the kids were outside. Whenever Bill ate he would lie down and sleep for a while." Ronny Wamboldt went out to the shed Billy had built near the barn. It had a stove and a bed in it. He was asleep in minutes. Jane was in the kitchen when Billy called to her from the bedroom.

"Come in here and give me a backrub," he demanded.

Jane went immediately to the bedroom.

"Shut the door and strip," ordered Billy. "I want to screw ya."

As Jane undressed, she glanced over her body. Ugly bruises and welts were visible on her upper left arm between the shoulder and the elbow, and on her left leg from her hip to her ankle. She shivered involuntarily, remembering the beating she'd received several days earlier. She'd been in bed and Billy had the stereo playing full blast so no one could sleep. Between songs she called out to him politely,

"Hon, could you please turn the stereo down a bit?"

Billy peered into the bedroom.

"What's the matter? Is the music bothering you? Is it keeping you awake?"

"Yes, hon, it is."

"Just a minute, I'll fix that."

Jane looked up seconds later to see Billy enter the bedroom with the metal portion of a vacuum-cleaner hose. Cringing, she lay on her right side against the wall. When the first blow landed, she put her left arm up to protect her head. He struck her over and over with the pipe.

"Don't tell me what to do in my fucking house, you

tramp!" he shouted. "I'll kill you. I'll give you something to complain about, and it won't be music."

Jane couldn't shake the image of that beating as she got into bed with Billy. She prayed he wouldn't take long. He climaxed quickly and rolled off her.

"Get the fuck up, old woman, you've got work to do," said Billy, pushing her away.

Jane dressed and went outside to check the clothes on the line. They were dry. She brought them in and had begun ironing them when Margaret Joudrey came to the door.

"Hi, honey. Is Billy home?"

Jane pointed to the bedroom. Margaret Joudrey walked over and looked in.

"Bill, are you awake?" she asked.

"Ya. What the fuck do you want?" said Billy with a grunt.

"You really hurt me by what you said to me in front of Roger last evening, and I want you to know that. I can't fight you alone, so this morning I called Stan's people in the States and they're going to help me fight you. And I called the police and reported you for shooting at my trailer, and they're investigating it."

Billy Stafford jumped up from the bed.

"Get the fuck out of my house and don't ever step foot in here again!" he shouted. "You fuckin' old bag, you don't scare me one little bit!"

Margaret Joudrey turned quickly and left the house with Billy yelling after her.

"You'd better have a good day, you old cunt, because you'll never live to see another one."

Jane Stafford saw the telltale signs: the flushed face, the bulging eyes, and the foam forming at the sides of the mouth. She went over to the table and sat down. Allen and Darren were lying down. Ronny Wamboldt came into the house. Billy told him to get ready to go into town and looked over at Jane.

"Give me some money, old woman, I'm going to town."

"I can't give you any, hon, I've only got enough to

pay the truck insurance when it comes due at the end of the month."

Billy stared at her fiercely.

"What's the matter with you? Sitting there with nothing to do, eh?"

Billy reached for a pile of clean laundry, carried it outside, and threw it in the dirt and mud. He carried the clothes back into the house and threw them around the kitchen floor.

"There now, you fuckin' slut, that should give you enough to do until I get back."

Jane felt nauseated as Billy approached, slapped her across the face, and spat on her. Without a word, he went to her purse on the kitchen cupboard and opened it. "He took whatever money was in it, and they were gone. I just sat there and looked at the mess all around me. The kids got up as soon as Bill left. They were hungry, so I made them something to eat. They looked so sad and pleading. I got out the washing machine and began washing all those dirty, muddy clothes all over again. By then, it was cloudy and rainy and I was a nervous wreck, wondering when they would be home and what shape they'd be in."

Ronny Wamboldt remembers he and Billy stopping in Milton to pick up a quart of rum at the liquor store. They had finished most of the bottle and a marijuana joint by the time they returned to Bangs Falls in time for supper. They drank the rum straight from the bottle without mix, or, as Ronny Wamboldt describes it, "raw" and "that alone." It was about six-thirty when they arrived back at the house. Jane heard the truck's stereo before they came into view. "I could hear it playing full blast. Even before I saw them I knew they were drinking. I don't remember if they ate supper or not. I know they had one drink each to finish off the bottle of rum." Jane did the dishes while Billy and Ronnie sat at the table.

"Did you put that can of gas in the shed, dummy?" asked Billy.

"Yes, sure did," answered Wamboldt.

"I got the truck filled up and I got five extra

gallons," said Billy, addressing Jane. "I charged them at Myles Whynot's garage. You can pay for it when you go into town tomorrow."

Jane noticed Billy seemed contented.

"Well, old woman, see what my horoscope is for today."

Jane looked it up in the book he kept. Billy was pleased with himself when she told him it said it was his lucky day. She was also an Aquarian, but she thought that it certainly hadn't been her lucky day.

"Get ready, old woman," declared Billy, "you're going to drive Ron and me down to Leona's."

Jane remembers it was raining and foggy when the three of them went out to the truck. Billy noticed the five-gallon can of gas was still in the back of the truck.

"Lookit, dummy, the gas is still on the truck."

Wamboldt got out of the cab and took the gas to the shed.

Leona Anthony lived about five miles from the Staffords on the River Road towards Charleston. The road was a mess. The frost was coming out of the ground and, with all the rain, it made driving very difficult. Billy had the stereo wide open, so loud they couldn't hear each other talk. A mile or two along the road, Billy, who was sitting in the middle of the cab, nudged Jane with his elbow.

"Pull over!" he shouted above the music. "I want to smoke a joint!"

Jane sat silent as Billy and Wamboldt shared the marijuana. She felt like she was in a deep well that she could never climb out of. The image of her sons' pleading looks wouldn't leave her mind. "I just kept seeing them in front of me and my thoughts drifted back to the previous spring. Bill was on the boats at sea. Allen had a girlfriend who lived just over the road from where we lived. Her father didn't want Allen around because of Bill's reputation. One Saturday night she told Allen she couldn't see him anymore. Allen came home about 10:30 P.M. He was fifteen years old then. I was already in bed because I had to work in the morning. Allen hollered in at me, 'Good night, Mom. I

love you.' Next thing I heard was the alarm. I got up
and got Darren and myself ready to go. When we went
out I was astonished to see my car was gone. I ran back
into the house to tell Allen that someone had stolen my
car. I was even more shocked to find Allen was also
gone. I went over to Marie and Morton's and I called
my boss and asked him if he could come and pick me
up. He did. When I got to work I called the RCMP and
asked if they knew anything about Allen or my car.
Constable Buchanan said he would come out to work
and pick me up and take me to get my car. It was a
party line and that's all he would say on the phone. He
came and picked me up."

"Mrs. Stafford, we picked up Allen driving your
car," said the policeman. "He was drinking and wouldn't
tell us anything, so we put him in jail for the night. We
were hoping you would get in touch with us this
morning. I think your son has a problem, but he won't
talk."

The RCMP turned Jane's car keys over to her and
let Allen out of jail. The boy was quiet, sullen on the
drive home.

"Why did you take my car?" asked Jane softly.
"Where were you going?"

Allen looked her in the eyes with the same pleading look she was to see again and again.

"Mom," he said quietly, "I took your car and I was
driving to Liverpool to the wharf. I was going to put the
pedal to the metal and drive right off the wharf, into
the ocean and just die."

Jane felt tears welling in her eyes. She wanted to
reach out and hug her son.

"Mom, we aren't living," continued Allen. "We
aren't alive. We're just like robots—we just exist."

Jane knew her son was right, and felt panic and
frustration as she sat in the cab of the truck at the side
of the road in the rain with the stereo blaring while
Billy and Wamboldt passed a joint back and forth. "I
couldn't deny what Allen said back then, any more than
I could deny the look on his face when we left the
house earlier that evening. Well, we got to Leona's.

Ron was drunk and stoned by that time. Leona was at home with her sons, Leslie and Timmy. I think we played cards but I can't really remember. They drank beer. I had one—I never finished it. They also smoked some dope and I had a puff or two when they passed it to me." Billy did most of the talking, which centred on deer hunting and animals. At about 8:30 P.M., he declared it was time to go home. Ronnie Wamboldt staggered into the truck. Again, Billy sat in the centre and Jane drove. "From the time we got into the truck Bill never shut up," recalls Jane. "The stereo was playing full blast and he was ranting and raving above the noise." The focus of Billy's abuse was Margaret Joudrey.

"When Margaret turns her lights off down there tonight, it'll be lights off for her, for good!" he shouted. "I got five gallons of gas in town today and I'm going to dump it all around that fucking trailer and watch them burn. They'll never get out. Can't you just see Margaret with her game leg and Roger with his bad heart, running around trying to get out. They won't have a chance."

Jane stared straight ahead, trying to manage the wheel on the treacherous road while Billy went into a fit of laughter, which she describes as "his evil laugh." He stopped laughing abruptly and stared directly at Jane.

"And I'll deal with that son of yours at the same time. I've waited a long time to deal with him. I might as well clean them all up at one time."

"He went on like that the whole way home, and just before we pulled into the driveway, he fell asleep. He could fall asleep anytime, anyplace, at the drop of a hat. All he had to do was close his eyes and he was asleep."

Allen watched television when Jane and Billy left for Leona Anthony's. "I watched *Fame*," he recalls, "and when that was over figure skating was on, so I didn't watch that. I went to bed." Darren had watched some television with Allen but was sound asleep when Jane pulled into the driveway. Allen woke up when he heard the truck. Outside it was foggy and raining and very dark. Ronnie Wamboldt staggered from the truck into the house and passed out. Allen heard him come in and went back to sleep. Billy, meanwhile, was asleep or passed out in the truck, with Jane behind the wheel beside him. A tape continued to play on the stereo in the cab of the truck. Jane stared straight ahead. It was one of Billy's rules that she had to remain in the truck until he woke up and gave her permission to enter the house. The beatings and the mental anguish, which had become more intense in the previous months, had taken their toll on her body and her mind. Her nerves were frayed and her weight, normally 140 pounds, was hovering just above one hundred pounds. Her eyes seemed blank and distant and had a haunted look about them. Because of the weight loss her clothes didn't fit properly. Her self-esteem was nonexistent, and she had no desire to buy new clothing that would fit. She could see no future.

"I just sat there and the words . . . everything that he had been saying, just started sinking in . . . Margaret . . . Allen. What was he going to do? I just said, 'To hell with it, I'm not going to live like this anymore.'"

Jane beeped the horn. Allen heard it but ignored it. He thought Billy might be fighting with his mother, causing one of them to hit the horn accidentally. He got out of bed and went to the door when he heard a second beep. Opening the door, he peered out, saw his mother, and approached the truck. He remembers it was raining and the truck was parked about ten feet from the door to the house. The driver's window was rolled down.

"Get the gun and load it," said his mother simply.

Allen shrugged and returned to the house. He chose a twelve-gauge, single-shot shotgun, one of seven guns Billy kept on a rack in Ronny Wamboldt's bedroom. He also kept an ammunition box full of rifle shells under the bed. Shotgun slugs and shells were kept in a belt hanging on the gun rack. Allen wasn't quite sure if his mother really wanted the gun. He thought Billy might have wanted it. "A lot of times they

Jane with her younger sisters, Sandy and Mona.

Jane at age fifteen.

Jane's son Allen from
her first marriage.

Jane's son Jamie from her
first marriage.

The turnoff to Bangs Falls and River Road.

The Stafford house at Bangs Falls.

Jane and Billy in happier days.

Jane with Darren when he was a few months old.

Billy with Darren.

Billy with his gun.

Ronny Wamboldt and Billy Stafford asleep in the Stafford living room after heavy drinking.

Margaret Joudrey was like a mother to Jane Stafford until
Billy's death.

Andrea Wamboldt, Jane's best friend and estranged wife of Ronny Wamboldt, who lived with the Staffords.

Billy's truck with his body in the cab.

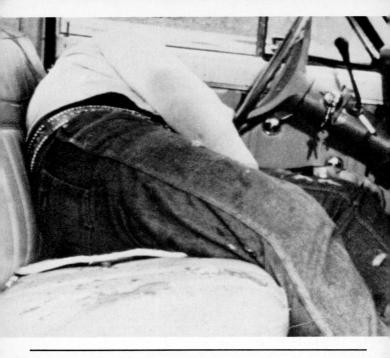

Billy's decapitated body slouched against the driver's door.

The Bangs Falls bridge from which Jane's son Allen and neighbor Roger Manthorne threw the shotgun used to kill Billy.

Gary Grant, the RCMP constable Billy Stafford hated the most.

Prosecutor Blaine Allaby.

Nova Scotia Legal Aid lawyer, Alan Ferrier, who defended
Jane Stafford.

The quaint Liverpool courthouse where Jane was sentenced to six months in prison after pleading guilty to manslaughter.

Jane Stafford awaits jury's decision on steps of the courthouse.

Jane, days before she went back to court for sentencing in February, 1984.

Darren in front of his grandparents' house in early summer, 1985.

Photos provided by CBC, Jane Stafford Hurshman, Brian Vallée, and the RCMP.

porch. He returned to Margaret Joudrey's trailer, with the garbage bag in hand, about half an hour later.

"What am I going to do with it?" he asked Manthorne.

"I don't know."

"Will you come with me while I throw it in the river?"

Manthorne refused to accompany him. Allen took the garbage bag to the bridge and threw it over the railing into the Medway. He returned to the trailer to await his mother's return.

Maurice and Gladys Hurshman's trailer home in Danesville is no more than a ten-minute drive from the satellite station. They arrived at the turnoff but saw no sign of Jane. Hurshman parked his car on the satellite road just off River Road. He turned out his headlights but left his parking lights on. They were there about ten minutes when they saw the lights of a car approaching from the direction of Charleston. Driving the car was Ronald Harlowe, who lived along River Road past the satellite station. He was returning home from Liverpool. "I took the 103 Highway and swung off on the River Road. When I got close to home just before the satellite road I noticed a car parked with just parking lights on, and he was parked in the satellite road. When he seen me coming, he shut his parking lights off and drove by me with no lights on. Harlowe recognized Hurshman's car and "I just thought it was odd that he drove by me with no lights on."

Harlowe continued up River Road past his own house to visit friends a quarter of a mile up the river. "But there was no one there, so I went right home." Jane Stafford, with Billy's body in the cab beside her, hadn't yet passed by, and Harlowe saw no other vehicles. He knew Billy Stafford and would've recognized the truck. He'd once stopped working on a scallop dragger because of an altercation with Billy. The dragger was the *Kathy and Susie;* the incident occurred shortly before Billy was charged with mutiny on that boat. Harlowe wasn't afraid of Billy, but he stopped working on the *Kathy and Susie* because the skipper,

Paul Minard, was a friend of his "and I didn't want to cause a problem there. Me and Billy getting in a racket on the boat wouldn't do anybody any good." Although he and Billy often argued, Harlowe considered him a friend. He was aware of Billy's mean streak, and although Billy was much bigger than he, he wouldn't back down from him. Billy often threatened him but never followed through. He remembered his last confrontation with Billy, when Billy threatened to hit him.

"You go ahead," challenged Harlowe. "I'll get you back even supposing it's in your sleep."

Billy knew Harlowe was serious, and that was the end of the argument.

Maurice Hurshman didn't realize it was Ronald Harlowe's car that had passed him on River Road. "When I got abreast of the car I realized that I didn't have my lights on, so I pulled them on." He drove into Charleston as far as the fire hall, where he turned and went back to the satellite road to wait for Jane. He waited a few minutes and began moving slowly back towards River Road. By this time, Jane had left the truck and was walking along the side of the road. "I saw the car coming from down the satellite road and I knew it was Mom. I knew the car. They stopped near the stop sign and I came up and got in the back on the passenger side."

"What's wrong, Janey?" asked Maurice Hurshman. "Why did you want us to pick you up out here? Did you have a fight or something?"

"Don't ask me anything," replied Jane. "Just leave me alone and please take me to your place so I can get cleaned up."

They drove in silence to the Hurshman home in Danesville. Jane could hear her parents' dogs, Zimby and Tina, barking when they pulled into the driveway. "Mom left the lights on in the trailer for the dogs. I told her to turn them off. Dad got out of the car but stayed outside the trailer. I went into the trailer in the dark and went right to the bathroom. I took the clean clothes from the green garbage bag. Then I undressed and had a bath. I cleaned up everything and put all of the stuff back into the same bag, including the towel and the facecloth. When I came out, the lights were on."

"Please take me home now," said Jane to her mother.

"I wish you would tell me what's wrong."

"I just don't want to talk about it."

Jane again sat in the rear seat with her parents in front.

"River Road is too bad to drive, take me around the pavement instead," said Jane. They drove along Highway 3 east through the town of Brooklyn, skirting Liverpool and along Highway 8, which for a time follows the course of the Mersey River past the town of Milton. They turned off the highway to 210 East, which took them to the Bangs Falls cutoff, like River Road at that time of year, a soggy, rutted, almost impassable dirt road. It was several hundred yards from the cutoff to the rear of the Stafford house. Maurice Hurshman made the turn to the cutoff, but Jane insisted he stop and let her out.

"I'll take you right to your door, Janey," he said.

"No. I'll get out right here."

She waited until her father turned around and drove off before she started walking. It was dark, and the rain continued to come down in a steady drizzle. The road was full of ruts. "I could feel the mud up to my ankles. I didn't have any boots on. I tried to follow the tire tracks but I couldn't see in the dark and I kept slipping into the muck. I walked along until I could see the light from Mr. and Mrs. Wood's place, and then I cut through the bush." The Woods were an elderly, retired couple. Jane did not want to chance them seeing her. It left her a nightmarish struggle through three hundred feet of dense, wet bush. Branches sprayed her with rainwater and scratched her face and hands when she brushed against them in the dark. She also had to contend with isolated patches of snow, which were crusty on top and sometimes couldn't bear her weight. Jane came out of the woods behind the Stafford barn and entered the house. On the kitchen table there was a note from Allen saying he was down in Margaret

Joudrey's trailer. Jane went into her bedroom and flicked her light on and off. "She knew when the light went on and off that I wanted her for something. It was a signal we had used for years." Margaret Joudrey, Manthorne, and Allen came up to the house together. Margaret and Jane hugged each other.

"Don't worry, everything will be all right," said Margaret.

Manthorne and Allen both noticed Jane seemed pretty shaken up.

"It's all over," said Jane. "I ain't going to have to put up with it anymore. I blew his fucking brains out."

Jane still had the garbage bag with her bloodied clothing, towel, and facecloth. Allen burned them in the woodstove, along with her purse, which had been in the cab of the truck when Billy was shot. They sat around the table talking in whispered tones for a time.

"We broke the gun down into three pieces and threw it in the river," said Manthorne. Allen told her about cleaning off the side of the house and throwing the rags and bloodied rocks into the river. Manthorne remembers having a cup of tea that was left in the pot on the stove, before he and Margaret left shortly before midnight. Jane put on her housecoat and sat on the edge of her bed. Allen came in and laid down on the bed.

"I don't know what's going to happen from here on in," said Jane softly. "I left the truck off the side of the road down by the satellite station."

Allen eventually fell asleep. He dozed off and on through the night. Jane didn't sleep at all. "I didn't really believe Bill was dead. When I got out of the truck I left the keys in the ignition. To me, he was going to drive back home. I sat there all night, just sat there. I knew he should be dead, with all the blood and everything, but I didn't really believe it. I just waited for that truck to come up the driveway." In the morning Jane went in and woke up Ronnie Wamboldt with the first light of day.

"Do you know where Billy is?" she asked.

"No, I don't know where he could have went," replied Wamboldt.

"He must have gone somewhere through the night."

"I don't know."

Wamboldt got up, washed up in the bathroom, had a cup of tea, and went out to the back shed and started drinking. Jane wandered around the house in a daze. She drank tea and smoked cigarette after cigarette. She was also taking Valium. "It was like a weird dream. Finally I got dressed and went down to visit with Margaret. I was just coming back from there when the police arrived. When they told me Bill was actually dead, I passed out. At that moment I really knew that he couldn't hurt any of us anymore. I must have passed out from sheer exhaustion and relief. Just the fact that he was gone. That he wouldn't be there anymore."

X

Staff Sergeant Peter Williamson assigned ten officers to the Billy Stafford case by the end of the first day of the investigation. As the day wore on, the evidence increasingly pointed to Billy's common-law wife, Jane Stafford. There was Billy's mistreatment of her and rumours of attempts to hire a hit man and of a twenty-thousand-dollar life-insurance policy. Williamson sent Corporal Howard Pike and Constable Archie Mason back out to the Stafford residence in Bangs Falls in the early evening of March 12, 1982. Jane's memories of the days immediately following Billy Stafford's death are blurred. The trauma of the event combined with heavy doses of Valium added to her confusion. She couldn't concentrate, and her thoughts were disconnected. But she clearly remembers closing the truck door with Billy's body propped against it inside. "It was foggy, cold, and raining," she said. "I remember feeling the rain hitting my face. I always loved the rain. As I walked the short distance across the road, a warm feeling came over me. I felt like I was being anointed with warm oil. As if I was being forgiven for what I'd done."

Jane also remembers fainting when Howie Pike told her Billy was dead. She remembers awakening on the sofa and telling Allen she didn't want to go to jail and leave Darren alone. She said she'd try to hide her involvement in Billy's death by telling the police Billy was involved in drug deals and Mafia hit men probably shot him. That's what she told Pike and Mason when they returned to her house that night. Pike said he and Mason talked to Jane for about an hour that evening and she appeared to be drugged, "almost as if she was in a daze, more or less, staring off into the distance."

The next day, a Friday, Lamont Stafford drove Jane to the hospital, where a doctor prescribed Valium for her. Meanwhile, the police were picking up leads that deepened their suspicion that Jane was heavily involved in Billy's death. Most important were comments by friends of a fishing boat crewman, Beverly Taylor. Taylor was at sea the night Billy Stafford was killed, but when he landed two days later, he contacted the RCMP when he learned they wanted to talk to him. By the night of March 13, Peter Williamson decided it was time to bring Jane Stafford into the Liverpool detachment for questioning. Armed with a search warrant, Archie Mason and five other RCMP officers descended on the Stafford house shortly after midnight. "I don't know how many Valium I had consumed at that point," said Jane. "I don't know what all took place that night." With Mason were Constable Robert Hillier, who was continuing to secure exhibits in the case; Auxiliary Constable Andrew Baker, who was to stand guard at the house through the night; Constable Susan Ivany, from the RCMP Bridgewater detachment; Corporal Ron Pond, a veteran officer brought in from the Yarmouth detachment to aid in the investigation; and Constable Blair

McKnight. Pond and McKnight were to interrogate Jane. Mason's job was to introduce them to her.

"Corporal Pond and Constable McKnight want to ask you some questions," said Mason. "And they might want you to return to the Liverpool detachment with them. I also have a search warrant to search your residence." Constable Susan Ivany noticed Jane "seemed to be in a state of some remorse or she was very subdued. She wasn't very energetic or vital." Corporal Pond remembers Jane was wearing a blue housecoat and was asleep on the sofa when they arrived. Susan Ivany, who was in uniform, accompanied Jane to her bedroom, where she dressed in a brown plaid shirt, blue slacks, and a brown corduroy jacket. Pond and McKnight were not in uniform. They accompanied Jane to an unmarked cruiser. When Jane walked past Constable Hillier he noticed she was "solemn, sedentary. As she walked past me her head was down and she didn't say anything to anybody that I heard. She seemed very quiet." Susan Ivany sat with Jane in the back seat. Pond was driving the cruiser, and McKnight sat beside him. McKnight, who was wearing blue jeans, a plaid shirt, and a jacket, turned to Jane when she entered the car and read her the standard caution. "You need not say anything. You have nothing to hope for, any promise or favour, and nothing to fear from any threat whether or not you say anything. Anything you do say may be used as evidence. Do you understand what I've said?"

"Yes," mumbled Jane, nodding.

They drove with Jane to the Liverpool detachment. With them was a bottle of Valium they'd seized from the house.

"We'd rather not engage in any conversation until we get to the office," advised McKnight.

"Can I smoke?" asked Jane.

"Yes."

Jane was taken to a small interview room. The room is about ten by twelve feet, with an eight-foot ceiling. The walls are covered with white Styrofoam. There's a green filing cabinet in one corner, a solid wood table in the centre, and two wood chairs. There are no pictures on the walls. The Styrofoam is designed to reduce echoes and outside noises. It was twelve thirty-five on Sunday morning when Jane entered the small room. Susan Ivany went into the room with Jane. They made small talk for about fifteen minutes. Then Blair McKnight entered and told Ivany to leave. He and Jane lit up cigarettes. He said she answered his questions slowly and didn't seem very alert. He thought she might be on tranquillizers. McKnight questioned Jane until 2:15 A.M. She stuck to her "Mafia" story. Susan Ivany came back into the room when McKnight left. She was checking for bruises, and she brought in a camera. "She didn't seem very unkempt," recalls Ivany. "She just seemed quite expressionless." Jane says Ivany told her to strip from the waist up so she could photograph her.

"Why don't I strip completely," said Jane defensively. "Then you can photograph all of me."

"That won't be necessary."

Ivany photographed a large bruise on Jane's left arm. She asked Jane how she got the bruise, and Jane explained it to her. Jane says no photographs were taken of the left side of her body, which was still black and blue from the beating administered by Billy with the vacuum-cleaner hose. The photograph that was taken didn't turn out and was never used in court. Susan Ivany left the room, and minutes later, at 2:38 A.M., Corporal Pond, dressed in a business suit, entered. He questioned Jane for more than two hours. "I was actually very sympathetic with her. I was obviously trying to get at the truth, but I was trying to be as gentle as I could to her under the circumstances." He said he was sympathetic because he'd heard a lot of stories about Billy Stafford "and possible motive for this incident." Pond told Jane the police knew of her attempt to hire Beverly Taylor to kill Billy. Jane wasn't swayed. Pond gave up at 4:50 A.M., and at 5:05 A.M. it was Blair McKnight's turn again. He was with her almost two hours until Pond returned at 6:55 A.M. He stayed only five minutes and then both he and McKnight entered the room. At no time was Jane told she was a suspect or under arrest. She declined when they asked her if she wanted a lawyer, insisting instead that she be allowed to see Lamont Stafford. Throughout she stuck to her Mafia story and said she wanted to go home because she feared the men who shot Billy might return and shoot her children.

Pond and McKnight spent about ten minutes together in the room with Jane, urging her to tell the truth. They believed that with the two of them telling her they didn't believe her she might be swayed and tell them what really happened. "No heavy tactics, nothing like that," said Pond. But Jane Stafford saw it differently. She remembers being drained and tired through the night, sometimes dozing off with her head resting on her hand between visits from the two police officers. She believes they were engaging in a game of "good cop-bad cop," with one being sympathetic to her and the other being aggressive and stern. At one point she said she was dozing off when Constable McKnight entered the room and told her he was aware she'd attempted to hire someone to kill Billy Stafford. He dropped a copy of the Criminal Code on the table in front of her.

"Here, read that," he said. "You can be locked up for fourteen years as an accomplice."

"I want to see Lamont," said Jane.

"Look," said McKnight, frustrated, "I'm getting tired, you're getting tired, we're all getting tired. So why don't you tell us the truth so we can all go home?"

Jane remained silent.

"Do you know what the people are doing out around Greenfield tonight?" he asked. "They're celebrating. Celebrating Stafford's death. Why don't you confess so you can go home and celebrate, too?"

"I want to see Lamont," repeated Jane. She felt close to Billy's father and believed he had the right to hear from her that she killed his son. She would tell him before anyone else. She hadn't done much talking during the years under Billy Stafford's reign of fear. She'd been beaten into unconsciousness, been shot at at close range with a high-powered rifle, had a knife held to her throat, and been degraded and humiliated. She thought it ironic that the police thought they could cajole her into talking. Their tactics steeled her resolve to remain silent.

Jane's throat was dry.

"Can I have a drink of water?" she asked McKnight.

"You wouldn't want to drink the water in this station," he said with a smile.

McKnight brought Jane a cold orange drink instead, and at 8:30 A.M. he brought her coffee and breakfast. At 8:40 A.M. Corporal Howard Pike drove to Hunt's Point to pick up Lamont Stafford.

Lamont Stafford was working outdoors when Pike arrived. Lamont cleaned up and changed his clothes before they left for Liverpool. They arrived at about 9:15 A.M. Jane asked to go to the washroom to clean up before meeting Lamont. She didn't know it at the time, but her father, Maurice Hurshman, was already in the station. He'd been picked up at his home that afternoon and had spent the night sleeping in a cell waiting to see his daughter. Jane met with Lamont for about twenty minutes in the interview room, and then her father joined them for another ten minutes. Staff Sergeant Williamson, meanwhile, had arrived at the detachment. Lamont Stafford, Maurice Hurshman, and Jane emerged from the interview room and went into a larger coffee room. Williamson followed them in and closed the door behind him. Jane, at that point, was still sticking to her Mafia story. The four of them sat around a table, with Williamson directly across from Jane.

"What can you tell us about this matter?" asked Williamson somewhat gruffly.

Lamont Stafford jumped to his feet.

"She's had enough of that garbage," he said. "If you want her to talk to you, then you talk right to her."

Lamont sat down and turned to Jane.

"Did you kill Bill?" he asked.

"Yes," replied Jane.

Williamson then sat back and listened while Jane described all of the abuse Billy Stafford had subjected her to. He interjected from time to time "to keep the flow of the conversation going." Jane's shoulders sagged with relief when she had completed her story.

"I feel a great weight has been lifted from me," she said.

Williamson gave her the standard police caution and had her repeat her story as he took it down. He left out her descriptions of Billy's abuses. That oversight prevented the statement from being introduced in subsequent court proceedings. Lamont Stafford remembers Jane "seemed to be in quite a dopey state, like she'd been taking a lot of tranquillizers or some darn thing." He held Jane's hand while Williamson took down her statement, and he consoled her when she wept at its conclusion. Williamson noticed Lamont didn't seem angry or upset with Jane when she admitted killing Billy.

In her statement to Williamson, Jane Stafford took sole blame for the death of her husband. She said she went into the house, loaded the shotgun, and went out to the truck and shot Billy. She said she drove the body to the spot it was found and walked the seven miles home along River Road. She said she threw the gun in the river and burned her clothes after cleaning up and changing. She made no mention of the actions of Allen or Roger Manthorne, nor did she tell of her parents' role in picking her up and later driving her to the Bangs Falls turnoff. Jane was relieved it was over and she'd protected her family and friends. Peter Williamson was also relieved. He had a confession, but he also felt a lot of sympathy for Jane Stafford. Jane was sipping a cup of coffee when she overheard him talking to fellow officers in the outer office.

"She deserves a medal," said Williamson. "She probably saved a couple of our officers' lives. He always had loaded guns. I'm sure we would've gone out there one day and he would've shot one of us."

Shortly after 11:00 A.M., Corporal Pike and Lamont Stafford helped Jane out to a police cruiser. She wanted only one thing—sleep. But first they drove her to the scene of the crime, to the satellite station, and back to Liverpool to reconstruct the events of the night Billy died. Corporal Stan Clarke was waiting with two divers when Jane arrived at the Bangs Falls bridge at 12:30 P.M. She walked from the car and pointed to a spot in the river where she claimed she threw the shotgun.

"Finally I got to go home," said Jane. "It was cold in the house and there was a real mess, with mud and dirt everywhere. I guess it was from the police searching the place. Everything was torn apart. The attic, the dresser drawers, the beds, the closets, and the cupboards—everything was a mess. I didn't know what had happened, and I didn't care. I walked through the mess, picked up a blanket, and lay on the bare mattress. I was totally exhausted."

A few minutes later, Darren came into the bedroom and stared at his mother. Jane lifted the blanket, and without a word he crawled in beside her. Jane held him close.

"Your father is dead," she said softly. "I killed him. He won't be coming home anymore."

Darren sat up and looked at her.

"He won't do this to you anymore?" asked the boy, flicking his hand back and forth, as if slapping her face. "He won't hurt us anymore?"

"No, baby."

"He's really gone, Mommy? Is he really gone forever?"

"Yes, baby, he's gone forever."

Darren wrapped his tiny arms around his mother's neck and hugged her.

"I'm glad, Mommy. I'm glad. Are you glad?"

On March 16, 1982, an information was sworn by Corporal Howard Pike charging Jane Marie Stafford with first-degree murder in the shooting death of her common-law husband, William Lamont Stafford. Jane was not arrested or jailed. Staff Sergeant Peter Williamson was convinced he had the whole story. His men were continuing their investigations, and Jane Stafford wasn't about to go anywhere. Jane remained heavily sedated, and her recollections of the next two weeks are minimal. "I don't know who came or went or how long I slept. I don't know what kind of a state I was in.

Someone cleaned the house up and took care of things because I certainly wasn't capable." She vaguely remembers the arrival of her sister Mona from Barrie, Ontario, and her sister Sandy from Ottawa. She also remembers seeking the services of a lawyer. The one she chose was Alan Ferrier, who worked in the Bridgewater office of Nova Scotia legal aid. She had met Ferrier several months earlier, when she was seeking advice on another matter. "A friend of mine recommended him and set up an appointment for me. He handed me a form to fill out to see if I qualified for legal aid." Ferrier told her at that time that her income was too high to qualify for legal aid.

"Gee, I never thought of getting your services without paying," said Jane. "I'm quite willing to pay."

"I can't do that," explained Ferrier. "Under the law, I can only handle clients who quality for legal aid. I can recommend someone who can handle this for you." Ferrier arranged an appointment with another lawyer. Jane was impressed by his forthright manner and now, facing a charge of first-degree murder, she decided it was Ferrier she wanted.

Alan Ferrier was thirty-one when Jane Stafford came to see him in March 1982. Even with a thick moustache he could have passed for twenty-four or twenty-five. Born in Edinburgh, Scotland, in May 1951, he has two older brothers and a younger sister. His father, an insurance salesman, immigrated to Canada when Alan was nine months old. The family moved to Nova Scotia, and Alan was raised in Dartmouth. He was a good student and spent his sixth, seventh, and eighth grades at Dartmouth Academy, then an exclusive school for boys. (It has since been bulldozed to make way for a condominium development.) Most of the teachers at the academy were either English or Scottish. Parents loved to send their children to the academy, because it was a throwback to the private schools in the old country.

At sixteen, Ferrier enrolled at Dalhousie University, graduating in 1970 with a degree in commerce. He was five feet, two inches when he started at Dalhousie and didn't have his first date for two and a half years "because I looked more like fourteen." At nineteen, his commerce degree wasn't much good to him because he wasn't old enough to sign legal documents or contracts. He decided to go on to law school, graduating at age twenty-three, the second youngest in his class. He spent two months articling at the Kentville office of Nova Scotia legal aid before moving to the Yarmouth office, where "I ended up with a murder and an indecent assault right off." When his boss moved to Ontario to open a civil litigation practice, Alan Ferrier, an articling student, was left virtually in charge of legal aid for three counties. The year was 1974, and he was earning $700 a month. "I was thrown into a lot of trials. It was a wonderful time. I learned a whole shitload of law." In the spring of 1975, he was admitted to the Nova Scotia bar. He moved to Bridgewater legal aid in January 1979. The Bridgewater offices are in a small, flat-roofed brick building that used to house the Bridgewater Public Library at the corner of Dufferin and Pleasant streets, halfway up the Dufferin Street hill. An oak stairway leads to the tiled floor second-storey office of Alan Ferrier. Under Nova Scotia law, Jane Stafford had an option of using the legal aid offices or a private lawyer of her choice. She wanted Alan Ferrier.

"Well, I think I qualify for legal aid now," said Jane when she met Ferrier again. "The police say I need a lawyer, and I would like you to handle my case. Will you do it?"

Alan Ferrier leaned back in his chair and half smiled.

"Yes, you sure do need a lawyer. Now do you want to tell me about it?"

Jane doesn't remember much of the conversation after that "except that he stopped me and asked, 'Are you on anything now?' I reached in my pocket and took out the pills from the doctor. He read the container and counted the pills. That's all I remember of that meeting."

It was obvious to Alan Ferrier that Jane Stafford was still distraught and very confused. He arranged for her to see a psychiatrist. To this day, Jane doesn't remember the psychiatrist's name. "I was really right out of it. I know he was in Halifax and I know my Uncle Jimmy and my sister Mona drove me there. I really didn't want to go. It was just like on TV. There were fancy dressed women in his office with lots of jewellery. They probably had nothing better to do with their time or money. I had to wait there with them. I had on blue jeans, and the sides were out of my sneakers. The fact that he was a man really put me off. When I was called in, the room was very dim. He told me to sit in a chair, but I refused. He had a couch across the room and asked me to go there. That did it. I couldn't stand it. I left. I think I might have told him I thought he was crazier than me. I was still heavily drugged. I don't know if that was it or not."

Jane's mind was swirling when she left the psychiatrist's office. She couldn't understand what was happening to her. Billy was dead. Everybody, including the police, were sympathetic towards her, and yet she was still facing a charge of first-degree murder. She feared she'd be locked up for life and, more devastating, she'd be separated from Darren. She decided to make a new confession to the police. She would say her son Allen shot Billy Stafford while he was pummelling her in the cab of the truck. Allen would be defending her. She would be free to be with Darren. Jane told her sister Mona she was changing her confession. Mona called Allen to tell him of his mother's plans. When the police came for him later at his grandfather's house, he told them he shot Billy Stafford. "I figured that's what Ma wanted," he said later.

On March 25, 1982, Jane Stafford, in the company of her lawyer, went to Staff Sergeant Peter Williamson's office at the RCMP's Liverpool detachment. There she signed a statement in which she said her son Allen had shot Billy Stafford after "he started beating me on the head. He kept pounding me on the head and my head was down by the steering wheel and somehow the horn blew. He was still beating on me when the next thing I remember was a gun blast." Jane Stafford and her son were arraigned on first-degree murder charges the next day. She was placed in a cell in the Queens County Jail in Liverpool. Later that night, Cyril Page, the diminutive high sheriff for Queens County, picked up Jane at the Liverpool detachment to transport her to the women's section of the Halifax Corrections Centre. Page, a former used-car salesman, was in his sixteenth year as sheriff. His wife, Pearl, accompanied him, as she always did when he was transporting female prisoners. It was a two-hour drive to the Corrections Centre. En route they stopped at the Queens County jail to pick up Jane's belongings. Jane sat alone in the back seat.

"Cyril, do you mind if I take my shoes off and try to rest some?" asked Jane.

"Suit yourself," replied Page. "You got the whole back seat. There's a blanket back there. If you want to make a pillow out of it, go right ahead." He remembers Jane mentioning that her son Darren was going to Ontario to be with her sister. Then she fell asleep. "I believe Jane slept pretty near the whole way to the Halifax Correction Centre. It was a terribly foggy night going to Halifax, and I was much more concerned with my driving than I was with really talking that night."

The Halifax Corrections Centre is a dreary red-brick building just off the highway on the outskirts of Bedford, Nova Scotia, just north of Halifax. The centre is a provincial prison designated to hold people serving jail terms of less than two years. It is also for prisoners awaiting trial or those on remand. The centre houses about 150 male prisoners and a maximum of twenty-four women. The women are housed in A Block. Cyril Page stopped his car in front of the jail's high, chain-wire fence and pressed the button on the two-way remote box, much like those at drive-through restaurants. He identified himself and told the main guard station he was bringing in a female prisoner. The gate slid open. Normally he would drive to the rear of the centre to the women's entrance, but it was late, and he brought Jane to the front door. Page removed Jane's belongings from the trunk of his car. His doors lock automatically, and Jane had to wait for him to unlock the rear door. She entered the centre with Page, their movements scrutinized by a guard sitting in a glassed-in control cage at the entrance.

"Immediately, a matron arrived and took Jane from me," said Page. "That's the last I saw of her that evening." Jane was taken through the drab entrance foyer, of cement block construction, painted light and dark shades of beige, with a tile floor. They walked through the visitors' area, an eight-foot corridor with two facing orange vinyl couches and two green chairs of the same material. The furniture was stained, and the stuffing was coming out in several spots. Once in the women's section, Jane was quickly processed, issued prison clothing, and locked in a cell. Most women prisoners were confined to one of two dormitory rooms, but trouble makers, newcomers, and those whom authorities believe might be threatened in the general population are placed in the cells.

The cells are in a U-shaped room with a guard station at the bottom of the U. A partial wall separates the two lines of cells, which have four cells in each line. The room itself has brick end walls painted an unappetizing green. The floor is grey-painted cement. The cells have individual steel doors. There is a common shower room beside the first line of cells. Each cell has its own toilet and metal bed. Four other inmates were playing cards in front of the cell row.

"What are you in for?" asked one of the women after Jane had been locked in her cell.

"I killed somebody," replied Jane softly.

The four continued playing cards and joking with each other and seemed to ignore Jane for a time. Then one of them turned to Jane.

"How did you do it?" she asked.

"I shot somebody."

"What did you shoot him with?"

"A shotgun."

They stared at Jane momentarily through the cell bars. Her weight, normally 140 pounds, had fallen to 100 pounds in her last brutal months with Billy Stafford.

"You don't look big enough to hold a gun, let alone pull the trigger," said one of the women.

They began joking amongst themselves again and then sang a song. The chorus included the words "she didn't know the gun was loaded."

The RCMP were not satisfied with Jane Stafford's latest statement on how Billy died. The physical evidence showed conclusively that she could not possibly have been in the cab of the truck when Billy Stafford was shot. They were relieved when Jane agreed to take a lie-detector test. On Saturday afternoon, the day after Jane's arrival at the Halifax Corrections Centre, Corporal Howie Pike arrived to take her to the Halifax RCMP headquarters, a squat, five-storey brick building. Jane sat on a chair near the commissionaire's desk at the front entrance while Pike went upstairs to see if the polygraph operator was ready for her. Cathy Merrick, who worked with the RCMP telecommunications staff at headquarters, sat with Jane. She remembers that Jane smoked a cigarette and seemed nervous. In the ten minutes or so that Pike was gone, Jane overheard a police radio call about a baby found abandoned in a sleeping bag on the side of the road. "The baby was found dead. It was very cold outside and the baby died of exposure. I remember feeling very sad."

The RCMP always has two full-time qualified polygraph operators available from provincial headquarters in Halifax. The day Jane arrived, Michael Innes, whose territory included the western part of the province, was on duty. It's RCMP policy to keep polygraph operators on the job for about five years before moving them to other assignments. Polygraph operators require specialized training, and once qualified they are considered experts, often envied by their peers. But the job becomes a dead end as far as promotion opportunities, and the repetition and constant travel, integral to the job, become boring in time, particularly for officers with families. The five-year rule of thumb allows the force room for transfers and promotions, and it serves as a hedge against burnout.

Michael Innes had been a certified polygraph examiner for three years at the time Jane Stafford was brought in for testing. There is a saying in the polygraph trade: The instrument is only as reliable as the examiner who operates it. Michael Innes was considered one of the best. Today he is a sergeant at the RCMP's Kingston, Nova Scotia, detachment. He administered polygraph tests in Nova Scotia, New Brunswick, Prince Edward Island, and Newfoundland. He received his training on the polygraph at the Canadian Police College in Ottawa and upgraded himself at seminars in Saginaw, Michigan, and Winnipeg, Manitoba.

Jane didn't know it, but Innes had earlier spent sixteen hours in Liverpool, where he talked to her mother and gave her father, Maurice Hurshman, a polygraph test, which indicated he had nothing to do with Billy Stafford's death. Corporal Pike talked to Innes for a few minutes, and the two of them took the elevator down to the main entrance. Innes, a twenty-one-year veteran with the RCMP, is a slim six-footer, with strong cheekbones and deep-set blue eyes. Jane remembers him as "an easy-speaking man with a very nice smile." Innes accompanied Jane to the polygraph suite. They spent almost three hours together. "We mostly talked about me and my life. Then he took me into a room full of all sorts of weird-looking equipment." Innes could see Jane was quite nervous, and he did his best to set her mind at ease during what is called a pretest interview.

"When people speak to the police they normally don't tell all they know, perhaps because of our uniform," he explained. "At times people become scared when they see a uniform. And maybe they forget to tell the police the truth."

"I hope I don't detect some suspicion from you because I'm getting fed up with this," said Jane. "I came in here today to show you that I'm telling the truth. The rest of those guys didn't believe me."

"Look, I'm sorry, Mrs. Stafford, but my job here today is just to show you are in fact telling the truth, or if you're not telling the truth, to show you're telling a lie, so I'm very sorry if you're misunderstanding anything from what I've said."

The polygraph suite is carpeted and measures about ten by ten feet. During a test the drapes are drawn and the door closed to prevent interruption. The only sound, other than the voices of the examiner and the person being interviewed, comes from a heater by the window that keeps the temperature in the room at seventy-two degrees Fahrenheit, the ideal temperature for accurate testing. Jane arrived in the polygraph suite at 2:33 P.M., and the first test commenced two hours later.

Innes explained how the polygraph works and motioned Jane to sit in the chair, which has padded arms for comfort. "He began hooking wires and belts on me and he told me I had to keep very still. I was terrified. He assured me it wouldn't hurt but deep inside I didn't believe him. I remember thinking this must be what it's like when they put you in the electric chair. I thought this is what they're eventually going to do to me." The wires and belts included a standard blood-pressure belt or cuff that was attached to Jane's left arm. It measures rises or falls in blood pressure and heartbeat accelerations. Tubes attached around the upper and lower chest measure breathing or internal movement. They are placed over the clothing. Two small plates were attached to Jane's right hand to record sweating or "galvanic skin response."

The polygraph instrument itself was set off to Jane's right and behind her, out of view to prevent her from seeing any tracings that might upset her or ruin her concentration. Before commencing, Innes told Jane she didn't have to take the test, gave her the standard police warning, and asked if she wanted to have her lawyer present. He also had her fill out a form outlining her personal and medical history.

"It's my understanding, Mrs. Stafford, that you're here because on the night of March 11, 1982, your common-law husband, William Stafford, was found shot to death. As a result of that you're suspected by the police as possibly being involved," intoned Innes. "That's why you are here to take this test—to clear up whether you are involved or not involved."

Innes ran four tests on Jane; each involved ten questions. "Three are crime questions. We call those relevant questions. We ask three other questions, which are known lies or probably lies. We refer to them as control questions. And then we ask them four other questions—is your name so-and-so, etc. . . ." Upon completion of the tests, Innes took the results into another room to review and score them. He concluded Jane lied to him about who pulled the trigger on the gun that killed Billy Stafford. He returned to the polygraph room to confront her.

"When you came in here today you knew the truth and the good Lord above knew the truth," he said. "I didn't know what the truth was. Unfortunately, as a result of my polygraph test, I now know you haven't been completely truthful with me. You did pull the trigger on the gun that killed Stafford, didn't you?"

"Yes, I did it," said Jane. "I'm glad it's over. You wouldn't believe how bad he was to me."

"If I get Howie, will you give him a statement now?"

"Yes," said Jane softly.

Minutes later, Innes returned with Pike. Innes handed him a card with a printed police warning. Before leaving the polygraph suite, Jane grasped Innes by the hand. "She looked me in the eye and just held my hand for a while, and she thanked me very much and left. I thought she looked relieved." Pike escorted Jane to the elevator.

"I'm sorry for all the trouble I caused everybody," said Jane.

They went to a small office on one side of the main detachment office and sat at a table. Jane began weeping.

"Are you all right?" asked Pike.

Jane nodded and lit a cigarette. Pike waited while she composed herself.

Pike began reading from the card Innes had given him.

"You must clearly understand that anything said to

you previously should not influence you or make you feel compelled to say anything at this time. Whatever you felt influenced you, or compelled you to say earlier, you are not now obliged to say anything further. Whatever you do say will be taken down in writing and may be given in evidence. Do you understand?"

"I understand," said Jane. "I killed Billy. Everything I said earlier was the truth except that it was me who shot Bill—not Allen."

She gave a detailed statement, which Pike wrote down and she signed. They left the building and began the drive back to the Halifax Corrections Centre in Pike's unmarked steel-grey Ford.

"Would you like to stop for something to eat or drink?" asked Pike.

"No, thanks," said Jane. "I don't want anything. Just take me back to jail, where I can lie down and be alone in peace and quiet."

It was Saturday afternoon, March 27, 1982, when Jane Stafford was returned to jail. Two days later she was freed after a bail hearing at which her father posted a five-thousand-dollar bond. Allen, still charged with a first-degree murder along with his mother, was also freed on a five-thousand-dollar bond, posted by Jane's uncle, James Hurshman. Jane attempted to put her life back together as best she could as she waited for the next move by the justice system.

"After all that had happened, I stayed at Mom's for a while and then I decided I had to come home to Bangs Falls. It was something I had to do. I had to deal with it. And I did. I came home and I made a big fire in the fireplace outside. And everything that was here that was his or anything that I shared with him, I burned. That bed got burned just the same as everything else. I just burned and burned and burned . . . it seemed like forever. My neighbour Margaret Joudrey stayed with me that first night. I didn't know what kind of feelings I would have after coming back here for the first time. Sometime through the night I woke up. It was still dark, but it was coming on to morning. I can remember I was sweating, but I was cold at the same time. It was just awful. At that point I just didn't know—I wanted to be able to deal with everything. I wanted to be able to handle it inside, in my own way. I spent a lot of time praying and just sort of talking to myself. After a while there was a feeling of comfort, a real nice feeling. Whatever happened that night—I'm not sure, but there was a different feeling in that house from then on—peaceful. And I didn't find it hard to live there after that."

Jane resigned herself to whatever might lie ahead. "I just figured I'd probably go to prison. Whatever they decided they were going to do, they were going to do. And I didn't think about what was going to happen tomorrow. All I knew was that Bill wasn't going to be there. Prison couldn't be worse than the way I lived. When I went to the correctional centre for those few days it was almost like being in a motel. Somebody served you something to eat. You didn't have to get up. You had nobody telling you to do anything. Nothing could have been worse than when I lived with him."

On June 7, 1982, following a preliminary inquiry before Judge W.A.D. Gunn of the Provincial Magistrate's Court in Liverpool, Jane Stafford was committed to stand trial at the next sittings of the Trial Division of the Supreme Court of Nova Scotia at Liverpool. At the June inquiry, charges against Allen were dropped.

It galls Jane's lawyer, Alan Ferrier, that there was any trial at all. He was prepared to enter a plea of guilty to manslaughter on her behalf and let a judge decide what her punishment should be after hearing the life she was forced to lead. He believes that the local RCMP and Crown prosecutor were in favour of accepting the manslaughter plea, but the provincial attorney general's office turned down the idea because Billy Stafford was asleep when Jane shot him.

Ferrier believes the decision to proceed with a charge of first-degree murder was absurd, considering Staff Sergeant Williamson's remarks after he learned of the abuse Jane had suffered:

"He commented to his officers that she deserved a medal, and that she'd probably saved at least two police officers' lives. In the context of that kind of reaction, it's not surprising that he would accede to a suggestion of a manslaughter plea, because obviously he knew what Jane was up against. They appreciated Billy probably far better than most people did, and I think that the Crown on the local level and the police were prepared to be fair. Accepting the plea of manslaughter would allow some flexibility in the question of sentencing, and it would leave it for the trial judge to decide on the basis of all the evidence what would be an appropriate sentence. The difficulty with first- and second-degree murder is that the minimums are established and the judge has no control over that. Jane was charged with first-degree murder. She was looking at twenty-five years without parole. It's absolutely absurd to consider that kind of a punishment for her reaction to an enduring life of violence over five years that none of us would tolerate for five seconds. I think it's an irony that in telling the truth, she ended up creating great difficulties for herself. And I think that's an indication of how she was not thinking things out, as the Crown originally contended when they laid a charge of first-degree murder. Clearly she hadn't thought things out or she wouldn't have said Billy was asleep when she shot him. She could easily have lied or made up a situation, and it's doubtful that anybody would have disbelieved her in light of his character and the way he had treated her in the past."

In the weeks and months before her trial, Jane Stafford put her complete trust in Alan Ferrier. "My trust in him just grew and grew as time passed. To me, he was God-sent. He always laid everything on the line. I knew he would do his best for me." She was convinced she had the right lawyer when she saw him in action in court for the first time at her bail hearing. While awaiting a decision in a back room in the courthouse, they talked quietly:

"Jane, are you suicidal?" asked Ferrier.

The question surprised Jane.

"Are you asking me if I'm considering killing myself?"

"Yes, that's what I'm asking you."

"Hell, no. Maybe I was when I was with Bill, but no one is going to hurt me anymore—so why would I want to do that?"

Jane was smiling. Ferrier smiled and reached out and hugged her. "I knew at that moment that he really cared about what happened to me. At that point I put everything in his hands."

XI

The courthouse in downtown Liverpool can best be described as quaint. A small grey marble sign, with a black border and lettering, states "Court House Erected 1854." The sign sits adjacent to the building's black wooden double doors. Other than the doors and a narrow, grey wooden veranda along the front, the entire building is painted white. The single-storey structure has four large pillars, which crowd the sidewalk of the narrow street running in front. The low-peaked, elegant building somehow doesn't seem out of place on the quiet residential street where it's located, a block from Liverpool's main street. Inside, the judge's bench, with its high-backed, carved oak chair, sits in an alcove looking out over the courtroom. Matching jury boxes are to the right and left of the bench. The door to the jury room is to the left of the judge. Tables for the court clerk and recorder are directly in front of the bench. Behind them is a long table for Crown and defense counsel. Directly behind the counsels' table is a small press table. Seats for the public, seventy-five in all, are set up on either side of the courtroom at the rear. They are separated by a boxed-in foyer leading to the main doors and the street. The seats in the public gallery are auditorium-style, plywood and metal stacking chairs, which detract from the other carved oak furniture and railings.

It was in that old, historic building that Jane Stafford was to be tried. The case attracted nationwide attention, and the courtroom was packed every day throughout the trial. The trial began November 2, 1982, and ended November 20. It became an ordeal for Jane Stafford, who had lived such an isolated existence for so many years, to run a daily gauntlet of well-wishers and television and newspaper reporters scrambling for a quote. "Reporters were always waiting for me to arrive in the morning and again when I left at night. Thank God Alan was there to reassure me. He told me just to say 'no comment,' and that's what I did, day after day."

The public and media attention were there, not only because there was widespread sympathy for Jane Stafford in a community that knew what Billy Stafford was like, but also because the case seemed tailor-made as a battleground for the women's movement's struggle against male oppression. The task of young, aggressive Crown Attorney Blaine Allaby, on the other hand, was to convince the jury that Jane Stafford had no right to kill Billy simply because she was in a tough situation, and that the murder was planned and deliberate beyond a reasonable doubt.

Jane Stafford's case wasn't the only one on the docket when the Supreme Court session opened on Tuesday morning, November 2. The first order of business was to select a grand jury. That process moved quickly, and the grand jury retired to consider if there was enough evidence to proceed against Jane Stafford. The jury took less than two hours to decide there was enough evidence, which didn't surprise anyone. The Supreme Court session in Liverpool was scheduled to last two weeks. Alan Ferrier, Crown Attorney Blaine Allaby, and the presiding judge, Mr. Justice D. Burchell, quickly agreed the Stafford trial would take at least that long. In the afternoon a twelve-member petit jury, who along with the judge comprise the court, were chosen from the one hundred or so people summoned for jury duty. One juror, Doris Whynot, subsequently stepped down when it was revealed that she knew Jane Stafford and might not be impartial. The case proceeded with eleven jurors.

After selection of the jury, Jane Stafford was arraigned on the charge of first-degree murder. She pleaded not guilty. It was to be Friday, the fourth day of the trial, before the jury got to hear any evidence in the case. Wednesday and Thursday were taken up with *voir dire* matters, in which Allaby and Ferrier argued about what evidence was admissible. The public was allowed to listen to those arguments but not the jury. The media were also restricted from using evidence or arguments put forward in the *voir dire* sessions. Alan Ferrier won a victory of sorts when he successfully argued against the admission of Jane Stafford's first statement to police, given to Staff Sergeant Williamson in the presence of Lamont Stafford and her father, after she was detained all night at the RCMP Liverpool detachment. Ferrier argued, "The course of the evening was in fact designed to tire and frustrate a woman who is obviously very placid and quiet, who was under the influence of drugs, and it was a design on their part to create an atmosphere of sympathy, to give Mrs. Stafford the impression that they understood her. She was almost constantly with one police officer or another for a period of nine hours, from one o'clock in the morning until approximately ten. How would the average citizen react to that, far less a person who is on tranquillizers?"

Crown Attorney Allaby contended, "At no time was there any threat, promise, or inducement given to Mrs. Stafford, and I would submit that at all times she was dealt with in a reasonable, friendly, and in fact, on occasions, sympathetic manner." He said the Valium taken by Jane before midnight would have worn off before 10:00 A.M. the next morning. Ferrier said that to allow Jane's first statement into evidence "would in effect bring the administration of justice into disrepute" because of the way Jane was treated by police.

Mr. Justice Burchell said the conduct of the police

"does raise some questions in my mind. It has not been explained, for example, why it was necessary to take the accused into custody in the middle of the night. The question is . . . whether the police deliberately set about to deprive the accused of sleep so as to make her compliant under interrogation." He eventually concluded: "I'm unable to say that the methods employed by the police affected the operating mind of the accused, nor am I able to say that of themselves they offend standards of decency or offend the integrity of the judicial process." However, Justice Burchell accepted another of Ferrier's arguments, that Staff Sergeant Williamson chose not to include Jane's description of the brutalities Billy Stafford inflicted on her in the statement he took from her. Williamson testified he excluded the beatings from the statement because he felt they had nothing to do with the event, since they occurred in the past.

"I take a serious view of the question of whether the statement that has been reduced to writing was a complete statement of the disclosures of the accused," stated Burchell. ". . . If the prosecution decides to induce a confession it must take the whole of it together and cannot select one part and leave another. On that ground, rather than on the issue of freeness and voluntariness, I conclude that the statement should not be admitted."

Blaine Allaby won a behind-closed-doors legal victory when Burchell ruled that Jane Stafford's third statement, given to Corporal Pike after her failed lie-detector test, was admissible. "All the circumstances surrounding the taking of the statement were entirely circumspect and correct," ruled Burchell. "I'm referring, of course, to the conduct of the police, and I'm satisfied, I suppose I should add, beyond a reasonable doubt, that the statement was given freely and voluntarily and that it is the product of the operating mind of the accused."

The jury was finally returned to open court on Friday morning, November 5. Allaby's first witness was Beverly Taylor, the Riverport seaman who told his story of Jane approaching him to kill Billy Stafford in return for the proceeds from the twenty-thousand-dollar family insurance policy. Taylor told Ferrier during cross-examination he never once considered killing Billy Stafford.

FERRIER: Did you suggest or make any plans with Mrs. Stafford to set him up on a dope bust?

TAYLOR: We discussed alternatives. I asked her why she didn't go to the police. She said they couldn't help her. I asked her why she didn't go to the lawyers. She said she'd never run far enough to get away from him. And then I said, "Billy trucks dope back and forth on the gypsum boats. Why don't you have him put away for a couple of years?" . . . as I was leaving that day, she thought it was a pretty good idea, then she in later conversation said it wasn't. . . . Her reason was that there was another fellow living at the house at the time and if Billy got busted for dope then this guy would take the charge and Billy would still be there.

Allaby, the same morning, called two women to the witness stand who worked with Jane at the Hillsview Acres County Home in Greenfield. Gail Brewster, a part-time cook and domestic worker, used to fill in for Jane as cook on Thursdays and Fridays, Jane's days off. She described Jane as "a hardworking woman and very nice."

ALLABY: Did you notice any change in her in the last two or three months before she stopped working?

BREWSTER: Yes.

ALLABY: Could you tell us what you observed?

BREWSTER: Well, she was losing weight and she seemed to be, you know, like something was bothering her but I don't know what.

Muriel Oliver, an assistant matron at Hillsview Acres, also noticed Jane didn't seem to be herself.

OLIVER: Well, for maybe a month she seemed like she was worried or she just didn't seem to be herself.

ALLABY: And what made you think that? What led you to that conclusion?

OLIVER: Well, she was usually jolly and joking and

everything, and she just seemed to be quiet, you know, she just seemed to be quiet.

Both Brewster and Oliver remembered Beverly Taylor coming to the home to meet with Jane.

Ronald Wamboldt, who lived at the Stafford home for several months prior to Billy's death, was called to the stand by Allaby in the afternoon. From the Crown's point of view he didn't turn out to be much of a witness. An admitted alcoholic, Wamboldt remembered nothing, after midafternoon, of the events of the day of the shooting. The last thing he remembered was driving towards their home in the truck. The next morning he remembers Jane waking him up and asking if he knew Billy's whereabouts. He told her he didn't know and then "took my time getting up and dressed, went to the bathroom, washed. I think I had a tea . . . then I started drinking again."

If it was the Crown's intention to show benevolence on Billy's part for inviting Wamboldt to come and live in his house, the strategy backfired. Wamboldt said he accepted Billy's invitation to live at the Stafford house because he had no other place to go. He admitted under Ferrier's cross-examination that Billy often slapped and punched him and ordered him to do odd jobs around the house and in the yard and woods. Wamboldt's testimony gave the jury its first glimpse into how Billy Stafford ran the lives of the people around him. He told Ferrier that Billy often pointed loaded guns at him.

FERRIER: And did you ever give him good reason to point a gun at you?

WAMBOLDT: Never.

FERRIER: Because you wouldn't have said boo to him?

WAMBOLDT: No.

FERRIER: Has he fired shots at you?

WAMBOLDT: Not right at me, no. You see, if he did he'd never miss me because he was a good shot.

FERRIER: So he knew how to tantalize you and scare you?

WAMBOLDT: Right.

Wamboldt admitted Billy used his fists on him long before he moved into the Stafford home.

FERRIER: For a man that was your friend, he never really called you Ronny very much, did he?

WAMBOLDT: Not too often.

FERRIER: He called you dummy?

WAMBOLDT: Dummy.

FERRIER: So you were aware of his behaviour towards you but you went to live with him anyway?

WAMBOLDT: Yeah, stupidity.

FERRIER: If he told you to do a job around the house, you did it?

WAMBOLDT: Right.

FERRIER: What would likely happen if you didn't do it?

WAMBOLDT: I'd get another smash.

Wamboldt said Billy Stafford was particularly cruel to his son Darren, who was four years old during the time Wamboldt lived with them in Bangs Falls.

ALLABY: Did you ever see him strike or hit Darren?

WAMBOLDT: Yes.

ALLABY: How often?

WAMBOLDT: Oh, at least five times a day.

ALLABY: And how would he strike or hit him?

WAMBOLDT: Sometimes he'd take his fist...

ALLABY: And how hard would he hit him?

WAMBOLDT: Well you could hear it but it wouldn't knock him out, but you could hear it.

Wamboldt said Darren was a nervous child and "very afraid" of Billy Stafford. He said Billy often cuffed the boy at the dinner table, and he witnessed Billy force-feeding him several times.

FERRIER: To the point where he threw up?

WAMBOLDT: Right.

FERRIER: Into the bowl that he was eating out of?

WAMBOLDT: Yes.

FERRIER: And then be made to eat that thrown-up food again?

WAMBOLDT: Yes, he did.

During cross-examination, Wamboldt also told Ferrier about the punishment Jane took from Billy, even while playing cards.

FERRIER: And Billy wouldn't like the card that she played?

WAMBOLDT: Oh, yes, that's right.

FERRIER: And he'd cuff her?

WAMBOLDT: Right.

FERRIER: Punch her? With the back of his hand, is that what you're indicating?

WAMBOLDT: Like that, yes.

FERRIER: Knock her right off her chair?

WAMBOLDT: Right.

FERRIER: What happened to her? Did she get back up and keep playing cards?

WAMBOLDT: Yes.

FERRIER: Did she complain?

WAMBOLDT: No.

FERRIER: What would happen if she complained?

WAMBOLDT: She'd get it again, I imagine.

At Jane Stafford's June preliminary inquiry, Ronald Wamboldt testified that Billy Stafford often argued with his neighbour Margaret Joudrey and threatened, the day before he died, that "if she didn't straighten her ways up and mind her own business, that he'd take and burn her out . . . or blow her friggen head off." But at Jane's trial five months later, Wamboldt couldn't remember making the statement. Under questioning by Ferrier he said he'd managed to quit drinking from shortly after Billy's death until he testified at the preliminary inquiry in early June.

FERRIER: Would you say to this court that your ability to recall events on June fourth would have been better than it is today?

WAMBOLDT: Yes, quite a bit better.

FERRIER: Partly because it was closer to the events?

WAMBOLDT: Partly, yes.

FERRIER: And partly because you had stopped drinking?

WAMBOLDT: Yes.

FERRIER: Do you often get blackout spells when you're drinking?

WAMBOLDT: Yeah, I pass right out, yeah, quite often.

He said he'd been drinking quite heavily since the

FERRIER: Now those arguments were over the property?

MANTHORNE: Yes.

FERRIER: And you heard Mr. Stafford get into an argument with her, not very long before he died, about the property?

MANTHORNE: Yes.

FERRIER: Wherein Mr. Stafford said at one point, "You old lady, I'd like to burn you out"?

MANTHORNE: Yes, sir, he said that, yeah.

During re-examination, Allaby asked Manthorne if Margaret Joudrey was upset by Billy's threats. "Yes, sir, she was," he replied. All of that was crucial evidence for the defence, because the prosecution's next witness was Margaret Joudrey, and she'd turned hostile towards Jane Stafford from the moment she was ordered to give evidence at the June preliminary inquiry. It was a shock for Jane to see the woman "who'd been my friend and mother for six years, get on that stand and turn against me. I just hurt so bad inside. I felt like someone had taken their both hands and squeezed my insides." She listened as Margaret Joudrey told the court Jane had been like a daughter to her and that she got along well with her and Billy. She admitted having arguments with Billy but passed them off as "just foolishness."

ALLABY: Now do you recall shortly before he died there was an argument that you had with him?

JOUDREY: Oh, yeah, we had a little argument.

ALLABY: What was that about?

JOUDREY: Not much. Well, he was going to put pigs up there, a pig yard, and I didn't want the pigs up there.

ALLABY: And why didn't you want them there?

JOUDREY: Because they stink.

ALLABY: And what about the title of property lines? Was there an argument with him over that?

JOUDREY: Well, sometimes he used to go over the line and I used to go up. He made a big cement thing to put a tree or something in and I said well if anything happened and somebody else got the land, you know, he couldn't put it there.

ALLABY: So where did he put this with respect to his own land?

JOUDREY: Still put it there.

ALLABY: But you felt it wasn't on his land?

JOUDREY: It wasn't on his land, it was down below the mark.

Margaret Joudrey painted Billy Stafford as an overgrown loudmouth whom she liked to argue with and had no fear of. She said Billy sometimes gave Darren a slap on the buttocks but "I never seen a mark on Darren from Bill." Jane couldn't believe what she was hearing when Joudrey said she saw Jane beat Darren with a broomstick after he'd run away. Images of Billy Stafford breaking a mop handle in two and beating Darren until he was covered with welts filled her mind. That was the day Billy shot at her while she was out in the yard and ordered her to come in and clean up the mess. He also punched her when she began to cry after seeing Darren lying in his own blood and feces. When she cleaned the boy up, they picked up Margaret Joudrey at her trailer and went for a ride as if nothing happened. Now, in the courtroom, she stared in disbelief at her neighbour, who said she couldn't remember all the details but "she took that stick and she laid it on his little bum and I was afraid. And he had black and blue spots for quite a while afterwards. But I've never seen none from Bill."

ALLABY: What about Jane? Have you ever seen her with any black and blue spots?

JOUDREY: No, only her eyes, and that's natural because I think that's the way she is.

ALLABY: Did she ever complain to you about any treatment from Bill?

JOUDREY: Oh, yes, she complained but I didn't pay any attention to her. I heard so many lies that . . .

ALLABY: What type of thing would she complain about?

JOUDREY: Oh, Bill done this and Bill done that.

ALLABY: What do you mean by this and that?

JOUDREY: I didn't pay any attention to her.

Jane said she has never touched Darren with anything other than her hand and the only time she spanked him in front of Margaret Joudrey was when, at age two or three, she found him down by the river.

"He'd run off and taken all his clothes off. I was scared he could have drowned. I put him over my knee and spanked him. That was it. I'd never hurt my child."

The courtroom became a verbal battleground when Ferrier cross-examined Margaret Joudrey. She was belligerent and several times had to be ordered by Mr. Justice Burchell to answer Ferrier's questions.

FERRIER: The biggest problem you had at your place was the fact that Mr. Stafford always objected to your ownership of the property?

JOUDREY: Well, I don't know what that's got to do with this, I ain't going to answer that.

FERRIER: Mrs. Joudrey, you'll answer that question.

BURCHELL: Yes, you have to answer any questions that are put to you, Mrs. Joudrey.

FERRIER: The biggest problems between you and Mr. Stafford were that he told you you didn't own the property you were living on?

JOUDREY: No, not necessarily.

FERRIER: That's what he told you, Mrs. Joudrey. Isn't it?

JOUDREY: Oh, yes, but what in the heck is that?

FERRIER: And is it not true that the man that owned that property was Stanley Joudrey?

JOUDREY: That's right.

FERRIER: The man you lived common-law with?

JOUDREY: That I ain't going to answer. I don't have to.

FERRIER: My Lordship?

BURCHELL: Yes, you have to answer that, Mrs. Joudrey.

JOUDREY: Okay, yes.

FERRIER: Stanley died without a will, isn't that correct?

JOUDREY: That's right.

FERRIER: So in fact you do not own, legally, that property? You do not have legal title...

JOUDREY: I own it. Sure I own it.

FERRIER: You do not have a legal paper to that title?

JOUDREY: That's right.

FERRIER: And that's what Mr. Stafford used to rub in your face all the time.

JOUDREY: No, he didn't...

Margaret Joudrey said she didn't think details of her common-law marriage or the property where she lived were any of Ferrier's business. Mr. Justice Burchell immediately rebuked her. "Well, it's the business of this court and the business of the jury, Mrs. Joudrey. It's not for you to say."

Contrary to Roger Manthorne's testimony, Margaret Joudrey said she wasn't crying when she hugged and comforted Jane Stafford the night Billy was shot.

FERRIER: So if Roger Manthorne said you were crying, he'd be lying?

JOUDREY: Well, I don't know why he'd say I was crying, because I wasn't crying.

She also disputed Manthorne's testimony that she was upset by Billy Stafford's threat to burn her out. "So if Roger Manthorne told this court that you were upset by the remarks that Billy Stafford made to you, he'd be lying about that, too?" asked Ferrier.

JOUDREY: No, I don't think he'd be lying too much about that because Roger doesn't know too much.

FERRIER: Roger lives there?

JOUDREY: Sure he stays there.

FERRIER: He's got two eyes in his head?

JOUDREY: I know he's got two eyes. He'd be a funny-looking thing if he didn't.

FERRIER: He can see what's going on, can't he, Margaret?

JOUDREY: Roger don't pay any attention to what's going on.

Ferrier pointedly asked Margaret Joudrey why "you say all these wrong things about Jane and nothing about Billy." She said her feelings towards Jane "ain't the same as what it used to be." She said her feelings changed after she had to testify at the preliminary inquiry.

FERRIER: Things have changed now, haven't they?

JOUDREY: That's correct, because she got me mixed up in this and there's no need of it.

FERRIER: How did she get you mixed up in-it?

JOUDREY: Well, she's got me here, ain't she?

FERRIER: Now what you're telling this court is that now, today, you don't feel anything for that woman?

JOUDREY: That's right.

FERRIER: But on the night that Billy Stafford was shot,

Mrs. Joudrey, that woman was still your daughter, like a daughter to you?

JOUDREY: Well, yeah, I still liked her.

She told Ferrier she was mad at Jane "because I'm at an age now where I shouldn't be mixed up in anything. I've never been in the law before." She said she never talked to Jane after the June 4 preliminary. "I never had no more to do with her after that because I don't want to get in no more trouble. I'm in thick enough now."

Margaret Joudrey insisted that she and Billy Stafford were great friends who had occasional arguments. "We played cards," she said, "and I learned him to play yammy and we played that. Then they say Bill and I didn't get along. Well, heck, we was together mostly all the time, he was down home or I was up there."

FERRIER: So why would he do these things to your property? Why would he deliberately put something on your side of the property?

JOUDREY: Well, she knew the line as well as he did.

FERRIER: But Billy put it there. Billy was the head of the household, right?

JOUDREY: I suppose so. In fact, I'd say so.

FERRIER: And your idea is that when there's a man, he should be the head of the household?

JOUDREY: That's right.

FERRIER: And Billy made the decision to put something on your property line—and did it?

JOUDREY: That's right. He wasn't hurting nothing.

She told Ferrier that Jane once told her she hated Billy. Under re-examination, Blaine Allaby asked her when Jane made that statement. "Oh, Lord, I don't know," responded Joudrey. "I'm a woman, I don't keep run of the time and I don't keep run of the days and I don't keep run of the months."

ALLABY: Would it be weeks, months, or years?

JOUDREY: Oh, it wasn't years, maybe months.

Jane Stafford's mother and father were called to testify on the afternoon of Monday, November 8. Like other Crown witnesses they'd been banned from attending the trial until it was their turn to testify.

Maurice Hurshman said when he picked his daughter up near the satellite station on the night of the shooting and brought her to their trailer home in Danesville to clean up, "she looked like she was in shock. Her eyes was sticking right out, popped, she just looked straight ahead . . . if she turned, she turned her whole body. . . . I said, 'You should stay for the night,' and she said she had to go home. She was going home if she had to hitchhike. So I said, 'I'll drive you home,' so me and the wife we, that's what we done." He said Jane wouldn't answer any questions about what was wrong and he didn't learn about Billy Stafford's death until the next day. Hurshman told Ferrier during cross-examination he hadn't seen much of Jane after she left home in Winnipeg as a teenager.

FERRIER: Is it fair to say that your relationship with your daughter was not all that close?

HURSHMAN: That's right, yeah. . . . We never got to see each other that much, only if she'd phone sometimes and see how things were.

Both Maurice and Gladys Hurshman said they had no idea how serious Jane's situation with Billy Stafford was. Both of them said they were frightened of Billy after he attacked Maurice Hurshman and damaged their home. Gladys Hurshman said Billy "jumped up and plowed him one in the face and knocked him back against the window and broke the window out; and kicked the door in and hauled it off the hinges, and then Jane stepped in and he doubled up his fists and plowed her back against the wall." She said they didn't see much of Jane after that incident. She denied that she had any problems early in her own marriage.

Following Gladys Hurshman to the stand was Constable Robert Hillier, the first of seventeen police and medical witnesses to be called by the Crown. Hillier, with the RCMP Liverpool detachment, was in charge of exhibits during the investigation into Billy Stafford's death. His duties included accompanying the body from the scene of the shooting to Queens General Hospital, where at three-fifteen on the afternoon of March 12, 1982, he placed it in a cooler in the basement. He secured the hinged door of the cooler with two padlocks until the following morning, when he transferred the body to the morgue at Victoria General Hospital for an autopsy. Hillier also helped gather exhibits from the Stafford residence. He was there with several other officers the night Jane was taken into custody for questioning the first time. "When Mrs. Stafford was leaving the living room, walking through the kitchen, her younger son was seated at the table and she walked over to him and picked him up and gave him a hug before she left."

Corporal Philip Campbell, a forensic firearms examiner with the RCMP's Crime Detection Laboratory in Halifax, gave a lot of technical evidence of the workings of the type of gun that killed Billy Stafford. He concluded the Coey model 840 twelve-gauge, manufactured in Coburg, Ontario, was held at a range of less than six inches "and it could have been contact." He said the slug would have a velocity of sixteen hundred feet per second as it left the muzzle of the gun. "And if one has a contained vessel such as the skull, it would cause the skull to explode. The flesh around the wound would be burned. The flesh in that area would exhibit what's called a monoxide pink appearance. The oxygen is taken out of the blood and the tissue, in the combustion of the powder, and forms a monoxide colour, a very characteristic colour."

Constable Susan Ivany testified that she accompanied Jane Stafford to the Liverpool detachment just after midnight on March 14. She said she photographed a bruise measuring three and a half inches long and an inch and a half wide on her arm. She learned later the photographs had turned out poorly and she didn't get to see them.

Corporal Ron Pond, one of the two RCMP officers who interrogated Jane through the night of March 14, said she was picked up around midnight because "things started to come together throughout that day and up until an hour or so before midnight. We sat down and went over what we had and with my experience with anything serious, it's best to keep going when you are hot on the trail. Things were on a roll, so we thought we better keep pushing at it trying to get to the bottom or to the truth."

When the trial resumed on the morning of November 10, a Wednesday, Alan Ferrier asked to speak to Mr. Justice Burchell before the jury was brought in. He was upset by reports in the local media. Ferrier said he didn't want to overreact but said there were a number of inaccuracies in the reporting. He was particularly concerned with a report on the local radio station, CKBW, and in the Halifax *Chronicle-Herald*, that linked the evidence of a bruise on Jane Stafford's left arm to the effects of the recoil of a shotgun being fired. "The impression that was given as a result of the reporting of the evidence was to connect in some way the evidence of the bruising and the evidence of Corporal Campbell about recoil," complained Ferrier. Mr. Justice Burchell agreed with Ferrier that there'd been "no connection in the evidence. When I read it I twitched, reacting the same way you are to it." Ferrier asked the judge to caution the press but warned he'd ask for a publication ban if that type of reporting continued. "I accept his comments as being significant," said Burchell, "and I think the caution he has requested should be given by me at this time and I do so."

Jane Stafford, wearing blue slacks, a sweater, and a light brown jacket, looked up as the jury filed into the courtroom to listen to its fourth full day of testimony. The first witness was Constable Blair McKnight, who with Corporal Pond had interrogated Jane in the early-morning hours of March 14. He was followed by Staff Sergeant Peter Williamson, who read the statement given to him by Jane on March 25 when she said her son shot Billy. During cross-examination Williamson outlined his dealings with Billy Stafford over the years:

WILLIAMSON: He was a violent man.

FERRIER: And were other members of your detachment advised to deal with him carefully?

WILLIAMSON: Yes, I left instructions that if we were ever to respond to a complaint at Billy Stafford's that they were to go armed.

FERRIER: And were you aware that he had some propensity towards guns himself?

WILLIAMSON: Yes, he had made threats against several of my members.

FERRIER: And when did he do that?

WILLIAMSON: Over the ensuing years, depending on which member had come in contact with him.

FERRIER: What was his general attitude towards the police?

WILLIAMSON: He hated us.

FERRIER: Were you aware of any specific prosecutions against him?

WILLIAMSON: I remember he was charged with mutiny in Lunenburg. I know he'd been charged with several charges under the Lands and Forests Act for jacking deer. We investigated him on a number of occasions for intimidation of his neighbours out in that area. We suspected that he was dealing with drugs, that he was using drugs, and that he was pushing drugs. . . . Over the years we keep track of all the complaints that come in on an individual, and I would say that the average person would probably have three or four entries on a card, and that's over a period of maybe twenty years. He had three full cards.

Ferrier asked Williamson if he was sympathetic towards Mrs. Stafford.

WILLIAMSON: I made some comments that I sympathized with the way she was living.

FERRIER: And you had become aware of alleged abuse?

WILLIAMSON: Oh, I was aware of it.

FERRIER: And did you not in fact say to her that she deserved a medal?

WILLIAMSON: No, I didn't say that to her because . . . that would be condoning the action that she took. But I made that statement . . . to other policemen.

FERRIER: And you're sure, absolutely sure, that she may not have heard that comment?

WILLIAMSON: She may have heard it but it wasn't directed at her.

FERRIER: All right. Now at that particular point did you

also say she probably saved at least a couple of police officers' lives?

WILLIAMSON: Yes... That man had threatened many of our members, and from our investigation we went into the house and checked his guns and each one of the guns were loaded and hanging on the wall.

FERRIER: And you didn't believe at that point that your feelings about Mrs. Stafford were unfounded?

WILLIAMSON: No, they were really founded.

FERRIER: And you weren't really surprised to hear all of the personal abuse that Mrs. Stafford had undergone?

WILLIAMSON: No, not in the least.

FERRIER: I realize, and I'm not suggesting to you that you condoned it, that you condoned anything... but you did have a considerable amount of sympathy for Mrs. Stafford at that point?

WILLIAMSON: I did.

The Crown's final witness was Corporal Howard Pike. He identified the barrel of the shotgun used to shoot Billy Stafford. It was retrieved from the Medway River on June 3, the day before the preliminary inquiry. Divers were unable to retrieve it before that. "At the time in March the river itself was quite high from the spring flooding and the current was too strong for the divers to stay in the fast current. We had to wait until the water level went down in the river." Pike described his dealings with Jane Stafford from the time he and Archie Mason informed her of Billy's death to his taking of her signed statement after meeting Sergeant Michael Innes for the polygraph test.

Pike read the statement to the court. "Question: What can you tell me about Billy Stafford's death on March the eleventh, '82? Answer: I killed him. Where and how did it happen? Answer: In the truck in our yard in Bangs Falls. We arrived home and Ronny went in and went to bed. I just sat in the truck because Bill was asleep or passed out or something. I waited a little while, I don't know how long, maybe twenty minutes or half an hour. I beeped the horn a couple of times and Al came to the door. I just told him to get me the gun and load it. He came back out with the gun and by that time I had gotten out of the truck. I got the gun from Al and he went back inside. I just laid the gun over the driver's window and pulled the trigger. It was just a big mess. I was covered with blood and stuff. I went to the door and I laid the gun on the ground and I told Allen to get me some clean clothes and put them in a garbage bag. I told him to go down to Margaret's and call Nan [Gladys Hurshman] and have her meet me down by the satellite station. I told him to clean the place and get rid of the gun and that Roger would help him, and to tell Margaret that everything would be all right, that he wouldn't hurt her no more. I got in the truck and drove down to where you found the truck. It took me quite a while driving down because I was scared. I parked it and got out and took my clothes and went across the road and went down until I hit the pavement. Then I seen the car lights coming down the satellite road. I knew it was Dad's car because we used to own it one time. I don't remember if I told them I shot Billy or not. I just told them to leave me alone and to take me home until I got cleaned up. They took me over to the trailer in Danesville. Mom left the light on in the trailer for the dogs and I told her to turn them off, and Dad got out of the car but he stayed outside. I went in and it was dark, and I went in the bathroom and took off my clothes and put them in the garbage bag. I took a bath. I cleaned everything up and put all of the stuff back in the same bag, including the towel and facecloth. I made sure everything was cleaned up and when I came out the light was on and I asked Mom just to take me home, so they did. When we got to the Bangs Falls Road, I told them to let me out and I would walk the rest of the way. I went as far as the streetlight and cut up through the woods and went over to my place. When I went in I had the bag of stuff and I put everything in the stove. There was a note on the table from Allen and he said he was down at Margaret's. I checked on Darren and I knew Ronny was still sleeping 'cause I heard no sound from his room. I flicked the light on and off 'cause Margaret can see it from her trailer. A couple of minutes later they all come up and

Margaret just hugged and kissed me and said everything would be all right. Then Roger told me that they broke the gun down and threw it in the river. Roger and Margaret left shortly and I got my housecoat on and I went to bed and Al came in the same bed. I told him I didn't know what was going to happen from here on in. I didn't know. I told him where I had parked the truck, then we hardly spoke anymore. He dozed off and on through the night. I never slept at all. In the morning around daylight I went in and woke Ronny up and I told him Bill must have gone somewhere through the night. He didn't know nothing. I just sat around and drank tea and smoked and Ronny and Allen were outside. I went down to Margaret's and when I came back out the police arrived."

Pike said that Jane, after giving the statement, "appeared to be more relaxed than any other time that I had seen her. I think she made words to the effect that she was sorry for what had happened, for all the trouble that she had caused, and she was glad that it was finally all over."

At the end of the morning session on Wednesday, November 10, the Crown rested its case and the trial was adjourned to 2:00 P.M. the following Tuesday. The six-day break was necessary because the following day was Remembrance Day and Mr. Justice Burchell had to travel to Windsor, Nova Scotia, to open a Supreme Court session there at the beginning of the week. When the trial resumed Tuesday afternoon, Alan Ferrier briefly addressed the jury and called Gladys Hurshman as his first witness. Jurors and spectators were surprised to see her take the stand, since she'd already testified.

FERRIER: You've given evidence previously in respect to this matter?

HURSHMAN: Yes.

FERRIER: And at that point in time in the trial you gave evidence with respect to questions by me regarding your relationship with your husband?

HURSHMAN: Yes.

FERRIER: In respect to that, can you now tell the court

whether or not there was a period of time in your marriage that was tumultuous?

HURSHMAN: Yes... when Jane was growing up we were in New Brunswick, like we moved around a lot... Winnipeg and Germany.

FERRIER: And can you tell the court what kind of problems you had in your marriage at that point in time?

HURSHMAN: There was a lot of drinking problems and fighting and things like that.

FERRIER: And how severe was the drinking problem at that point in time?

HURSHMAN: Quite a bit. Quite a lot.

FERRIER: And who had the problem?

HURSHMAN: My husband.

FERRIER: And how did he treat you during these times of heavy drinking?

HURSHMAN: There was some rough times, fights... well, just more or less slapped around.

FERRIER: Now can you tell the court whether or not this would take place in front of the children?

HURSHMAN: Yes, oh, yes.

FERRIER: And do you recall specifically how Jane would react to those incidents?

HURSHMAN: Well, sometimes if it got too bad she'd take the two smaller ones out, out in the room or somewhere around.

FERRIER: Why did you not indicate to the court that there was these problems between you and your husband when you were on the stand previously?

HURSHMAN: Well, I didn't want to cause any trouble between my husband and myself. I mean, he's not, he don't drink now.

FERRIER: And how would you characterize your relationship now with your husband?

HURSHMAN: Good.

Under cross-examination by Blaine Allaby, Gladys Hurshman insisted the reason she didn't admit to marital problems in her previous testimony was to protect her marriage. "I didn't want to cause any trouble between my husband and me."

ALLABY: What made you change your mind?

HURSHMAN: . . . I just figured I might as well tell.

ALLABY: Did anybody tell you you should tell?

HURSHMAN: No.

ALLABY: Did you feel it might help Jane's position if you . . .

HURSHMAN: Yes.

ALLABY: So that was the main reason you've changed your story? Because you feel it will help Jane?

HURSHMAN: Yes.

The courtroom went very quiet when Alan Ferrier called his next witness, the accused, Jane Marie Stafford. She'd dreaded this moment for weeks. The fear intensified once the trial began. Although she was closer to her parents than ever before and her sisters Sandy and Mona were in town to provide moral support, Jane often felt alone and depressed. "I couldn't think, and my sanity was wearing very thin. I just drifted from day to day waiting and wondering when it would all end. There were times I was so frightened I didn't think I'd make it through the coming day."

To help her make it through the trial, Jane kept to a loose routine. Allen and Darren were living with her at home, and in the mornings she was up early to make their breakfasts. Allen caught his bus by 8:00 A.M. Jane took Darren the short distance to Marie and Morton Joudrey's at eight-thirty, when she left for the courthouse. After school Darren stayed with the Joudreys until Allen or Jane arrived home.

"When we were all home," recalls Jane, "I'd make supper and the three of us would discuss our day. All I would say about court was whether I thought it was a good or bad day. In the evening I bathed Darren and let him play or watch TV until 7:30 P.M. When he was in bed I did my daily household chores. I don't care much for television, so I read a lot and listened to music when the house was quiet in the late evenings. Sometimes Mom and Dad or my sisters would visit for a while. On Saturdays and Sundays or other days when there was no court I would drive to the beach alone and walk for hours. Sometimes I went to Mom and Dad's for supper and then I'd go home to my music and my quiet."

Jane also developed a routine during the long days spent sitting in the courtroom, where her life was being dissected bit by bit before the media and the public. She was encouraged and heartened by the onlookers who packed the courtroom each day. Friends and strangers wished her well, and that helped hold her together. During the morning and afternoon recesses she drank coffee and smoked cigarettes in a back room, often in the company of Alan Ferrier. She ate lunch with her friend Andrea Wamboldt or at Gramma Mill's house.

Always in the back of her mind was the knowledge it would soon be her turn to take the witness stand. As the day approached she began having nightmares. She lost more weight, and her pale blue eyes were accentuated by the dark circles brought on by lack of sleep. "I was terrified," recalls Jane. "I had two main fears—that they would show me pictures of Bill's body. That was the main fear. I didn't know until I read it in the newspaper, after my preliminary, that he was decapitated. I never knew where I shot him and I never asked. The other fear was that I would get a mental block and just sit there and forget everything I had to say. I wasn't really frightened by all the people in the courtroom. They helped me get through each day."

Alan Ferrier did his best to ease his client's fears about taking the witness stand.

"You've got to pretend the only people in the courtroom are you, me, and the prosecutor," he told her over coffee. "Just tune everyone else right out."

Jane is a religious person, and she believes it helped her. "I know I had God inside me. Only people who have felt his presence can understand what I mean by that. I can't express it in words, I just know that he was constantly with me."

Jane approached the witness stand with her head bowed. She appeared frail and vulnerable. Even with the hush in the courtroom she could barely be heard as she spoke in a sometimes inaudible monotone. Several times during her testimony, Mr. Justice Burchell asked her to speak up. Slowly, Ferrier guided her through her early years and her first marriage. Jane characterized those years as rough ones.

"Dad drank a lot," she said. "Most of the time he was drunk. He went to work that way and came home that way. Fighting. Hollering." Her first husband drank a lot but wasn't violent. "He lost his work and everything through drinking. The last three or four years I was with him he didn't work." Jurors and spectators craned to hear her words when Jane related the horrors of her life with Billy Stafford.

FERRIER: What did you do about these assaults, anything?

JANE: No, I didn't. I just carried on about my business. He would tell me it was my fault, anyway. Whenever I did get a beating he would always tell me it was my fault. I was the one who started it... you hear it so much, after a while you begin to believe it." For more than two full hours Jane recited a litany of physical and mental abuse that Billy inflicted on her and other members of the Stafford household. The jury also heard how Jane was sexually abused and forced into bestiality and how when she dared complain Billy beat her and on one occasion forced her to drink a glass of his urine. Jane told about her unsuccessful attempt to hire Beverly Taylor to kill Billy Stafford.

FERRIER: At that point in time, Mrs. Stafford, can you tell the court whether or not you wanted Mr. Stafford dead?

JANE: Yes, I wanted him dead. I hated him. He was a maniac.

FERRIER: Why didn't you leave him?

JANE: There was no leaving him in my mind. I told him once before that I was going to leave him and he said he was never going to be a third-time loser. He said, "Wherever you go, old woman, you'll be back." And he said you'll bring that bastard of a kid back with you. He said because I'll just start with your mother and your father and your sisters, and he said, until you come back. So there was no way, no way.

Jane Stafford was still on the stand when the court adjourned for the day at 4:45 P.M. Mr. Justice Burchell told Jane, "Since you are in the process of giving your testimony at this trial, you mustn't discuss the case with anyone between now and when we resume tomorrow morning at nine-thirty." That instruction would seem reasonable and logical to any observer, but for Jane Stafford it was devastating. "I had to leave the courtroom without seeing Alan Ferrier before I left. I was not allowed to talk to anyone because I was still under oath. I still don't understand that. I felt awful—deserted. I had to go home and think all night about having to come back in the morning and take that stand again. My nerves were like live wires. When I arrived the next morning, it was as if Alan was reading my thoughts. He looked around and for a brief moment we made eye contact. He smiled to reassure me and I knew by his eyes he was saying, 'You can do it, Jane, I know you can.' I was on the stand another two and a half hours."

Jane testified that Billy's treatment of her and others got worse as time went on, and the worst time of the day was suppertime. "It was just an ordeal to have supper."

FERRIER: Who prepared supper?

JANE: I did, when I came home from work.

FERRIER: Now during this time what would Mr. Stafford be doing when you came home from work? What would he be up to?

JANE: I'd say three quarters of the time he was drunk or smoked up, sitting around hooting and hollering. He was usually hollering before I got in the door. Just anything that came into his head. He was always ranting and raving. Always had money to drive around, go places, do things.

FERRIER: Whose money was he using during this time period?

JANE: Oh, whenever I had any left he would take that, but that wasn't usually very much.

FERRIER: So where did he usually get his money?

JANE: Selling dope.

FERRIER: Are you personally aware of that?

JANE: Yes, I know that.

Ferrier asked Jane what kind of a relationship she had with Margaret Joudrey.

JANE: A very good one. She knew everything that was going on for the last five years that I lived there. She was the same as a mother to me.

FERRIER: And what kind of things would you confide in her?

JANE: Everything, she was the only one that I had any contact with. We lived out there and except for Margaret and where I took Darren to the baby-sitters, I never visited anybody's house. . . .

FERRIER: When you did have contact with people, was it alone or with Mr. Stafford?

JANE: He was generally with me. One day a week I would get to come to town, to do errands, to pick up groceries and such, go out and visit his mother and father. Had a certain time to do everything and had to be home by a certain time.

FERRIER: And going back to Mrs. Joudrey, how did she appear to you to be reacting to Mr. Stafford's accusations about the land?

JANE: She was as scared of Bill as everybody else out around there. She probably hated him more than I did.

FERRIER: You've heard her give evidence in this matter?

JANE: Yes, I have.

FERRIER: What do you think of the position that she's taken now?

JANE: Well, until we had the preliminary I didn't know that she'd be like that. She was the last person I ever expected to go like that.

FERRIER: Why do you think she's not supportive of you now?

JANE: Oh, she figures I can get her in some kind of trouble or take her land. I don't really know what reason she's thinking. I don't know.

Ferrier asked Jane to compare the relationship she had with Mrs. Joudrey to the relationship she had with her own parents. Jane said her relationship with Margaret Joudrey was "much closer. I didn't have much contact with Mom and Dad. Margaret was about the only one around that I talked to. At that time she was closer than my own mother."

Jane testified that on the night she shot Billy he was hollering and very angry on the way to visit Leona Anthony's. She said he called Margaret Joudrey an old bag and said "she was worried last night. He said her light was on all night. He said she won't have to worry about seeing the light shine down there no more after tonight. He said he was going to burn her out. And he kept this up pretty well the whole way." After leaving the Anthony house, "He started right in on the way back. He told me about the Mounties being out to visit Allen. He said when he got done with Margaret he would deal with him, too, might as well clean everything up in one night." Ferrier asked Jane about the statement she made to Sergeant Williamson claiming that her son Allen shot Billy Stafford. "Why did you lie at that point, obviously to me and to Sergeant Williamson?"

JANE: ... The RCMP and all the people seemed good and sympathetic and they talked like they understood but I was still charged with first-degree murder. And I didn't really think anybody would believe just how we lived in that house. How bad it really was. I was still at that point taking the tranquillizers or nerve pills. I wasn't even thinking... when I come in and told all of this I didn't even think to tell Allen the story I was going to tell. I didn't even know I was going to tell it at that point. I didn't want to go to jail. I didn't want to be away from Darren.

FERRIER: Now what made you think that Allen was going to give the same story as that?

JANE: I don't know. I didn't even consider that fact.

Under cross-examination, Jane admitted to Allaby that in addition to attempting to hire Beverly Taylor to kill Billy and twice considering shooting him herself, she once asked Billy's eldest daughter, Sharon, from his first marriage, to help her kill him. Sharon Stafford had moved to Nova Scotia from Ontario to live for a time.

ALLABY: Do you remember talking to Sharon Stafford about getting some chemical?

JANE: Yes.

ALLABY: What was that about?

JANE: I asked her to get me some dope or something.

ALLABY: What for?

JANE: That would kill a person.

ALLABY: And why did you want it?

JANE: Well, I figured I could give it to Bill.

ALLABY: How many times did you mention it to Sharon?

JANE: I think I asked her on a couple of occasions.

ALLABY: What did you tell her you wanted it for?

JANE: She knew what I wanted it for. I told her, for her father.

Jane, under questioning by Allaby, said she wasn't aware that a shelter for battered wives existed in Halifax.

ALLABY: You never inquired about any way the situation could be relieved other than by killing Billy?

JANE: If I'd have left there would have been a lot more people killed than Bill.

ALLABY: That was your feeling?

JANE: That I knew.

Alan Ferrier, during re-examination, asked Jane "whether or not on the eleventh of March of 1982 that you had any thoughts of killing Mr. Stafford prior to the time that you were in the truck?"

JANE: No, I didn't. I didn't think I had guts enough to do it.

Ferrier also asked Jane if Billy ever told her anything about killing anybody. "Yes, he did. He told me he couldn't fish out of Liverpool. That's when he went to Lunenburg. When the boat went out, the *Enterprise*, the crew was aboard, and he said how Jimmy LeBlanc and him had argued. He said Jimmy went into the galley to make a mug up, and he said shortly after he went in behind him and he threw him overboard. And nobody on that boat would talk either. It was the same as the mutiny, nobody would talk. They knew he done it."

Jane's body sagged with relief when Mr. Justice Burchell thanked her and told her to step down from the witness stand. "I was finally finished but I was drained." The major fear she carried through all of her testimony during cross-examination had proved unfounded. "It never left my mind—at what minute are they going to make me look at those pictures." As for the Crown's questioning, Ferrier had prepared her well. "He told me to take my time and think of my answers before I spoke. Sometimes I thought so long, I couldn't remember the question. He also told me if I couldn't remember an answer or didn't know it, to tell them so. I tried so very hard to do everything right. I know the judge and the Crown kept telling me to speak up, over and over again. But to me it seemed like everything I said had an echo. I could hear myself well. The questions seemed to be nonstop. They just kept coming at me. Sometimes I never had time to finish one before they asked me another." Jane returned to her chair a few feet to Ferrier's left. The relief was obvious in her face.

Following Jane, Ferrier called three experts to the stand to talk about her mental condition. The first was Dr. Rosemary Sampson, a clinical psychologist from Halifax, who had interviewed and tested Jane six weeks before the trial. She had tested her for verbal, general, and performance IQs and found all three scores "within the normal range of intelligence. Considering her educational level, her occupational status, the time that she has been away from school, she answered and dealt with the test quite well." Dr. Sampson testified she found Jane to be extremely depressed "with many defenses. In other words, she has ways of keeping herself pretty well encased as it were." Jane also sees herself as a victim and has "an extremely low self-concept. She's an extremely anxious person, very guilt-ridden. I think she's an emotionally immature woman whose life history reflects poor interpersonal, particularly heterosexual, relationships. She presents a pattern of anger which has continually been internalized, which eats away at the person. I think that type of a person would very often think of suicide, but she had a moral strength in her that would not act upon that, unless really pushed to the extreme."

As Jane was subjected to increasing stress, said Dr.

Sampson, "her ability to deal with situations lessens, but I would surmise that her planning ability, even in the best of times, is problematic . . . she would maybe start out thinking on something and then not really see what the end point was going to be." Dr. Sampson told the court that when she presented Jane with material she could identify with, "the stress made her thinking, her way of acting, more fuzzy—more illogical." Under cross-examination, Dr. Sampson told Allaby she thought Jane was aware of what she was doing when she pulled the trigger and killed Billy Stafford. Allaby also questioned Jane's motives in implicating her son Allen in her second statement to the RCMP.

ALLABY: Does it surprise you that she would try to indicate that her son was responsible for what she had in fact done?

SAMPSON: I think it's pretty much in keeping with the extreme stress that she was under, and afterwards the extreme shock. . . .

ALLABY: But is there not a protective maternal instinct that would say to her, "No, you don't do this, you don't blame it on your son, your child"?

SAMPSON: . . . Her confusion was to the point where she was amnesic, she doesn't remember certain things. She was sort of at the ultimate of her stress level and her thinking became more confused, more fuzzy, and she wasn't thinking properly.

ALLABY: Is what she did consistent with her personality, killing Billy Stafford?

SAMPSON: I don't believe so.

ALLABY: Once he was dead and she realized he was dead, would there be a reaction, perhaps relief, almost an elation?

SAMPSON: I wouldn't predict that to be so. I think she would just be so disbelieving of what was going on and I think her confusion level would be even increased.

Dr. Carol Abbott, a Halifax medical doctor specializing in psychiatry, testified that she had assessed Jane after three meetings with her in May and June. She said Jane appeared to be older than her stated age and "she was extremely nervous and tense. I described her affect as being flat rather than depressed, though I think one could call it depressed as well. . . . The situation that she'd been in for the last five years of her marriage had been one of overwhelming stress, both physical and mental . . . I think it affected her in terms of her passivity, which we see to the alleged abuse . . . she could never predict when he was going to react the way he was, and I think it's this unpredictability that made it difficult for her to feel that she could do anything to control the situation."

Dr. Abbott said Jane told her she initially trusted Billy Stafford "and I don't think she looked beyond that . . . I think outwardly she was compliant. I think outwardly she went along with him, and I don't think that she felt at any time that she could express any of her feelings towards him because of the risk of provoking him, and I think this was constantly there. Even when he was away I think that she felt it even then, there was the fear that it would get back to him. So that although she suppressed or repressed or denied her feelings, these were the defense mechanisms with which she dealt with the stress at that time."

FERRIER: Can you tell us whether or not she has any aggressive tendencies in her personality?

ABBOTT: I can't think of any that come to mind. I think that there is no history, to my knowledge, of violent behaviour in her personality . . . in fact it was the opposite, her behaviour was far more likely to be compliant and passive.

FERRIER: How did you assess her ability to put thoughts together in a structured way?

ABBOTT: That's a difficult question to answer. I think that she can put thoughts together. I think she reacts to situations as they come up. I think that she does not look at the consequences and in this respect her judgement is limited, it's limited to the effects of her immediate reactions.

FERRIER: You've heard her evidence with respect to the events of the night in question. Can you tell us whether or not it appears to be consistent with, or inconsistent with, a well-thought-out plan of deliberate, cold-blooded murder?

ABBOTT: No, I think it's quite inconsistent with a deliberate plan that is well thought out and what you call cold-blooded murder.

Dr. Abbott said she thought Jane was protective of both Darren and Allen. When she implicated Allen in one of her statements to police, it was "an example of the fact that she had no idea of the consequences of her action, and hadn't realized the implications of it for both herself and for other people close to her." She said she didn't think Jane had ever been close to her parents, and Margaret Joudrey "was probably one of the only resources that she had in terms of someone that she could share some little amount of feeling with."

FERRIER: Did you note whether or not there was suicidal tendencies in terms of your examination of her?

ABBOTT: Yes, she told me that she had considered suicide at times during the last years that she spent with her husband. She told me that she never carried out anything about it because of her fear of leaving her small son to suffer further abuse.

When Ferrier asked Dr. Abbott if she thought Jane was strong-willed or weak-willed, she said, "in some ways one could say that she's been a strong person to stay in such a situation for as long as she did, which I think most people would consider not endurable. I think to stay in a situation that is such a bad one involves having pretty strong defenses to be able to withstand it, so in some ways one can say that she has strength. Well, there are weaknesses, too. I mean her weaknesses in terms of her passivity, in terms of her inability to exercise judgement beyond the immediate situation, inability to see other ways out of this situation, to see other resources that might be available."

Dr. Abbott said she had to qualify her analysis because Jane's situation was so unusual in that she felt totally blocked because of Billy's intimidation and believed "that this man had the ability to carry out his intimidation. So I think in one way, one can see these as weaknesses," but that should be qualified because "there were very good reasons why this lady couldn't get out of the situation she was in."

FERRIER: Are you saying that she did not have the strength to get out of it but she had the strength to endure it?

ABBOTT: . . . Initially she thought that maybe the situation would improve. I think that as the years went by she lost hope of the situation improving, and I think increasingly felt a sense of hopelessness and helplessness about it. Along with that goes difficulty feeling that there is any future, an inability to see that things can be any better for herself. I think she suffered a tremendous amount of loss of self-esteem, loss of any kind of personal integrity in this situation. We've heard some of the abuse that she talked about, and I would think it would be extremely hard to maintain any kind of sense of personal integrity, any sense of one's own effectiveness in that situation.

FERRIER: Would there be a similarity in the sense of being psychologically imprisoned?

ABBOTT: I think that's one way of putting it. I think that's a very good way of putting it, of feeling, as I think someone has already used the term "encased," shut in without being able to see any escape.

The stress on Jane Stafford was at its peak the night she shot Billy, said Dr. Abbott, and when it became no longer endurable she saw only one way out. "I think she felt there was a threat to the lives of people that were very dear to her and I don't think that she had much doubt that there was a very, very high chance of her husband carrying through his threats. She knew he had the ability to do that and had made the plans to do it."

Alan Ferrier's final medical witness, Dr. John Dimock, was an expert in forensic and child psychiatry from the Royal Ottawa Hospital, where he's director of the Family Court Clinic section. Dimock is also an assistant professor of psychiatry at the University of Ottawa and has an extensive background in child abuse cases. He was also a member of the Ottawa Committee on Battered Wives. He concluded that Darren was subjected to a moderate degree of "emotional if not physical abuse. I asked him to reproduce some diagrams that I drew and he did two or three of them fairly successfully, but then it came to the diamond and he did not complete that successfully, and he reflexively and immediately flinched away from me, taking sort of evasive action. And I was most amazed by seeing that, and I obviously asked him why he had done that and he quite spontaneously, without any provoking on my part, said he wasn't allowed to get things wrong or else his father would give him a clip or would strike him."

Dr. Dimock interviewed Darren in Ottawa in the summer of 1982, while the boy was staying with Jane's sister Sandy. Darren played with the toys the doctor had in his office. One was a toy truck that Darren said was like his father's truck. The boy told him his father was always hollering at him or hitting him, on one occasion hitting him in the mouth. On another occasion he pointed a gun at him. Darren was five years old at the time he was interviewed.

Dr. Dimock testified he asked Darren what three magic wishes he would like to make "and he would tend to talk to me about wishing to be like me, and wishing to have all the toys that I had, and that kind of response. He asked for some toys very much like mine, he asked for some paper and pencils because there were paper and pencils there and we were drawing...and then his third wish was that he was big and his father was small and that he could have hit his father. He seemed quite pleased with that last wish and smiled to himself afterwards."

Dr. Dimock said that as Darren relaxed in his presence over ensuing visits he seemed to become quite aggressive. "I see that often in children who are subject to emotional problems, who will show aggressiveness as really an expression of their sadness, of their depression." He recommended Darren receive further psychiatric care. He also interviewed Jane and was familiar with the abuses she'd been subjected to. He said it wasn't unusual that she didn't know about the existence of the home for battered wives in Halifax "and anyway these institutions are underfunded and over-crowded."

FERRIER: Is your evidence indicating in your experience with battered wives that there tends to be a self-isolation about the problem?

DIMOCK: There's a lot of shame, a lot of fear, a lot of personality traits in the wife herself, which all associate themselves with that particular syndrome. I believe it is a syndrome. It's certainly different in some cases than others, different reasons for staying in a marital situation. But certainly these wives, the wives that I've seen, tend to isolate themselves, will keep things secret for many years in some kind of almost unreal hope that things will improve, which they sometimes do, you know, if maybe the alcohol abuse ceases or...

FERRIER: How important would it be to Mrs. Stafford that her mother had been subjected to abuse by her husband and stuck it out and survived?

DIMOCK: There's certainly an aspect of learned behaviour. She'd seen a similar kind of thing occurring. Really she used to sort of shepherd the other kids away into another room perhaps when things were getting hot. And this kind of reaction to abuse again is sort of quiet acceptance because of the hopelessness of the situation. That certainly explains to me a lot of what was going on even in their own marriage.

The doctor said the sexual abuse Jane was subjected to is not unusual in terms of bondage and the use of an artificial penis and vibrators. "The bestiality aspect, the use of the dog, I've seen on occasion but I think when that kind of behaviour is involved then one is really involved in a very serious sadistic type of a relation-ship." Under cross-examination, Dr. Dimock said he believed Jane was trying to remove Billy's body as far away from Darren as she could when she drove it down River Road the night of the shooting. He doesn't be-lieve she did it to avoid detection. Following Dr. Dimock's testimony, the court recessed for twenty-five minutes. Jane Stafford felt uneasy as she listened to the evidence from the three doctors. She didn't understand some of the terminology but she felt much of it was negative.

Her spirits lifted when she went to a back room off the main courtroom and saw Alan Ferrier smiling. He was proud of the job she had done on the witness stand. He hugged her.

"I know how hard that was for you, but you did it," he said.

Jane sat down and lit up a cigarette.

"I left out so much that I should have said."

"You did just fine."

"I had trouble keeping my train of thought."

"It was okay. It was okay. We're almost there."

"I'm so scared, Alan, I'm so scared."

Jane went back into the courtroom and sat, head bowed, as she had through most of the testimony. Ferrier's next five witnesses were neighbours or acquaintances of the Staffords from the Bangs Falls area. Marsha Freeman told of finding a bullet hole in her home after Billy Stafford was fined and put on probation after she had complained to police that he tried to run her down while she was walking down a road with her baby in a carriage. Another neighbour, Marilyn Fisher, testified about Billy threatening her at her home after she complained to police that her dog had been shot. "He looked like a wild man. His face was red. His eyeballs was bulging out of his head. Like I said, he scared me." Victor Westhaver testified that during a social call at the Stafford residence Billy Stafford punched him and then shot at him and a friend as they fled his house. Calvin Anthony told the court he perjured himself at a trial in which Billy Stafford was charged with jacking deer.

FERRIER: And as a result of the evidence that you gave at that time, can you tell us whether or not Mr. Stafford was acquitted or convicted?

ANTHONY: Acquitted.

Ivan Higgins related Billy's unprovoked attack on him when he was invited with his wife and child to the Stafford house by Billy, who'd purchased a wood-burning stove from him. He told of running from the house in his bare feet after Billy struck him for no reason. After Higgins's evidence the court adjourned until the following morning, Thursday, November 18, 1982. It would be the day Ferrier wrapped up the case for the defense.

His first witness was Leona Anthony, who testified she once saw Billy hit Jane with his fist in an unprovoked attack while she was visiting them. She verified that Billy, Jane, and Ronny Wamboldt came to visit her house the night Billy was shot. She told Allaby she saw Jane with bruises "different times." Ronny Wamboldt's brother, Gene, testified he knew Billy for twenty years and "he had an awful temper, he'd fly off the handle some quick." He said he warned his brother not to stay with Billy Stafford because he was going to get himself in trouble. He agreed with Allaby that Billy Stafford was a bully—but if you stood up to him he'd leave you alone.

Andrea Wamboldt, Ronny's estranged wife, said she witnessed Billy abuse and physically assault Jane "a good many times." She also related how Billy went into a rage and put a gun to her head in the Stafford kitchen when she came to visit Jane from Ontario. "He just come running out of the bedroom with the gun and pointed it right at me, right between my eyes." Andrea Wamboldt said Margaret Joudrey witnessed many of the same abuses she saw Billy inflict on Jane. "I say Margaret Joudrey knows pretty well everything that went on. She pretty well done everything Billy told her to do. I think she was scared of Billy." Allaby asked her if she was aware how Billy treated Ronny Wamboldt.

ANDREA: Yes.

ALLABY: Did that upset you?

ANDREA: No, because Ron always hated him. I don't know why he even bothered with him, myself.

ALLABY: But it didn't bother you the way that Billy treated him?

ANDREA: No, because I figured he should have stayed away from him.

The last two witnesses Ferrier proposed to call were Billy's first wife, Pauline Stafford, and common-law wife Faith Hatt. The Crown objected to their testimony, and the jury was sent out while counsel argued the matter before Mr. Justice Burchell. After some deliberation he ruled in favour of the defense and had the jury called back into the courtroom. "Mr. Foreman, members of the jury, in this case the accused has admitted firing the shot that killed her husband. One of the matters in issue is the state of mind of the accused at the time in question. You've heard evidence to the effect that her state of mind was affected by abuse she had suffered at the hands of the late Mr. Stafford. Some doubt as to the veracity of her evidence on the matter of abuse has been raised and in particular by the testimony of Margaret Joudrey. The defense now proposes to introduce evidence as to Mr. Stafford's treatment of several other persons with whom he, in the past, has lived in a marital relationship. The purpose of that evidence is to show that it was the habit of Mr. Stafford to abuse women with whom he had such a relationship. It will be suggested by the defense that if the deceased had a disposition to abuse his legal wife and a former common-law wife, then evidence of such a disposition should be viewed as corroborating the testimony of the accused as to abuse suffered by her. It is therefore in relation to the question of whether evidence of the accused as to abuse suffered by her was truthful, that the evidence you are about to hear is being allowed to come before you. You must not lose sight of the fact that the real issue is the state of mind of the accused at the time in question, and you must not lose sight of the fact that it is the accused and not Mr. Stafford who is on trial."

Faith Hatt, who lived common law with Billy for two years, said she became a nervous wreck because of his unpredictability and fled to Calgary when she was three months pregnant. She said Billy was "like a mad dog... He actually frothed at the mouth when he'd come after me."

Billy's legal wife, Pauline, said she was with Billy from 1962 to 1968 and had five children by him. "He beat me quite often with anything he could get ahold of. A beer bottle, broom handle, his fists mostly." She also described how he abused the children from the time they were babies. She fled to a cousin's home in

Ontario with her children while Billy was out on the boats.

The defense rested its case and the court adjourned until 2:00 P.M., at which time Alan Ferrier addressed the jury. He made reference to Section 37 of the Criminal Code, which outlines self-defense. It states: "Everyone is justified in using force to defend himself or anyone under his protection from assault if he uses no more force than is necessary to prevent the assault or the repetition of it. Nothing in this section shall be deemed to justify the wilful infliction of any hurt or mischief that is excessive having regards to the nature of the assault that the force used was intended to prevent."

Ferrier said that section of the code "may be a relevant consideration for you to deal with in this matter. We have a situation where the deceased had indicated to Mrs. Stafford an intention to burn out Mrs. Joudrey and to deal with her son Allen. The consequences of that action, of course, could be just property damage, or bodily harm, or perhaps even death. Her view of that particular threat at that point was that it was serious and real, and that it could, in fact, be carried out when Mr. Stafford woke up. You will have to consider whether or not her actions at that point were more forceful than what was necessary under those circumstances. You will have to assess whether or not you believe at this stage that he was indeed going to carry out that very intended act."

But Ferrier's main argument was directed at convincing the jury to bring in a verdict of guilty of manslaughter rather than first-degree murder. He quoted Section 215 of the Criminal Code: "Culpable homicide that otherwise would be murder may be reduced to manslaughter if the person who committed it did so in the heat of passion caused by sudden provocation. A wrongful act or insult that is of such a nature as to be sufficient to deprive an ordinary person of the power of self-control is provocation for the purposes of this section if the accused acted upon it on the sudden and before there was time for his passion to cool."

Ferrier told the jury that Jane shot Billy Stafford as an impulsive reaction to what he said to her. "If you were thinking about a deliberate and planned murder and you wanted to get rid of the body, would you drive it down the road and stop it on the side of the road where it would definitely be found the next morning?" he asked. "Would you allow the gun belt to stay on the wall of your own home with the one slug missing for three days until the police finally came to your house and it was still there in the same condition it was before? How much thought went into this? I suggest to you, not very much. In fact, her actions are consistent with not thinking at all. Her only thought was to get rid of this mess. Get rid of this body and then I'll go home. Those actions are much more consistent with somebody who was just simply acting on the sudden, at the moment, hasn't carefully planned it out. Hasn't carefully thought out the consequences of what she has done. She reacted out of a protective nature which has been described to you by the psychiatrist, her feeling of responsibility towards the people who were around her and to Mrs. Joudrey."

Ferrier said Margaret Joudrey admitted she was upset with Jane because she had to testify in court. "She doesn't like Jane anymore. From a woman who was like a mother to an enemy, just like that. Her motives, quite frankly, make her a suspect witness. I would suggest to you that her evidence is absolutely useless."

Billy Stafford's first two wives, said Ferrier, lived terrible lives with him but they were able to escape. Billy, meanwhile, was getting worse and worse, "more violent and more unpredictable as time went on. So we had a man that was even worse, if that can be possible, than the kind of man that those two women had to deal with years ago. His basic makeup, his basic personality, never changed, he just got worse, and worse, and worse. This case generally requires you to consider the syndrome of a battered wife. That feeling of putting up with incredible abuse but staying for reasons that made absolutely no sense to a person who was outside of that relationship. It's easy for us to say, 'well, *we* wouldn't be imprisoned under those circumstances,' but first of all we are not Jane Stafford. She is Jane Stafford. And we are not Billy Stafford, either. And we don't know what it was like to live in that household. We don't know what it was like to be subjected to the kind of violence and abuse and sadomasochistic sexual practices that would drive anybody over the wall. And that evidence is a plain reflection of the kind of man he was. He liked to abuse people that he could control.

"I would suggest to you very, very strongly that the issue of provocation is substantial enough in this case to raise a doubt, and I want you to know that the law is that the Crown must disprove provocation. It is not for the defense to prove it. The Crown must establish that this murder happened and, without any doubt, without provocation. If you have any doubt whatsoever about provocation, you must exercise that in favour of Mrs. Stafford, and as a result it is acquittal on the charge of murder and a guilty finding on manslaughter. I urge that on you in the strongest way after hearing all of the evidence that you have heard.

"Jane Stafford was a prisoner in that home. If you were unlawfully imprisoned under those circumstances, if you were, if I might use the example, if you were a Jew in Auschwitz and you saw the boys coming to take your mother away to the oven and you had a chance to stop it, no matter what the consequences to yourself, you would react immediately, promptly, and you would do what you could to help without the thought of consequences to yourself. That's how she reacted that night.

"I would ask you to consider all of the evidence very, very carefully . . . and bring in a verdict of manslaughter only."

In his summation to the jury, Blaine Allaby said the Stafford case was important from the point of view of the law and "from the point of view of a lot of women out there who are considered battered wives. It is a problem which is much in the news in our society today and it's a problem which you are confronted with very directly. I am not going to stand here and suggest to you Billy Stafford was a saint. In fact, I think on a scale of one to ten, he'd be on the lower end. He was not a nice person. He was a difficult person. He was a bully and I think the evidence clearly establishes that, but Billy Stafford, unfortunately, perhaps, is not the one who is on trial. It is Jane Stafford who is on trial, and Jane Stafford is on trial for first-degree murder.

"My learned friend and the psychiatrists perhaps suggest that Jane Stafford was not mentally capable of formulating a foolproof plan . . . but anybody who commits murder and is charged, has not had a foolproof plan because they were charged. If the plan was foolproof, nobody would know about it. First she was going to get somebody else to do it for her and he wouldn't. Then rather than actually perform the act herself directly, she was going to do it by chemical poisoning, and finally she realized that if this was going to be done she had to do it herself. The Crown is suggesting that she waited for the opportunity and on March eleventh the opportunity arose. He was passed out in the truck, he was asleep, she could get the gun, she could kill Billy Stafford, which she wanted to do. She indicated in her own evidence she hated him, she wanted him dead, and I think the evidence establishes perhaps that that feeling had been there for at least a year and a half. She had it in her mind that she was going to kill Billy Stafford at some point.

"The whole thing may not have been a perfect plan, but as I say, perfect plans don't end up in court. The Crown is suggesting that she was waiting her chance and she took it on this particular night and what she did was planned and what she did was deliberate.

"I don't think anybody is questioning the fact that she had one hell of a life with that man but she is also a very interested party and some aspects of her evidence are corroborated, others aren't. Really there are only two people who know what happened in the truck that night on the way home. Was the story about burning out Margaret true? Those are things that you have to decide and make your determination on.

"The Crown is suggesting to you that first-degree murder is what this was. We may sympathize with Jane Stafford in her situation, but the law is the law, and what do we say to people out there? I would submit that in this case we have to say we sympathize but what you did was planned and deliberate, was not provoked, and was first-degree murder."

The trial was adjourned Thursday afternoon following Blaine Allaby's summation to the jury. It resumed the next morning with Mr. Justice Burchell's charge to the jury. He lived up to his reputation for meticulously reviewing the testimony of the witnesses. In this case there were forty-six witnesses, and his charge, including an explanation of the law, took seven and a half hours. His discussion of the law included a look at Section 37, the defense of self-defense. After reading the section he said the jury would have to decide whether for the "purpose of defending those under her protection, the killing of Mr. Stafford was objectively or actually a matter of necessity. So you must look at the means employed in self-defense and decide whether those means were necessary. In addressing that question, of course, you may take into account what you know about the character and disposition of Mr. Stafford. . . . You should understand that the law of self-defense proceeds from necessity, from the instinctive and the intuitive necessity to preserve one's self. Under no circumstances may that defense be raised as a cloak for retaliation or revenge. The use of force in self-defense should come as a matter of last resort. It's justified only where there are no other reasonable means to prevent the assault. If you have any reasonable doubt as to whether the accused acted in self-defense as I've defined it, you will find the accused not guilty of murder or of any other offense because if that is your finding or if you have a doubt, a reasonable doubt, as to self-defense, then the Crown will have failed to prove that the homicide was culpable, because a homicide committed in self-defense is not a culpable homicide."

Mr. Justice Burchell told the jury it could return

one of four verdicts: guilty of first-degree murder; guilty of second-degree murder; guilty of manslaughter; or not guilty. He explained in detail how each verdict could be reached. It was 5:30 P.M. before he completed his charge and the jury retired to begin deliberations. They took time off for dinner at 6:30 P.M. and continued deliberating until shortly after midnight. During the evening they requested that the testimony of Jane's son Allen be played back to them. The jury was sequestered in a local hotel overnight, returning to continue their deliberations the next day.

Jane Stafford had arrived in the courtroom at 9:00 A.M. Friday morning. Her heart pounded as she watched the jurors file into the jury room, closing the door behind them. Her stomach was tight, her nerve ends raw. "Alan Ferrier talked to me for a while, telling me to keep cool. But my whole life was being determined behind that closed door. The courtroom was filled, wall to wall, with people. There was noise and confusion all around me. I'd walk around a bit; sit a bit; and smoke one cigarette after another. I kept thinking of what Alan had told me, 'The longer the jury is out, the worse things look.' I didn't leave that courtroom until 12:45 A.M. I was exhausted. My head was pounding. I couldn't concentrate on anything. When I came out of the courtroom Mom and Dad were waiting outside." Jane went to them and hugged them.

"Is it over for tonight?" asked Maurice Hurshman.

"Yes, it's over for tonight."

"Can you come home with us now, Janey?"

"I can go home, but I'm not. I have to remain in town, where I can get to the courthouse quickly if a verdict is reached before 9:00 A.M. tomorrow morning."

Maurice Hurshman didn't understand. "Dad was hurt and couldn't understand why I didn't want to go home. I didn't even try to explain. I walked away and got into my car with my sister Mona and my friend Andrea. I thought back to when the court had adjourned the night before, on Thursday. Everything that could be done, had been done. The rest was just legal talk. As I was getting ready to leave the courtroom that evening,

Alan took me aside and said, 'Well, Jane, it's done. There is no more we can do. When you come to court tomorrow, bring your bag with you. You may need it. Say your good-byes before you come tomorrow.' I never told Alan, but my bag had been packed and in my car since day one of the trial. Well, on Friday morning I said my good-byes to Darren, to Allen, to my family. I told Darren, 'I might not be home anymore, so you be a good boy and you grow up and be as proud of your mommy as she is of you. I love you, babe,' and I sent him off to school. I said to Allen, 'I love you dearly— please always know that and please forgive me all the hurts that I've caused you. Don't worry about anything. Grampy has a letter and he knows everything that I want done. You will all be looked after.' I just could not go back to Dad's that Friday night. My mind couldn't handle any more hurt. Saying good-bye to everyone again in the morning was just too much for me. I wanted to go where there was no talk of tomorrow, no sad faces, no nothing. . . ."

Jane, Mona, and Andrea Wamboldt went to Sid Tollimore's house in Liverpool. "He's a good friend of Andrea's. Mona drove us there. I didn't want to talk to anybody. Mona could sense it, and she decided to drive home to Dad's for the night." She and Jane looked at each other as she was about to leave.

"I'll be here to pick you up in the morning," said Mona.

"I love you, sis," said Jane, hugging her. "Thanks for understanding. Now go home and try to make Dad understand."

When Mona left, Jane poured herself a drink and went into the living room and switched on the stereo. "I put on the earphones and let the world pass on by. I fell asleep there on the floor. I was awake very early— waiting for Mona to come."

Mona picked up Jane and Andrea, and they were back at the courthouse by 9:00 A.M. The jury filed in and resumed its deliberations at nine-thirty. Jane's mother and dad were sitting in their car when she arrived with Mona. Jane went over to them. They wanted to be with her in the courtroom when the jury returned its verdict.

"Is it all right for us to go in?" asked Maurice Hurshman.

"I'll check to see if you're allowed," said Jane. She returned moments later and told them they could be in the courtroom. They walked in together. "There were already a lot of people gathered. The news media were setting up their equipment outside, and everyone was hustling around. I didn't know what to do with myself. People kept coming up and wishing me luck and making comments as people do when they are trying to be nice but don't quite know what's appropriate to say. I smoked and smoked. Mona was like my shadow. She was with me through it all. Besides being my sister, she is one hell of a friend. Alan wasn't in the courtroom when I arrived that morning. He told me he wouldn't be back until the jury reached a verdict. He was within five minutes of the courthouse and would come as soon as they called him to say there was a verdict."

The jury interrupted its deliberations to ask Mr. Justice Burchell to clarify pertinent sections of the Criminal Code once again. Jane Stafford was frightened. She was facing twenty-five years without parole if they found her guilty of first-degree murder. She glanced at her watch over and over, counting the minutes—the hours. "They were out too long. I was sure I was going to prison for the rest of my life." By 11:00 A.M. Saturday morning it had been seventeen and a half hours since the jury first began its deliberations, including a dinner break the evening before, and they took the night off to sleep. At 11:30 A.M. the jury announced it had reached a verdict.

"For nearly three weeks I dragged myself in and out of that courtroom," recalls Jane. "I was terribly thin and run down. I didn't have any clothes that fit me properly, and I had no urge to buy any. In fact, I had no urge to do anything. Nothing really mattered. I was mentally and physically exhausted. I often forgot when I last ate or when I had more than a couple of hours' sleep at a time. Yet when court was called to order for that last time, for that crucial moment, every fibre of my being came alive. I sat in my usual spot about four feet from Alan, but this time he reached out and pulled my chair close to him and put his arm around me."

"Hang in there, Jane," he said. "It's almost over."

Jane showed no outward emotion. "I sat there like a statue. My heart was pounding so hard I thought that everyone else could hear it. The jury filed in. I looked at each of their faces as they took their seats. I had no idea what they were thinking." The court clerk rose from his chair in front of the judge.

"Mr. Foreman, have you reached a verdict?" he asked.

"Yes, we have."

"Do you have your indictment?"

"Yes, I do."

"Would you hand it to me, please?"

"Oh, I'm sorry," said the jury foreman. "We didn't fill it out ourselves. We thought that was to be done here."

"No, you must write it inside and bring it to me."

"I didn't . . . do you need all the jurors for that?"

"Perhaps you should," interjected Mr. Justice Burchell.

The jury filed out of the courtroom. Alan Ferrier got up from his chair and paced across the floor and back. Jane Stafford sat motionless. "I said a silent prayer, 'Please, Lord, no more delays. Let all this end.' I couldn't take any more." The jury returned to the courtroom within minutes.

"Mr. Foreman, have you reached a verdict?" asked the clerk.

"Yes, we have."

"Would you pass me the indictment, please?"

The foreman passed the folded paper to the clerk.

"Mr. Foreman, what was your verdict?" asked the clerk.

"Not guilty."

There was bedlam in the courtroom. Jane was standing, her legs feeling rubbery, when the verdict was announced. All around her there were tears of joy, laughter, and shouts of "Praise the Lord." "Every emotion possible was felt in that courtroom at that moment, yet I couldn't move. I was in shock. I said to myself, 'Thank you, Lord, for the miracle you just performed.' I couldn't believe the verdict. Alan had prepared me for the worst. I didn't know how to accept the best. I'd never once allowed myself to believe the verdict might be not guilty. I killed someone and they were telling me I was free to go. I didn't know how to react. Then everyone was around me, hugging me, shaking hands. It was too much." Alan Ferrier guided Jane into the back room where they had spent so many breaks during the trial. There were papers to be signed. Jane could see he was happy with the verdict, but she sensed something was troubling him.

"You should seriously consider packing up and moving away from here," said Ferrier. "Start a new life."

He paused a moment and looked at Jane.

"There is a possibility that this verdict may be appealed," he said.

"If it is, does that mean I have to go through all this again?"

"Yes, it probably does."

Jane was devastated.

"If there is an appeal, I could never go through all this again—I won't."

"Slow down, I'm only assuming there might be an appeal. If it does happen, I'll do everything possible to prevent you going through this agony again."

"What should I do?"

"I think you should go to Ontario, like you talked about."

"All right, I'll do it."

They walked back into the courtroom. There were still a lot of people milling about. Jane sat down. Alan Ferrier approached her.

"Well, lady, what are you waiting for?" he said. "You're free to go."

Jane looked up at him and smiled.

"Look, mister, I walked in this courtroom with you, and by golly, I'm leaving the same way."

They walked out together to face a barrage of reporters. "When they asked me how I felt, I answered in one word, 'super.' But in the back of my mind I felt it wasn't over yet."

Juror Daniel Smart, who worked for a Liverpool hardware store, said after the trial that the jurors found the Stafford case to be very emotional. "When she was on the stand . . . it was very hard to sit and listen to, because she said some things that people shouldn't have to say to other people. And it was hard for her. I was relieved when it was over, and I felt we came to the best decision that we could. Did she plan to murder him? That was the question. First-degree murder. And there was no way it was proved to us that she actually planned it. There was no way we could come to that decision without any doubts at all."

Alan Ferrier believes the single piece of evidence that probably affected the jury the most was that concerning Billy Stafford's treatment of Darren at the dinner table. "Many people say a woman deserves it. Many people say if she doesn't like it, she can get out. But when it comes to a child being abused, I think that's where they draw the line. And certainly in this case, the single most gruesome particular was that Billy force-fed this young fellow to eat at the same rate he did. If it caused him to vomit, he would simply place the vomit back in his plate and force him to eat it again. And I recall that perhaps that was the only time during the trial in which the jury reacted with just a sickening response to, and everybody in the courtroom did. I think that one single gesture was an indication of how brutal a man he could be."

Ferrier says there's no question that Billy's character was of key importance in the case. "I don't think anybody would dispute that. Some people say that's wrong, that the victim's character shouldn't be on trial. But in some cases it's necessary, and in some cases it's obviously more important than the character of your client because even if your client is charged with shooting... as Jane was in this case, her individual act of violence paled by comparison with the continuous acts of violence that this man perpetrated against her and her child."

Some feminist organizations heralded the jury's verdict as a legal breakthrough of sorts for battered women. They saw it as a symbolic victory in the campaign against wife-abuse and a sign of changing public attitudes towards battered women. Others hoped the decision would prompt other battered women to come out of the closet. Dr. Christine Simmons of Women Against Violence Against Women, a national feminist group, thought the case was perhaps a confirmation that the legal system was finally prepared to protect women from battery.

Alan Ferrier didn't see the Jane Stafford verdict as setting any sort of precedent. "I don't see this verdict having consequences for other cases. Jury trials are not precedents for anything. It doesn't even set a social precedent. Battered women don't have a license to blow the heads off the men who abuse them just because Jane Stafford got off. You simply won't find many situations in which a jury will say it was okay for a person to kill someone. This was a special case. And I think the verdict does show that our system of punishments isn't flexible enough to take into consideration abuse like this."

There were other reactions to the verdict. Local reporter Vernon Oickle, who covered the Stafford case for the Liverpool *Advance,* said that a lot of people thought she was a heroine, but Wayne MacKay, a professor of criminology at Dalhousie University, took a different view. "Some people have applauded the Stafford jury victory as a successful quest for justice," he wrote in the February 1983 issue of *Atlantic Insight.* "Few people would suggest that Jane Stafford deserved a severe criminal penalty. She was clearly a victim of her tragic circumstances and did not have many realistic options. However, those factors would normally relate to the severity of her sentence, not to establishing whether she committed the crime. Is the moral of the

Stafford case that an abused wife can kill her abusing husband (even when he is not immediately threatening), without engaging in the crime of murder?... It's hard to find much sympathy for Billy Stafford. But are such people fair targets for vigilante justice at a local level? There is obviously a place for the jury in our criminal system. It gives flexibility to the law. However, in its quest for justice in the individual case, a jury should not be permitted to distort principles. Whatever one thinks of the result in the Stafford case, it is difficult to support on the basis of principle. The meaning of this morality play is at best confusing and at worst disturbing. Jane Stafford was the person on trial, but it was Billy Stafford who was found guilty."

XII

When Jane Stafford and her sister Mona left the Liverpool courtroom shortly before noon on November 20, 1982, they were speechless. "We just stared at each other," said Jane. "No words were appropriate. Then as she drove a ways we said a prayer together. It was one my sister Sandy wrote for me after Bill's death: 'May we ever have grateful appreciation of our blessings and opportunities; strength and courage for whatever the day may bring; wisdom for our problems and decisions; faith for our disappointments and sorrows; no annoying regrets of yesterday; no undue concern for tomorrow; kindness, patience, and sane cheerfulness and unselfishness; in all things—to all people, amen.'" They drove to their parents' Danesville home. When the car pulled into the yard, Darren ran out to meet them. He jumped into Jane's lap before she could get out of the car.

"Mommy, I heard about you on the radio. You don't have to go to jail. You can stay home with me and be my mommy forever."

The telephone rang continually with well-wishers offering congratulations. "Finally I had to go and lie down, I was so tired. That evening Mona and I went to a tavern to celebrate. A lot of people who attended the trial were there, and we had a nice time." The next day, Sunday, Jane, Darren, and her father drove Mona to the airport. Jane, Darren, and Allen would be following in two weeks' time. "After we came home from the airport, I had supper with Mom and Dad, and then Darren, Allen, and I went home. I wanted to spend a quiet evening with them, like a family. The next day Darren and Allen went to school. I was busy answering the telephone all day. Friends, strangers, everyone called. I got fed up with it all and jumped in the car and went to the beach for some peace and quiet. I sat wondering about the future. I realized I was free, really free for the first time in my whole life. It was all new to me. The questions kept going around and around in my head. What was I supposed to do now? I didn't want to go back to my old job. How was I going to support myself and the boys? Here I was, free, and I didn't have a clue what to do about it. Then I started thinking about the things I used to dream about. Ever since I was a little girl I wanted to be a nurse or an interior decorator. I decided on nursing. At that point they were just thoughts and dreams. I also thought about the move to Ontario. I was so confused. I never had to think for myself before. I really didn't know how. It was astonishing how many things I didn't know how to do. Mom and Dad came to visit that evening, and we decided I would pack up and move away. I'd leave the first week in December. From then on I didn't have time to think, to reason things out. I'd taken the phone off the hook when I came home from the beach, and when Mom and Dad left, I replaced it." It rang almost immediately.

"Hello, are you Jane Hurshman?" said a male voice.

Jane was surprised because only one of her uncles referred to her as "Hurshman," and it wasn't his voice.

"Yes," she replied.

"Well, you don't know me. I'm Alan MacDonald."

"That's the line I've been getting from everybody. What do you want?"

"Before you hang up on me, just listen for a minute, please. I'm making this call for Fred. He's right here beside me, and he wants to talk to you. But before I go, I'd like to congratulate you. Everyone here in this joint has been following your trial and rooting for you. Here's Fred."

"Hi, lady, how are ya. I used up all my calls for the month so my buddy Mac used one of his to call you for me."

"That was very nice of him. Tell him I said thanks for both of us."

The call was from Kingston Penitentiary in Ontario. Alan "Mac" MacDonald was a lifer in jail for killing a policeman and a taxi driver in Dartmouth, N.S. in 1975. Mac, as Jane came to know him, called on behalf of his friend, but it was he and Jane who began corresponding. "After that call I received a letter from Mac. He became a very special part of my life. Although he was in prison I came to have complete faith and trust in him. Our letters became more and more personal. I poured my heart, soul, and feelings out to him."

On December 2, 1982, less than two weeks after Jane was found not guilty, she, Allen, and Darren left by train for Ontario. Mona met them at Union Station in Toronto and drove them to her home in Barrie, sixty miles north of Toronto. The house was small and had only one bedroom. "Mona and her husband, Ed, were very good to us. But they weren't used to having kids around, especially on a permanent basis. The boys and I slept on a mattress on the floor in what was their dining room. It was very crowded. I got the boys enrolled in school and I went to the local college to inquire about a nursing course. I couldn't get in right away. As the days went by I got more and more depressed. I was in a whole new world. I didn't know anyone, and I didn't know the area. I was scared and confused. I had many mixed feelings. Everything was happening too fast, and I didn't know how to cope. I couldn't adjust, and I was withdrawing inside myself." Things got worse on December 15, less than two weeks after Jane's arrival in Ontario. Alan Ferrier telephoned to say that the Crown had launched an appeal in her case.

"Be prepared to be served papers by the RCMP," said Ferrier. "Send them to me by registered mail as soon as you receive them. It's not necessary for you to come back here at this time. I'll let you know when it's necessary." Jane's depression deepened as she envisioned going through another long trial and possibly being sentenced to years in jail. The day after Ferrier's call, an RCMP officer delivered the notice of appeal to Jane. He was dressed in street clothes and drove an unmarked car. He introduced himself and handed Jane the papers.

"I'm really sorry to have to give this to you," said the officer. "I can't see what they hope to gain. Every officer across the country has followed this case, and it should have ended when you were acquitted."

Jane thanked the officer and he left. "I just stood there staring at the piece of paper in my hand. I couldn't believe it was all happening again. I couldn't handle another trial. I hadn't even time to recover from the first one. My mind was like an overloaded circuit. I wanted to go home. I felt like I had to run away. I didn't want to be in Ontario anymore. I wanted to be home, where I knew what was happening. I telephoned Alan but he told me he didn't want me to come back yet. Then I called Mom and Dad. They wanted me to do whatever Alan advised. Mona wanted me to stay, but everything inside me was screaming, 'Go back!' Again I felt like a lost little girl, not knowing which way to go or where to turn. It was total confusion. I felt deserted."

Life brightened for Jane when she, Mona, Ed, and

the children went to Ottawa to celebrate Christmas with her sister Sandy's family. "It was the first Christmas I'd spent with my sisters in eighteen years and the only one I can really remember. After Christmas, I made up my own mind: I was going home, and no one was going to tell me I couldn't. In the second week of January I moved back to Nova Scotia." Jane's house in Bangs Falls had been up for sale since the previous April. "I went back to the house and stayed there, even though it was still for sale. I was more at peace with myself, and Darren was happier. He'd had trouble adjusting in Ontario." Jane went to see Alan Ferrier about the appeal. He told her it could drag on for a long time and suggested she get on with her life. Jane did just that. She upgraded her high-school education and prepared to enter a nursing course at the nearby Lunenburg Regional Vocational School in Bridgewater. She tried not to think about the upcoming appeal of her case. Meanwhile, her correspondence with Mac, the Kingston inmate, intensified. He also called on the first Monday of every month. "He became part of my life," said Jane. "He gave me the strength to go on day after day. At my most down and depressed times he could cheer me up."

Spring turned to summer and summer to fall as Jane waited for word of the appeal of her verdict. In September she enrolled in a course for nurses' aides. Finally the word came down: The appeal would be heard in Halifax in the Appeal Division of the Supreme Court of Nova Scotia on October 20, 1983. Jane knew it was coming, but with a date set, it became more real. "I was very down. Now I knew it was really happening." She was at school the day news came that an appeal date was set. At noon an announcement came over the public-address system asking Jane Hurshman to go to the main office. She was handed a large box of flowers. She walked back to class and opened it. It was a dozen long-stemmed roses. They were full and beautiful. Jane thought that Alan Ferrier must have sent them.

"Come on, Jane, read the card and tell us who they're from," urged one of her classmates.

The card read:

> To a very special lady
> Who is feeling down today
> Well Janey, hold your head high
> This man is cheering for you
> Love always
> Mac xoxoxo

Jane says she'll never forget Mac's thoughtfulness. "I know I must sound crazy, caring for a person I never met, nor probably ever will, but we had an affair of the heart and mind. He always sent me beautiful cards and nicely written letters."

The Crown's appeal was heard in Halifax, with Alan Ferrier arguing on behalf of Jane Stafford, and Blaine Allaby and Kenneth W. F. Fiske for the prosecution. The court reserved its decision, and it wasn't announced until six weeks later, on November 30, 1983. The Crown won its appeal. The verdict of the jury was set aside, and a new trial was ordered for Jane Stafford. The written decision came from Supreme Court Justice J.A. Hart and was endorsed by four other judges.

Besides allowing the appeal, the court mildly reprimanded Mr. Justice Burchell for spending so much time going over the evidence for the jury at the trial. "Surely this is not the task of a trial judge," said Hart. "There are twelve members of the jury who have heard the evidence and have the right to refresh their memories from the record, if necessary. . . . Nothing can be gained by a lengthy repetition of the evidence in detail except fatigue on the part of all concerned." Hart said both the prosecution and the defense brought out a lot of evidence about the character of Billy Stafford. "Much of this was unnecessary and indeed inadmissible unless it was relevant to a defense that could properly be put to the jury. It served only to create sympathy for the respondent and for this reason should have been excluded."

On Section 37, the defense of self-defense, Hart said Burchell's instructions to the jury "were broad enough to say that a person is justified in killing anyone who has threatened them and is likely to carry out such a threat. I do not believe that Parliament intended such an interpretation of the section." He went on to say there was no assault actively under way against Jane Stafford when she shot and killed Billy Stafford, who was "passed out or sleeping in the truck. . . . In my opinion no person has the right in anticipation of an assault that may or may not happen, to apply force to prevent the imaginary assault. The jury should not have been permitted to consider a possible assault as a justification of her deed, and Section 37 of the code should not have been left with them. Since the jury was improperly instructed on the law relating to the offense alleged against the respondent and since that improper instruction may well have permitted them to reach a conclusion that would not otherwise be open to them, I would allow the appeal, set aside the verdict of the jury, and order a new trial upon the original indictment."

News of the appeal and new trial received national attention. Alan Ferrier told the Toronto *Globe and Mail*, "the Crown went after her for first-degree murder, the penalty being twenty-five years without parole, yet its own agents said on the stand that she should get a medal." He said he initially advised Jane Stafford to plead guilty to manslaughter, which meant the punishment would be determined by the judge who would have heard evidence of the abuse she was subjected to and psychiatric evidence about the state of her mind. "She was prepared to go to jail for a couple of years. But the attorney general's office evidently did not want to be seen to be engaging in plea bargaining on a murder trial, and they made the decision to go for first-degree murder and to let the jury decide. Now they're not too pleased with what the jury decided."

Ferrier didn't realistically expect Jane to be acquitted. He couldn't have read the jury during the trial.

"Reasonably I think we expected that the best we could do would be to have a manslaughter verdict. The fact we got more than we expected, in hindsight, may have caused more problems than it solved. The use of the self-defense argument in the case was borderline. It was a situation where a man was asleep and generally the courts have not accepted that anyone is acting in self-defense if somebody's immobile when you act." Another problem, says Ferrier, was "a reaction at the time of the acquittal that this somehow was a license for women to go out and kill their husbands and then allege years of abuse or whatever." Less than three weeks after Jane Stafford was acquitted, a woman in neighbouring New Brunswick shot her forty-four-year-old husband in the head. The woman was charged with second-degree murder. During the trial her husband was described as an introvert with a serious drinking problem who repeatedly beat his wife and children. It took the jury slightly more than an hour to find the woman not guilty. That case was also appealed.

Exactly two months after Jane Stafford used a shotgun to put an end to her years of humiliation and abuse, many male Liberal and Conservative members of Parliament laughed and guffawed loudly in the House of Commons when they were told that one out of ten women in Canada are battered by their husbands. When New Democrat MP Margaret Mitchell asked about the report there were gales of laughter, amid which one unidentified MP joked, "I don't beat my wife. Do you beat yours?" The laughter outraged women across the country, prompting many of them to complain bitterly to their MP's about their lack of response to women's issues.

"I thought it was absolutely disgusting that the men MP's would be laughing and almost condoning the fact that men can beat their wives," complained Mitchell. "If I had asked about a man beating up another man they wouldn't have laughed at all. That's what the laughter meant to me."

Judy Erola, then minister responsible for the status of women, was quick to respond to the laughter. "I do

not find it amusing. Neither do the women of Canada."
Lucie Pepin, president of the Advisory Council on the
Status of Women, immediately wrote to every member
of Parliament, enclosing a fact sheet on battered wives.
"I'm really appalled they consider violence among 52
percent of the population a laughing matter." Three
days after the incident, on the third attempt, MP's gave
unanimous consent to a motion assuring women that
they consider the issue of family violence to be extremely grave. Conservative MP James McGrath said
his party "very much regrets what happened in the
house. We believe family violence is a very serious
problem in the country, probably more widespread
than is generally believed."

The incident underscored what a lot of feminists
had been saying for years—wife-battering was considered a joke by much of society. As insensitive as it was,
the laughter of the MP's did have some positive fallout.
Government money was soon being found for emergency shelters and transition houses, and the legal system
began to slowly harden its attitude towards wife-batterers.
In Ontario alone, $4 million was pumped into shelters
for battered women, and a message went down from
the attorney general's office urging police and Crown
prosecutors to crack down on wife-beaters. And more
reports came out and more studies were ordered.

One working paper, entitled "The Criminal Justice
System Response to Wife Assault," showed with cold
statistics and unemotional language the depth of the
problem and the uncaring attitude of the legal system.
It said domestic calls are the largest category of requests to police for help, even though less than 10
percent of incidents are reported to police. And between 40 and 70 percent of all violent crimes in North
America occur between married couples or those living
common-law. It found Canadian courts to be extremely
lenient with convicted wife-beaters, and jail terms were
rare. Typically, the court either suspends sentence and
releases the offender on probation, or he is given an
absolute or conditional discharge.

Although police are now more willing to answer

domestic abuse calls, arrest rates, the report found, are still too low for men who assault their wives. Crown attorneys still seem to give a low priority to wife-assault cases, viewing the problem as less serious than assault between strangers, while judges seldom send a man to jail because they are loath to break up a family.

Whatever progress was being made to help abused women, it was too late for Jane Stafford. Nothing was in place that she knew of during her years with Billy Stafford, and now she was facing a second trial for his murder. Christmas 1983 came and went, and still no date had been set for her new trial. Her life had become relatively normal. She was taking her nursing courses in Bridgewater and doing well. Darren was also doing well in school and no longer lived in fear, and Jane always had Mac's letters to look forward to. Their correspondence became more and more personal, and she kept his picture alongside those of her sons. She decided that she wanted to meet him in person and made arrangements to visit him during her coming March break. Prison officials in Kingston cleared the way for the visit and everything was set, but it was not to be.

The word came down from Halifax. The date for Jane's new trial was February 14, 1984—Valentine's Day and a month short of two years since Billy Stafford had been killed. Alan Ferrier knew that Jane Stafford did not want another lengthy trial. He also knew the Crown would now find it difficult not to accept a plea of guilty to manslaughter. He reasoned that a judge accepting that plea could not ignore the jury's not guilty verdict in her first trial.

"The jury's decision was important because it was a statement to the effect that we don't want to see her punished," Ferrier said. "That we have empathy for what she had to live through. The judge would have to be mindful of the fact that these people sat through the trial and saw all the evidence and their decision shouldn't be ignored. Their decision can only be represented now in terms of leniency, in terms of understanding and giving her a sentence that gives her an opportunity to start her life over again, to fulfill some of the goals that she has now."

Ferrier's instincts proved correct. The Crown this time readily agreed to accept Jane Stafford's plea of guilty to manslaughter. Explaining the change of heart, Crown prosecutor Blaine Allaby said that facts apparent before Jane's trial warranted a charge of first-degree murder. It was planned and it was deliberate. But as the evidence unfolded in the trial it became apparent that perhaps manslaughter was the proper charge. Jane was relieved that she wouldn't have to go through another lengthy trial, but she faced the uncertainty of sentence. The only certainty was it wouldn't be twenty-five years with no prospect of parole.

The night before her court appearance, Jane packed her small bag as she'd done so many times before and did her best to explain to six-year-old Darren that she might not see him again for a long, long time. It was a Monday. Her court appearance was Tuesday, and she had an exam scheduled for Wednesday at her school.

"I knew they were either going to lock me up or let me go. I wanted to write that exam on Wednesday. I'd done very well at school since the day I started in September. I studied hard and put everything I had into that course. Being able to concentrate so hard on something was great. I didn't have to think about all this legal stuff. The next day was just another date I had to meet. I'd deal with it when it happened."

Her friend Andrea Wamboldt stayed overnight with her in Bangs Falls, and the next morning Jane sent Darren off to school and they headed for Liverpool. They went to Andrea's apartment above Tompkins Market for a cup of tea before going to the courthouse. Andrea's eleven-year-old daughter Tammy was getting ready for school. It was about 8:15 A.M. when they arrived. Jane asked Tammy if she would go down to the store for her and pick up some Halls cough drops and a package of cigarettes. The girl returned with the cigarettes but no cough drops.

"Jim didn't have any Halls, so I didn't get you any cough drops," said Tammy.

"Thanks anyway, Tammy," said Jane. "They don't have to be Halls, but I'll pick some up when we leave."

Tammy left for school and about fifteen minutes later Jane and Andrea left the apartment and went down the covered exterior stairway at the side of the white building. Andrea was walking in front of Jane.

"Don't forget I want to get some cough drops at the store first," said Jane.

"I'll get them," said Andrea, turning towards the door.

Jim Tompkins was related to Andrea Wamboldt by marriage. He was in his midthirties and operated the store with his wife. As usual, he had arrived first at the store. His wife would join him later after tending to their two young children. When Andrea entered the store she looked to the rear, near the meat counter where Jim Tompkins could usually be found at that time of the day. She couldn't see him and he didn't respond when she called his name. As she turned to check along another aisle, her foot struck something. She looked down. It was Jim Tompkins' hand. He was lying on his back, dead. A rifle lay across his body. He'd shot himself while in a sitting position on the floor.

Andrea Wamboldt ran quickly from the store just as Jane was approaching. She quickly closed the door. Jane didn't understand the look of panic on Andrea's face.

"Don't go in there!" said Andrea. "Jim is on the floor, dead. He shot himself." The two of them ran from the store. Jane was terrified. "All I could hear was 'dead,' 'shot.' I thought, 'Oh God, what's happening?'"

"Go upstairs and wait!" Jane yelled to Andrea. "I'll send the police. Don't do anything. Just stay in your apartment. I'll send someone right up."

Jane jumped into her car and sped away. "I went right down Main Street like a maniac, not stopping for stop signs or anything. I kept thinking over and over in my mind, 'Oh Lord, this isn't real. This can't be happening to me.' Here I was on my way to court for murder and I find a dead man. How will I explain this one?' It was like a bad movie." Jane was ashen-faced when she pulled up in front of the old Liverpool courthouse. A small crowd had already gathered, and newsmen and television cameras were waiting for her arrival. She ignored their questions.

"Are there any policemen here yet?" she asked a journalist.

"I don't know."

Jane ran into the courthouse. It was empty except for Deputy Sheriff Michael Smith.

"Jim Tompkins just shot himself," she said to the startled Smith. "He's at his store, lying on the floor, dead. Andrea is waiting in her apartment for the police to come. Hurry and send someone right over."

Jane sat down and tried to calm herself. "I was a total ball of nerves. I was shaking so bad my chair was shaking. I prayed I wouldn't get mixed up in it." She reached into her purse and took out several envelopes. They contained Valentine's Day cards from Mac. "He'd sent me five cards, which he told me not to open until I left for court that morning. 'You'll know I'm with you when you read them,' he told me. I took them out and looked at them once again. I needed support and I got it as I read the cards over again. I could hear him saying, 'Chin up, Janey, walk tall, I'm right with you.'"

The courtroom was packed with spectators, including Jane's parents, by the time the clerk called the court to order and Mr. Justice Merlin Nunn took his seat on the bench. Jane's plea of guilty to manslaughter was quickly accepted. All that remained was to hear sentencing arguments from Blaine Allaby for the Crown and Alan Ferrier for the defense. All the players were aware the case was being watched with interest across the country. The case continued to be cited by women's groups, and Progressive Conservative MP Jennifer Cossitt had even tried to get the federal government to intervene to see that Jane Stafford didn't have to go back to court. She said, before the date for a new trial was set, that the decision by the Nova Scotia attorney general's office to appeal the jury's decision to acquit was horrendous. She told the House of Commons that Jane Stafford had "already received enough punishment—five long years of painful mental and physical punishment—and it appears that the department of the attorney general of Nova Scotia wants to punish her further. I believe, and I am sure everyone in this chamber would agree, this lady was more than justified in her actions to protect herself and her son from this terrifying onslaught of repeated assault."

Allaby called for a jail term to discourage others from taking the law into their own hands. Ferrier called one witness, Darren's longtime baby-sitter Marie Joudrey, who said she often saw bruises on both Jane and Darren. She said the boy was terrified of his father and would often run and hide when it was time to go home and he knew his father was there. In his address Ferrier said Jane would carry the mental scars of Billy's abuse for the rest of her life.

He asked for a suspended sentence and cited a Sudbury, Ontario, case as precedent. In that case a woman was charged with murder after shooting her husband in his sleep in 1980. As the story unfolded during her trial, the judge and jury heard of the beatings and degradation she and her children suffered at the hands of her husband. Before the case went to the jury, however, the woman pleaded guilty to the lesser offense of manslaughter, and the judge imposed a suspended sentence. Ferrier told Mr. Justice Nunn that the cases were almost identical and "she felt entrapped in much the same way as Mrs. Stafford."

He reviewed some of the sexual humiliations Jane was subjected to. "This was not a man. He was an animal. He indicated his power came from the devil." He said it was ironic that Jane was working in a nursing home, helping others, while being battered at home. Even the father of the victim was prepared to be bondsman for her. And the police said to one another, "This woman deserves a medal and has saved at least two police officers' lives." It had been extremely difficult for his client during her long trial to spell out from the witness stand her degrading and humiliating experiences. The acquittal and courtroom applause, said Ferrier, cannot be forgotten.

Mr. Justice Nunn said Jane lived a tragic life and Billy Stafford was a man on the outer fringe of a definition of humanity, but a human nevertheless. He said he did not subscribe to Staff Sergeant Peter Williamson's view that Jane should receive a medal for what she had done. He said Jane was "judge, jury, and executioner." Nunn said Jane was doing well in her certified nursing assistant's course and well on the road to rehabilitating her life and was not a danger to society but that there must be deterrence in the law and protection of society as a whole. "Wives," he said, "don't have the right to take the lives of their husbands." The case, he concluded, did not warrant a suspended sentence. He sentenced her to six months in jail and two years' probation with a recommendation that she be allowed to commute from jail to attend her classes and complete her nursing course.

Jane Stafford, who sat impassively during the hearing, felt only tremendous relief when Nunn announced her sentence. "It was finally over after two years of waiting, wondering with my life, my future on hold." Under Canadian law, Jane's six-month sentence meant that she could be out of jail in two months. "And I could finish my nursing course. It was super." She and Ferrier met in the back room of the courthouse for the last time. Ferrier had tears in his eyes as they hugged each other.

"Do you want me to appeal this sentence?" he asked.

Jane looked at him and smiled.

"Hey, smile, it's all over. Hell, no, I don't want you to appeal it. Just let me do my time and put all of this behind me forever. I'm so happy it's over."

Blaine Allaby was satisfied with Nunn's sentence. "She did take another human being's life. As the judge said, she acted as judge, jury, and executioner. I think in those circumstances a person has got to know if they're going to act in that way, then there has to be some price. Jane has paid a heavy price over the last two years and certainly well before that in the life she led with him. But the route she took is not the answer.

I think what the judge was saying is that you will be shown compassion by the courts, but there also has to be a price involved if that's the route you're going to take."

A lot of people around Liverpool took a different view, perhaps best summed up in an editorial by Jock Inglis in the Liverpool *Advance*. It read in part: "The Crown got its pound of flesh through the incarceration of Ms. Stafford, but at what cost to our judicial system? Obviously, the Crown was either afraid of losing the case the second time around, or like most who heard the evidence, felt that though she did take her husband's life, she had already suffered sufficiently. Otherwise they would not have plea-bargained. So Ms. Stafford was forced to go through another year of waiting, wondering whether she would spend the next ten years of her life in an Ontario penitentiary, only to find that the Crown would settle for the smallest of sentences. There are those of us who felt that the jury was the pillar of our judicial system, that once we were found to be innocent by a group of our fellow citizens we were free to go about our business. We know now that this is not so. We also wonder how, in the future, the Crown can expect we citizens to do our duty as jurors—to sit hour after hour, day after day, studying the testimony and finally to be told, once our verdict has been rendered, that no, our opinion was not really wanted after all, only that of the lawyers. What did the Crown really accomplish through this exercise? Did they prove to the citizens of Queens County, beyond a reasonable doubt, that Ms. Stafford committed a crime against our society? Did they show society that she deserved to be punished? Will the sentence stop others from protecting themselves from physical or emotional violence perpetrated by their mates? Did our society derive any meaningful benefit from the second trial? We think not."

Two weeks after Jane Stafford was sentenced to six months, pretty nurse Michele Jewell of Winnipeg was killed, her throat slit by a knife, just hours before she was to appear in divorce court. The twenty-five-year-old's husband, Michael, was charged with second-degree murder. Michele had been granted a restraining order against her husband at the time of her death. In a sworn statement she spoke of the fear she had that her husband might harm her. He'd threatened her, just as Billy Stafford had threatened Jane. Michele cited physical and mental cruelty as the grounds for divorce. She said reconciliation was impossible because of her husband's "abhorrent behaviour." Michele's dismembered body was found February 29, 1984. It had been packed into garbage bags and dumped on a northwestern Ontario farm owned by her husband's brother. As wife abuse goes, the case wasn't all that unusual. When there is death in "domestic disputes" it's the woman who dies in more than 90 percent of the cases. Michele Jewell took the legal way out. It didn't work. Death usually comes to a battered wife after one beating too many, one punch or one kick too many. Often the husband pleads guilty to manslaughter and the court accepts.

XIII

Jane Stafford was not afraid of jail. She considered it just another place to live, and her friend Mac had advised her in his letters how to get by, how to survive. She said her good-byes to Alan Ferrier and her family and was escorted to Sheriff Cyril Page's car waiting in front of the courthouse. His wife was with them. He drove her to the now-familiar Halifax Corrections Centre. This time it was daylight, and Page drove to the rear of the building. He took Jane into the guard's station. She sat on a chair while he handed the matron a commitment form. The sheriff left. Jane removed her jacket and was taken into the matron's office for processing. She was issued a pair of jeans, a blouse, sweater, panties, and bra as well as bedding, a towel, a facecloth, soap, and toothpaste. The matron filled out a card with Jane's medical history for the prison doctor and an "inmates' effects list." Valuables such as jewellery, cash, and wallet were put into an envelope. She was then moved through the guard station to the cell area. "My cell was about six feet by eight feet. It had a steel bed on the wall, a sink, and a toilet. Meals are brought in and you have to keep your own cell clean. There is no privacy at all."

Jane had to stay in the cells for four days before being placed in the general prison population. Guards from their glassed-in post control the shower, which is turned on in the cell area for a short period of time each night. On her first night in jail Jane was taking her turn in the shower with the curtain drawn when she heard a rough, mean-sounding voice.

"You Jane Stafford?" said the voice directly behind the curtain. Jane didn't have time to respond. "I'd like to know who the fuck you know or who the fuck you blew to get only six months for what you did?"

Jane was frightened. "I didn't know who was waiting for me behind that shower curtain. I didn't know what to say or how to react. Then some of Mac's advice came into my mind. He told me they would test me and that I had to stand up for myself or I'd be used and abused the whole time I was inside." Jane took a deep breath and yanked the curtain back.

"And just who the fuck wants to know?" shouted Jane, surprised at her own outburst. Judging by the voice, Jane expected to see a big woman before her. Instead, she had to look down at a frail ninety-pounder with curly red hair. They stood staring at each other, and then the woman started to laugh.

"I'm Pearl," she said. "I was just sentenced to ten years for shooting my old man. I was just wondering how come you got only six months for the same thing."

Jane had trouble to keep from laughing. Pearl was spending thirty days at the correction centre, awaiting transfer to an Ontario penitentiary. "That was my one and only unfriendly encounter, all the time I was in jail," Jane said. Back in her cell, Jane settled in for the night. The cell next to her was vacant, but there was a woman in the cell beyond that. She was attractive with long, dark hair. Jane guessed her to be in her late twenties. She was reading a book, but looked over to Jane a couple of times. Pearl was wandering around outside her cell, which was in the second bank of four, out of view around the other side of the U.

"You don't talk to her," Pearl said to Jane. "She's a fucking baby-killer." The young woman was Colleen Gottchall. She'd killed a young boy for whom she'd been baby-sitting. Some said it was the worst case of child-beating ever seen in the Maritimes. Gottchall was kept locked in her cell, unless no others were around, for her own protection. She'd been sentenced to twenty-five years without parole but won an appeal and was waiting to go back to court. Jane noticed the woman seemed to ignore Pearl's comments. Jane decided to talk to her.

"Did you really do what Pearl said?" asked Jane.

There was no response. Jane repeated the question. There was silence for a time. Jane was startled when the woman suddenly spoke to her.

"Do you like to read?" she asked.

"Yes," replied Jane.

"I've got lots of books here if you want to borrow one."

"No, thanks. I don't feel much like reading right now."

"Baby-killer!" shouted Pearl from her cell on the other side of Jane.

Gottchall ignored Pearl and continued talking to Jane. "She talked a lot about lawyers and how she didn't think too much of hers."

"Did you find it awful going in and out of the courtroom?" she asked Jane.

"What do you mean?"

"They took me in in handcuffs and people were

saying awful things to me. I had to have guards all around me."

"The courtroom I was in was small and I didn't have to wear handcuffs or anything like that."

"It was terrible..." said Gottchall, her voice trailing off.

Jane arrived at the jail on Tuesday. On Thursday she was permitted to drive to Bridgewater to attend classes and write her exam, a day later than scheduled. From then on she was permitted to attend her classes regularly. It meant four hours of driving each day. When she returned from school on Friday, Jane was moved into the general prison population. Including those in the cells, there were about twenty inmates in the women's block. Jane was assigned to one of the two dormitories, one with seven beds and the other with six. Three additional beds were set up in the medical room.

Shawna, a heavy-set black woman with reddish hair and light freckles, fancied herself the boss among the inmates, and nobody was about to argue with her. She weighed about 170 pounds and sported short Afro-style hair. She and another inmate shared the medical room. Several Cape Bretoners were in Jane's dormitory. They constantly argued or engaged in horseplay, making it difficult for her to study. On the Monday night following her first weekend in prison, Shawna told Jane to sit beside her in the dining room, a sign that she was accepted by the others, and more important, by the boss. Later, Shawna and some of her friends asked Jane to teach them to play Scrabble. Jane learned a lot of new words, most of them not to be found in any dictionary.

Shawna was serving time for assaulting a pregnant woman, who lost her child as a result of the beating. Despite her tough demeanour, Shawna had a compassionate side. When she saw Jane was having a difficult time trying to study in the dormitory, she offered to trade places with her so she could do her homework in the relative peace and quiet of the medical room. Jane's sole roommate was a pregnant teenager, serving time for break and entry.

Jane was up every morning at 6:00 A.M. and on her way to school an hour later. She was too early for breakfast but managed to down a cup of tea after making up her bed. "At school I bought my lunch at the cafeteria," said Jane. "By the time I got back to jail in the evening, supper was all over with. But the guards were good to me. They always saved some food for me. It was cold but at least I got something to eat."

The women's section of the prison included a drab but clean common room, of cement block construction, painted green and white with vinyl lounge chairs. There was television, a pool table, a bookcase, a record player, and a VCR machine in the room. Every second week a movie was brought in. Jane watched only one during her stay in the prison. It was a B-grade feature about a prison island where male and female inmates were left to fend for themselves.

"You talk about sex and violence," said Jane. "I couldn't figure it. They're supposed to be rehabilitating people and they show them trash like that."

Jane was subjected to a strip search each day when she left for school and again when she returned in the evening. Her prison garb was usually a pair of jeans and a pajama top. Each night she washed her school clothes in the laundry room. Jane's purse was also searched daily, and if she needed money for food, or to purchase something for Darren, she had to sign for it. She spent almost four hours a day driving to and from prison. When she wasn't studying in the evening she was writing, usually poetry. One poem, sent to a friend from prison, was called "Beauty":

I opened my eyes and faced the world
    The beauty was a wondrous surprise
I looked toward the sky—a beautiful blue!
    So splendid—the radiant view
I choked back a sob;
    But there was more to behold.
I turned to my left with a gasp of delight

There stood the majestic world in all its glory
Oh what a vision, so huge and free!
  A thrill of joy swept through me
I turned to my right, and beheld the ocean
  The waves performed a sensuous dance
There standing in the breeze
  I glanced around to see more
Utter silence held its mysterious beauty
  So untouched, so hidden
This wondrous sight that is forbidden to so many
  The beauty of it all must be told
There are so many beautiful sights out there
  For Darren and Allen, Jamie and I to behold.

Jane discouraged friends and family from visiting her in prison. She found it stressful to carry on a conversation through a screen. Other than inmates, guards, and schoolmates, Jane saw more of her father, Maurice Hurshman, than anybody. He usually drove to her school, or to the hospital when she later began on-the-job training. He always brought lunch, which they shared in the car as they chatted. Jane enjoyed the visits from her father. Sometimes he brought along Darren, Jamie, or her mom, Gladys.

The most difficult period of Jane's incarceration was the 1984 March school break. She wasn't sad about having to stay in jail over that ten-day period, but that was when she had planned, prior to being sentenced, to travel to Ontario to meet Mac at the penitentiary in Kingston. "They told me in jail I couldn't have any contact with any cons or ex-cons until after my parole period was completed," said Jane. "I had to write the hardest letter of my life, telling Mac I could have no more contact with him. He wrote back, so understanding, but I read the hurt between the lines. I didn't forget him and I never will. He was there for me when I needed support most."

Jane was assigned to train at Queens General Hospital in Liverpool, but one of her classmates, Joycelyn Priddle, agreed to switch, allowing her to train at Fisherman's Memorial Hospital in Lunenburg, forty-five miles closer to the prison. The location was closer, but Jane had to be at the hospital by 7:30 A.M., which meant being up before daylight to leave the prison by 5:30 A.M. Jane completed her shift at 3:30 P.M., which meant she had two hours to get back to prison or face the possibility of her privileges being revoked. Not once was she late.

Jane's training also included two weeks at a rehabilitation centre for psychiatric patients. It was there she discovered an unexpected plus, some answers about what made Billy Stafford tick. She'd carried the guilt of Billy's death for two years, during which she saw four psychiatrists but received no satisfactory answers. Each student at the rehabilitation centre was assigned a patient on a one-to-one basis. Jane admired her instructor, a psychiatric nurse who was aware of her background. At the end of her first week at the centre Jane found some answers. On that day, a Friday, she studied sociopathic personality disturbances, which included those who were antisocial, dissocial, sexual deviants, or drug addicts.

Jane decided Billy fit the antisocial category. There are eleven clues to help identify antisocial behaviour and personalities, and she believes all of them relate to Billy Stafford. Included on the list: little or no conscience; self-centred, poor judgement, and lack of restraint; doesn't learn from experience; no patience; ability to impress and exploit others; impaired interpersonal relationships; low tolerance for stress; rejection of authority; lies easily, rationalizes and projects guilt; irritates, disappoints, and distresses others; inability to understand and accept ethical values.

"I could relate to all of these clues in Bill's personality," said Jane. "All during class I kept silent. I just sat there absorbing it all. I felt like someone just gave me a million dollars."

Jane couldn't wait to get back to prison to think out all she'd learned. It was raining heavily when she left the rehabilitation centre. She was thinking about what she learned and took a wrong turn, ending up on a toll bridge for the city of Halifax. She was trapped in traffic and couldn't turn around. She was panicking about losing her privileges and her school year by the time she reached the toll bridge. She explained her plight to a sympathetic attendant, who called for a bridge patrolman. Traffic was stopped in both directions on the bridge to allow Jane to turn around. She drove fast to make up the time she had lost, and she arrived before her deadline.

"I spent the whole weekend putting all I learned into logical order," recalls Jane. "I finally came to the realization that I didn't have to carry all that guilt around inside me. I was finally able to put a label on Billy Stafford and bury him once and for all. It took me two years to do that. The guilt is gone but the terror of how I lived will remain forever in my memory."

On April 14, 1984, Jane Stafford, eligible for parole after serving one third of her sentence, returned to prison from her classes. It was an overcast, grey, rainy day. She was told by prison authorities that her release papers had come through. "I just had to sign them, pick up my belongings, and I could go," said Jane. "I ran out of there, still in my nurse's uniform with the rain hitting my face. I ran to the gate. It seemed like I waited forever for it to open for the last time."

Jane looked back to the guardhouse, wondering if the officer on duty had forgotten she was there. The guard was waving to her and smiling from behind the glass. He pressed the button to open the gate, and Jane heard his voice over the speaker:

"Good luck, Jane, be happy."

Epilogue

Jane Stafford is no more. Upon her release from jail she called Alan Ferrier and asked him to take the legal steps necessary to change her and Darren's surname to Hurshman. It was Jane Hurshman who graduated as a fully qualified nursing assistant in June 1984. On graduation day Jane was presented with a gold pin awarded to the best all-around nurse's assistant at Fisherman's Memorial Hospital. Today Jane lives in the Maritimes with Allen and Darren and sees a lot of her other son, Jamie. She has a good job in a rehabilitation centre and she's attempting to get into a college to take courses to permit her to work in transition houses for battered wives. She was released from parole on August 14, 1984, and her probation period ends on August 14, 1986. Jane requested that three of her poems appear in this book:

To My Parents

You are my parents, who together as one
Have given me my life to live
I want to thank you, Mom and Dad
For all that you have done,
I want to say, I love you both
And I love you both as one.

To My Sons

My sons, I know your fears
I know your dreams,
I can't promise you everything—
But I can promise you that I'll always support you,
I'll always comfort you and encourage you,
I'll always accept and care for you—

Trust me that I'll never abandon you
Trust me that I'll never harm you
No matter what, I'll take care of you
No matter what, I'll always love you!

To Mac

I just want to say—Let me love you,
Not according to any how-to books

Or by someone else's set of rules
But simply for who you are, and how you are with me.

And please love me
Not for what I ought to be
Or for what I might be molded into
But for what I am here and now.

Don't expect me to be someone all good and giving—
Someone who could never disappoint you
Or someone too right to be real
And too perfect to be me.

I'm just as human as anyone I know
And very proud and thankful that you are also
You are a very special person in my life,
And I love you.

At an August 13, 1985, meeting of the Queens County Council, six of eleven councillors voted against providing a $6,400 grant for a proposed transition house to aid battered women in Queens and adjoining Lunenburg County. Two male councillors were particularly vocal in their opposition.

Councillor Joe Rogers said he couldn't see a need for such a facility and that such facilities become vacation spots for some women and entice them away from their homes and families. And Councillor Laurie Smith said nowadays women bring on their own troubles. He said what some women need today "is a good kick in the backside."

A local newspaper, *The Advance*, published in Liverpool, supported the transition house in its editorials. And reports of the August 13 meeting brought a spate of angry letters to the editor deploring the actions of council. One of the letters was from Jane (Stafford) Hurshman. She said she was appalled, particularly by the remarks of Councillor Laurie Smith.

"Unless this man has himself lived in an environment of domestic violence," she wrote, "I don't think that he has the right to say that 'in some cases all they simply need is a kick in their backsides.' If this man had any idea of what he was talking about he would know that once a woman takes that first kick it is the start of an act of violence against her will. It is a terrible way to have to live; a life of suspense and fear, when you wonder at all times when the next act of violence is going to occur.

".. . I think that the councillors who are against this should be ashamed of themselves. I do not know how many thousands of dollars my trial cost the taxpayers, but I am sure that most of the public in Queens County would be in favour of this transition house. . . . Some councillors feel that expense of another costly trial, which could happen . . . I pray that in the near future these same councillors who now oppose this motion will have a change of heart and realize just how desperately this transition house is needed."

Councillor Laurie Smith did recant and a month later backed a motion to provide funds for the transition house, which will open in 1986. Other communities, including the town of Liverpool, supported the transition house and were ready to proceed with it without participation by the Queens County Council. Councillor Joe Rogers retired from politics and did not run in the October 19, 1985, municipal elections. Councillor Laurie Smith ran again but was defeated.

Appendix

Following is a list of transition houses and shelters in Canada for battered women. It was provided by the National Clearinghouse on Family Violence in Ottawa. For security reasons, no addresses are included. If emergency accommodation is needed, call the nearest transition house or shelter. Many have twenty-four-hour crisis lines. For immediate protection, call the police.

NORTHWEST TERRITORIES

Emergency Family Centre
Fort Smith
(403) 872-2378

YWCA of Yellowknife
Yellowknife
(403) 920-2777
873-4767

YUKON

Kaushee's Place
Whitehorse
(403) 668-5733

ALBERTA

Calgary Women's Emergency
   Shelter
Calgary
(403) 245-5901
   245-4442

Calgary YWCA Residence
Calgary
(403) 263-1550

Discovery House
(second-stage housing)
Calgary
(403) 277-0718

Sheriff King Home
   for Battered Women
Calgary
(403) 266-0707

Camrose Women's Shelter
Camrose
(403) 672-1035

Dr. Margaret Savage
Women's Crisis Centre
Cold Lake
(403) 594-5095

W.I.N. Houses I and II
Edmonton
(403) 479-0058

Unity House
Fort McMurray
(403) 791-7505
   743-1190

Odyssey House
Grande Prairie
(403) 532-2672

Yellowhead Emergency Shelter
   for Women Society
Hinton
(403) 865-2599

Harbour House
Lethbridge
(403) 320-1881

Lloydminster Interval Home
Lloydminster
(403) 875-0966

Medicine Hat Women's
  Shelter Society
Medicine Hat
(403) 529-1091

Central Alberta Women's
  Emergency Shelter
Red Deer
(403) 346-5643

A Safe Place
Sherwood Park
(403) 464-7233

BRITISH COLUMBIA

Marguerite Dixon House
Burnaby
(604) 525-3223

Chetwynd Women's Resource
  Centre
Chetwynd
(604) 788-3793

Ann Davis Transition House
Chilliwack
(604) 792-3116
      792-0727 (After hours)

Cranbrook Safe Homes
Cranbrook
(604) 426-8407

Mizpah House
Dawson Creek
(604) 782-9176

Meope Transition House
Fort St. John
(604) 785-5208

The "Y" Women's
  Emergency Shelter
Kamloops
(604) 374-6162

Central Okanagan
  Emergency Shelter Society
(Kelowna Women's Shelter)
Kelowna
(604) 763-1040

Ishtar Transition Housing
  Society
Langley
(604) 530-9442

Cythera House
Maple Ridge
(604) 467-9966

Mission Transition House
Mission
(604) 826-7800

Haven House
  Nanaimo
(604) 754-7123

Nelson Emergency Shelter
   Programme
Nelson
(604) 352-3504

Emily Murphy House
North Vancouver
(604) 987-1773

Haven Homes
Parksville
(604) 248-2093

Port Alberni Transition House
Port Alberni
(604) 724-2223

Port Coquitlam Women's
   Transition House
Port Coquitlam
(604) 464-2020

Phoenix Transition House
Prince George
(604) 563-7305

The Prince Rupert Transition
   House
Prince Rupert
(604) 627-8588

Amata Transition House
Quesnel
(604) 992-7321

Nova House
Richmond
(604) 270-4911

Shuswap Area Family
   Emergency (S.A.F.E.)
   Society
Salmon Arm
(604) 832-9616

Sunshine Coast Transition
   House
Sechelt
(604) 885-2944

Surrey Emergency Shelter
Surrey
via Emergency Services
(604) 576-8636
      588-0188 (crisis line)

K'san House
Terrace
(604) 635-6447
      638-9982

W.I.N.S. Transition House
(Women in Need Society)
Trail
(604) 364-1718

Monroe House
(second-stage housing)
Vancouver
(604) 734-5722

Powell Place Sanctuary for
   Women
Vancouver
via Emergency Services
(604) 668-3111

Vancouver Rape Relief and
   Women's Shelter
Vancouver
(604) 872-8212

For Vancouver area, see also
Burnaby, North Vancouver,
Richmond, and Surrey.

Vernon Women's Transition
   House
Vernon
(604) 542-1122

Victoria Women's Transition
   House
Victoria
(604) 385-6611

The Cariboo Women's
   Emergency Shelter
William's Lake
(604) 398-6831

MANITOBA

Westman Women's Shelter
Brandon
(204) 727-3644
      727-4504
1-800-862-2727

Dauphin Crisis Centre
Dauphin
(204) 638-8777

The Portage Women's Shelter,
   Inc.
Portage La Prairie
(204) 239-5232

Aurora House Crisis Shelter
The Pas
(204) 623-5497

North W.I.N. House
Thompson
(204) 677-2723
      778-7273 (crisis line)

Morden-Winkler Committee
   on Family Violence, Inc.
Winkler
(204) 325-9956

Baldwin House
Winnipeg
(204) 783-7129

Native Women's Transition
   Centre
Winnipeg
(204) 586-8487
      586-8488

Osborne House Crisis-Shelter
   for Battered Women
Winnipeg
(204) 775-8197

Manitoba Committee on Wife
   Abuse crisis line
(in effect as of April 15, 1983)

Anywhere in Manitoba, call
   toll-free 1-800-362-3344

In Winnipeg, call 942-3052

NEW BRUNSWICK

Foyer d'Accueil Vallée
   Lourdes
Bathurst
(506) 548-2350

Maison Notre-Dame
Campbellton
(506) 753-4703

Centre de Dépannage
Edmunston
(506) 735-6859
   735-3971

Women in Transition, Inc.
Fredericton
(506) 455-1498

Cross Roads for Women/
  Carrefour pour Femmes
Moncton
(506) 382-2002

Hestia House, Inc.
Saint John
(506) 642-2493

Fundy Region Transition
  House
St. Stephen
(506) 466-4485

Accueil Sainte Famille
Tracadie
(506) 395-2212

NEWFOUNDLAND (including LABRADOR)

Transition House
Corner Brook
(709) 634-4198

Labrador West Family Crisis
  Shelter
Labrador City
(709) 944-7800

Haven of Hope
St. Johns
(709) 726-5026
   726-0393

Transition House
St. John's
(709) 753-1461

NOVA SCOTIA

Bryony House
Halifax
(902) 422-7650

Chrysalis House
Kentville
(902) 582-7877

Tearmann House
New Glasgow
(902) 752-1633

Cape Breton Transition
  House
Sydney
(902) 539-2945

Juniper House
Yarmouth
(902) 742-8689

ONTARIO

Atikokan Crisis Centre
Atikokan
(807) 597-2868
    597-2086
    597-4239

Yellow Brick House
Aurora
(416) 773-6481

Women and Children Crisis
    Centre
Barrie
(705) 728-6300

Grant House
Beaverton
(705) 426-9959

Mississauga Family Resource
    Center
Blind River
(705) 356-7800

Brantford YM-YWCA
Brantford
(519) 752-6568

Nova Vita Women's Shelter
Brantford
(519) 752-4357

Leeds and Grenville
    Interval House
Brockville
(613) 342-4724

Family Crisis Shelter
Cambridge
(519) 653-2422

Lanark County Interval
    House
Carleton Place
(613) 257-5960

Chatham Kent Women's
    Centre, Inc.
Chatham
(519) 354-6360

Women in Crisis
Cobourg
(416) 372-0746

Maison Baldwin House
Cornwall
(613) 938-2958

North York Women's Shelter
Downsview
(416) 635-9630

Avoca House
Eganville
(613) 628-2522

Elliot Lake Women's Crisis
    Centre
Elliot Lake
(705) 461-9868

Women's Habitat
Etobicoke
(416) 252-5829

Three Oaks Foundation
Foxboro
(613) 967-1857

Geraldton Family Resource
  Center
Geraldton
(807) 854-1529

Survival Through Friendship
  House
Goderich
(519) 524-6245

Guelph/Wellington Women in
  Crisis
Guelph
(519) 836-5710

Pavillion Transition House
Haileybury
(705) 672-2128

Good Shepherd Women's
  Centre—Martha House
Hamilton
(416) 523-8895

Hamilton Wentworth Native
  Women's Centre
Hamilton
(416) 522-1501

Hope Haven
Hamilton
(416) 547-1815

Inasmuch House
Hamilton
(416) 529-8149
       529-8140

Maison Interlude House
Hawkesbury
(613) 632-1131

Toll-free line for area code
  613: 1-800-267-4101

Habitat Interlude
Kapuskasing
(705) 337-1122

Kingston Interval House
Kingston
(613) 546-1777

Anselma House
Kitchener
(519) 742-5894

Family Center—Mission
  Services of London
London
(519) 433-0641

Sisters of St. Joseph—
  Residence for Women in
  Need
London
(519) 679-9570

Women's Community House
London
(519) 439-4543

Haven House
Manitoulin Island
(705) 377-5160

Mattawa Family Resource
  Centre
Mattawa
(705) 744-5567

Halton Women's Place
Milton
(416) 878-8555

Interim Place
Mississauga
(416) 271-1860

Niagara Women in Crisis
Niagara Falls
(416) 356-5800

Crisis Centre North Bay
North Bay
(705) 474-1031

Nipissing Transition House
North Bay
(705) 476-2429

Hillside House
Orangeville
(519) 941-1433

Auberge
Oshawa
(416) 728-7311

Higgins House—Y.W.C.A.
Oshawa
(416) 576-8880

Interval House of Ottawa-
    Carleton
Ottawa
(613) 234-5181

Maison d'Amitié/Amity House
Ottawa
(613) 234-7204

Women's Centre (Grey-Bruce,
    Inc.)
Owen Sound
(519) 371-1600

Bernadette McCann House
    for Women, Inc.
Pembroke
(613) 732-3131

Crossroads 1
Peterborough
(705) 743-4135

Crossroads 2
Peterborough
(705) 743-8922

Ernestine's Women's Shelter
Rexdale
(416) 746-3701

Women's Interval Home of
    Sarnia-Lambton
Sarnia
(519) 336-5200

Women in Crisis Home
Sault Ste. Marie
(705) 759-1230

Emily Stowe Shelter for
    Women
Scarborough
(416) 264-4357

Sioux Lookout Family
    Resource Centre (F.R.C.)
Sioux Lookout
(807) 737-1438

Women's Place, Inc.
St. Catharines
(416) 684-8331
        684-4000

Women's Place
St. Thomas
(519) 631-9800

Optimism Place
Stratford
(519) 271-5550

Sturgeon Falls Family
    Resource Centre
Sturgeon Falls
(705) 753-1154

Genevra House
Sudbury
(705) 674-2210

Beendigen Native Women's
   Crisis House
Thunder Bay
(807) 622-5101

Community Residence
Thunder Bay
via Social Services
   Department
(807) 623-2711, ext. 2430

Faye Peterson Transition
   House
Thunder Bay
(807) 623-6600

Canadian Mental Health
   Assoc.
Family Resource Centre
Timmins
(705) 267-7109

Anduhyaun House
(native women's shelter)
Toronto
(416) 920-1492

Evangeline Residence
(Salvation Army)
Toronto
(416) 762-9636

Interval House
Toronto
(416) 924-1491

Nellie's
Toronto
(416) 461-1084

Red Door
Toronto
(416) 469-4123

Stop 86
Toronto
(416) 922-3271

Street Haven
Toronto
(416) 967-6060

Toronto Community Hostel
Toronto
(416) 925-4431

Walpole House
Toronto
(416) 923-5266

Women in Transition, Inc.
Toronto
(416) 967-5227

Women's Habitat of Etobicoke
Toronto
(416) 252-5829

For Toronto area, see also
   Etobicoke, Mississauga,
   and Scarborough.

The Chadwic House
Wawa
(705) 856-2848

Women's Place (Welland &
   District), Inc.
Welland
(416) 788-0113

Hiatus House
Windsor
(519) 252-7781

Women's Emergency Centre,
   Inc.
Woodstock
(519) 539-4811

Maria's Unity House
City of York
(416) 654-9568

PRINCE EDWARD ISLAND

Anderson House
Charlottetown
(902) 892-0960

QUÉBEC

La Passerelle
Alma
(418) 668-4671

La Maison Mikana, Inc.
Amos
(819) 732-9161

La Maison des Femmes de
la Côte-Nord
Baie-Comeau
(418) 296-4799
296-4733

Maison Fafard
Baie St.-Paul
(418) 435-2550
435-3520

Auberge Camiclau
Chambly
(514) 658-9780

Centre Féminin du Saguenay
Chicoutimi
(418) 549-4343

Horizon Pour Elle, Inc.
Cowansville
(514) 263-5046

Maison Halte Secours, Inc.
Dolbeau
(514) 276-3965

La Rose des Vents de
Drummond, Inc.
Drummondville
(819) 472-5444

Maison de Transition et
d'Hébergement familiale de
Fermont
Fermont
(418) 287-3833

Centre des Femmes de
Forestville
Forestville
(418) 587-2533

Pavillon Marguerite de
Champlain
Greenfield Park
(514) 672-8501

Centre Mechtilde
Hull
(819) 777-2952

Maison d'Accueil la Traverse
Joliette
(514) 759-5882

La Parados
Lachine
(514) 637-3529

La Bouée Régionale
Lac Megantic
(819) 583-1233

Le Toit de L'Amitié
La Tuque
(819) 523-7829

La Maison le Prélude, Inc.
Laval
(514) 682-3050

La Jonction Pour Elle, Inc.
Lévis
(418) 833-8002

Carrefour Pour Elle, Inc.
Longueuil
(514) 651-5800

Halte Femmes Haute-
Gatineau
Maniwaki
(819) 449-2513

La Gigogne
Matane
(418) 562-3377

La Passerelle
Mont Laurier
(819) 623-1523

Assistance aux Femmes de
Montréal
Montréal
(514) 270-8291

Auberge Transition
Montréal
(514) 481-0495

Inter-Val
Montréal
(514) 933-8488

La Dauphinelle
Montréal
(514) 598-7779

La Maison du Réconfort
Montréal
(514) 932-9171

Le Chaînon
Montréal
(514) 845-0151

L'Escale Pour Elle
Montréal
(514) 351-3374

Maison d'Hébergement
d'Anjou
Montréal
(514) 351-6134

Maison Marguerite
Montréal
(514) 932-2250

Multi-Femmes
Montréal
(514) 523-1095

Secours aux Femmes
(shelter for immigrant
women)
Montréal
(514) 727-6871

La Maison d'Hébergement de
Pabos
Pabos
(418) 689-6288

La Maison la Montée
Pointe au Pic
(418) 665-3981

La Maison Unies-vers-femmes
Pointe-Gatineau
(819) 568-4710

Centre Femmes (Y.W.C.A.)
Québec
(418) 683-2155

Expansion-Femmes de
   Québec
Québec
(418) 692-4471

La Maison d'Accueil Kinsmen
Québec
(418) 688-9024

La Maison des Femmes de
   Québec
Québec
(418) 692-4315

Maison de Lauberivière
Québec
(418) 694-9316

La Débrouille
Rimouski
(418) 724-5067

Maison des Femmes du
   Grand-Portage
Rivière du Loup
(418) 867-2254

L'Auberge de l'Amitié
   Roberval, Inc.
Roberval
(418) 275-4574
        275-2195

Alternative Pour Elles
Rouyn
(819) 797-1754

West Island Women's Shelter
Roxboro
(514) 620-4845

Le Centre d'Hébergement
Shawinigan
(819) 537-8348

L'Escale de l'Estrie, Inc.
Sherbrooke
(819) 569-3611

La Source
Sorel
(514) 743-2821

Havre l'Eclairci
St.-Georges de Beauce
(418) 227-1025

La Clé sur la Porte
St.-Hyacinthe
(514) 774-1843

Le Havre des Femmes
St.-Jean-Port-Joli
(418) 598-9647

Le Coup d'Elle Inc.
St.-Jean-sur-Richelieu
(514) 346-1645

Maison d'Ariane
St.-Jérôme
(514) 432-9355

L'Ombre Elle
Ste.-Agathe des Monts
(819) 326-1321

Maison Hélène Lacroix
Ste.-Foy
(418) 527-4682

Maison d'Accueil le Mitan,
Inc.
Ste.-Thérèse de Blainville
(514) 435-3651

La Gitée
Thetford Mines
(418) 335-5551

Résidence de l'Avenue A
Trois-Rivières
(819) 376-8311

Maison d'Hébergement Le
Nid pour Femmes victimes
de Violence
Val d'Or
(819) 825-3865

L'Accueil du Sans-Abri
Valleyfield
(514) 371-4618

Centre d'Hébergement
l'Entre-temps
Victoriaville
(819) 758-6066

Centre Amical de la Baie
Ville de la Baie
(418) 544-4626
544-7490

Maison des Femmes
Ville-Marie
(819) 622-0111

SASKATCHEWAN

Moosejaw Transition House
Moosejaw
(306) 693-6511

Battlefords Interval House
North Battleford
(306) 445-2742

Pesim Waskayikan Interval
House
Prince Albert
(306) 922-2100

Regina Native Women's
Residence Resource Centre
Regina
(306) 543-1212
545-2062

Regina Transition House
Regina
(306) 569-2292

Interval House, Inc.
Saskatoon
(306) 244-0185

Shelwin House
Yorkton
(306) 783-7233

ABOUT THE AUTHOR

Brian Vallée was born in Sault Ste. Marie, Ontario. He is a journalism graduate from Michigan State University. He has worked on newspapers in England, the United States, and Canada, including *The Toronto Star*.

Today, Vallée is a producer with the Canadian Broadcasting Corporation's current affairs television program, *the fifth estate*, where he has worked since 1978. He did some of the research and was associate producer for the ninety-minute documentary, *Just Another Missing Kid*, which won an Oscar at the 1983 Academy Awards. He recently completed work on a new novel, *Robard*, and is currently at work on a new book.

SEAL BOOKS

Offers you a list of outstanding, non-fiction, and classics of
Canadian literature in paperback by Canadian authors,
available at all good bookstores throughout Canada.

The Mark of Canadian Bestsellers

SIX BY
W. O. MITCHELL

His first book, WHO HAS SEEN THE WIND, is a Canadian classic. A work of brilliance, sheer beauty, and rare perception, this tells of a child's search for "the ultimate meaning of the cycle of life."

In JAKE AND THE KID Mitchell shows his special skill in capturing the peculiar individuality of his characters. This is the story of a hired man and a ten-year-old boy and their homely, whimsical adventures.

THE VANISHING POINT presents the complex dilemma of native peoples and the well-meaning whites who try to help them. Much of the power of this novel lies in the rendering of the Indian characters, authentic and strong.

Remarkable for its descriptive beauty, humour, and original characterization, THE KITE is written with vitality and affection, and will warm the reader's heart in its presentation of time and old age.

What begins as a dream of boyhood in HOW I SPENT MY SUMMER HOLIDAYS ends in a nightmare of corruption and insanity. Most somber of Mitchell's novels, this is a haunting, powerful tale of lost innocence.

With rollicking humour and spellbinding narrative, SINCE DAISY CREEK grips the reader with the tale of a man terribly wounded by a violent confrontation with an enraged grizzly. A darkly comic odyssey of a stubborn man's struggle to survive, to laugh, and to love again—a journey of the heart that probes both the raw passions and the sweet magic of living.

 Available in Seal paperbacks at all good bookstores throughout Canada.

Seal Books Bring You
Controversial and Timely Non-Fiction

LIFE WITH BILLY   The harrowing account of Jane Stafford's abusive marriage and how it drove her to murder.
With *Brian Vallee*   42239-X $5.95

WITCHES, PAGANS & MAGIC IN THE NEW AGE   An examination of the unprecedented revival of pagan religions.
By *Kevin Marron*   42380-9 $5.95

RITUAL ABUSE: CANADA'S MOST INFAMOUS TRIAL ON CHILD ABUSE   A behind-the-scenes look at the custody trial arising from allegations of satanism and sexual abuse. A precedent-setting case on child abuse in general.
By *Kevin Marron*   42250-0 $5.95

INTO THE AMAZON   A passionate record of a vanishing way of life on one of the world's greatest rivers; a personal narrative of the people including Chico Mendes; and a disturbing account of the devastation wreaked upon an area of the world that is key to the planet's survival.
By *Augusta Dwyer*   42421-X $14.00

CONSPIRACY OF BROTHERS   In 1978 small-town biker Bill Matiyek was shot dead in a local bar. Six members of Satan's Choice were sentenced to ninety years in prison. Did the bikers conspire to murder — or did the law conspire to convict them at any cost?
By *Mick Lowe*   42304-3 $5.95

The Mark of Canadian Bestsellers